Welcome to Multimedia

by Linda E. Tway, Ph.D.

MIS: PRESS

A Subsidiary of
Henry Holt and Co., Inc.

ISBN 1-55828-229-7

Printed in the United States of America

10 9 8 7 6 5 4 3

MIS:Press books are available at special discounts for bulk purchases for sales promotions, premiums, fund-raising, or educational use. Special editions or book excerpts can also be created to specification.

For details contact: Special Sales Director
MIS:Press
a subsidiary of Henry Holt and Company, Inc.
115 West 18th Street
New York, New York 10011

Trademarks

Acknowledgments

I would like to thank a number of people who assisted in various ways. Marla Weston and Bill Riedel served as creative sounding boards and offered technical advice where needed. Bill Riedel also critically read the manuscript, and tested the various exercises. Others who assisted in a number of ways and offered valuable input are my husband, Bill Magdych, my parents, Pat and Gene Tway, and Brian Staples at Microsoft Corp.

I am grateful to Kathleen Joyce, Development Editor at MIS:Press, for her suggestions and input, and to Laura Specht, Production Editor at MIS:Press, for her wonderful book design. Steve Blair at Asymetrix was both helpful and enthusiastic. And I thank my literary agent, Matt Wagner at Waterside Productions, for his general support and guidance.

Contents

Introduction

Multimedia is one of the most exciting technologies to emerge for the personal computer. Most everyone has heard of it, but many aren't sure what it really is. And if you're like many people, you probably want to know if you can get involved in multimedia. Well, the good news is that you can—and without investing a lot of money on a high-end computer.

This book is intended for anyone interested in understanding what multimedia is all about. Whether you just want to run existing multimedia software or you want to be adventurous and create your own multimedia programs, this book is for you. And you don't have to be a computer programmer to build your own applications. All you need is some special software, the right hardware, and a little time to read this book.

What You Will Learn From This Book

In the pages that follow, I'll explain what hardware and software you'll need to run multimedia programs, and what you'll need to develop interactive multimedia applications of your own. If you haven't yet bought a computer system, you'll learn what you should purchase. And if you already have a computer, you'll learn how you can upgrade your existing system for multimedia applications. In the second part of the book, I'll walk you through the development of an actual multimedia program—from the initial steps of creating simple text to the final stages of incorporating animation and sound. And to help you build your application, we've enclosed a working copy of Multimedia ToolBook, a well-known multimedia development package.

Although you may be tempted to skip the first part of the book and jump right into building an application, you'll find that the beginning chapters provide you with valuable information that will help you when you begin building your own multimedia program.

In addition, glossaries at the end of each chapter and the comprehensive glossary in Appendix A clearly define terms used in the text.

By the time you've finished this book, you'll not only have a good understanding of what multimedia is all about, but you'll also have the basic skills needed to develop multimedia software of your own—for fun, for work, or for profit.

> **Note:** This book focuses on the IBM-PC/XT compatible computer. However, those using a Macintosh computer will also find the information presented here valuable in understanding the world of multimedia.

Preparing Your Computer System

Part I of this book consists of five chapters that cover the basics of multimedia—what it is, what hardware and software you'll need, and finally, how to prepare your computer system to run and develop multimedia applications. If you want to learn more about computer basics, such as installing hardware components, you should read *Welcome to Personal Computers* by Chris Jamsa (another book in this series). It is a good source of additional information.

An Overview of Multimedia

In this chapter, you'll learn what multimedia is and the different ways multimedia software can present information to the user. We'll also take a look at the various components of multimedia. Finally, you'll learn the many different ways multimedia can be used to entertain and enhance the learning process.

What is Multimedia?

The term *multimedia* means different things to different people. Quite literally, it refers to anything that uses more than one way to present information. Whereas a musical recording uses only sound (and might be called "unimedia"), a music video is a type of multimedia because it communicates using sound and video. So chances are, if you talk to someone in the music industry about "multimedia," they will think you're talking about music videos.

In the computer world, multimedia refers to software programs that use more than one method of communicating information to the user—such as text and sound. Technically, multimedia on the PC is not as new as many think. The integration of text with graphics has been at the heart of many software applications for years. Any software that uses graphic images (such as charts and maps) to illustrate the text information displayed on a computer screen is an example of this.

However, more recently multimedia has come to mean more than the integration of text and simple graphics. It now encompasses sound and moving graphic images, sometimes called *animation*. Using this technology on an ordinary PC, we can simultaneously view windows containing text, still graphic images (such as a photograph), and an animated image, while listening to an explanation of what we are looking at on the screen. Multimedia thus greatly enhances the learning experience by involving more of our senses.

Imagine a software program designed to teach you to play tennis. On the computer screen (see Color Plate 1) is a window with text explaining how to serve the ball, another window that shows a diagram of the tennis court indicating where you should place the serve, and a third window that shows a moving video of a person making a serve to illustrate form. Meanwhile, a voice explains what to look for in the video. This is an example of how multimedia can be useful for teaching or training. It simultaneously uses four methods to teach you about the serve—text, graphics, animation, and sound. It would still be multimedia if it just used text and graphics or text and sound, but full multimedia applications can incorporate much more.

Components of Multimedia

The example given above illustrates four of the five components usually present in multimedia software, that is, text, graphics, animation, and sound. A fifth component, *interactive links*, integrates the whole program by giving the user a way to interact with the program and cause things to happen. Let's look at each of these components in more detail.

Text

Most everyone who has used a computer is very familiar with text. Text is the basis for word processing programs and is the fundamental information used in most multimedia programs. In fact, multimedia packages often involve the conversion of a book to computerized form, allowing the user to look up information quickly (without constantly referring to an index or table of contents). Later in this book, we will explore the various ways of including text in a multimedia application.

Graphic Images

When we speak of graphic images, we generally mean a "still" image such as a photograph or line drawing, such as the illustration of a tennis court. As humans, we are very visually oriented, and a picture is a powerful way to illustrate information—whether on a piece of paper or on the computer screen. Graphic images are therefore an important component of multimedia. A company's database of employees with names, addresses, and other information is much more effective when photographs of those employees can be displayed, too. As we'll see later, graphic files are larger than text files and consequently require more storage space on your computer. This is one of the reasons that multimedia applications require a large hard disk drive or equivalent storage capabilities such as a CD-ROM.

Animation

Animation refers to moving graphic images or "videos"—for example, the movement of a person making a serve. Just as a photograph is a powerful communicator, a small movie "clip" is even more powerful and is especially useful for illustrating concepts that involve movement. Other examples might be the movement of a horse during a gallop versus a walk, or the proper way to swing a golf club. These concepts are difficult to illustrate using a single photograph or even a series of photographs, and even more difficult to explain using text.

As you might have guessed, animation files require much more storage space than graphic files involving a single image. This often necessitates the use of a CD-ROM drive, as will be explained in Chapter 3.

Sound

Sound can substantially reinforce our understanding of information presented in other ways. For instance, a narrative might describe what we are seeing in a video of a horse's gallop and point out what to look for that makes it different from a horse's walk. This can further enhance our understanding of the difference between these two gaits. Although this same information could be conveyed using text, it is difficult to read explanatory text at the same time as watching a video.

Other types of information can't be conveyed effectively without using sound. It is nearly impossible to provide an accurate description of a lion's roar or a bird's call using words, and images aren't any more helpful. The incorporation of sound in a multimedia program can provide the user with information not possible using any other method.

As with animation, sound files are very large and require lots of disk space. In Chapter 3, you'll learn more about the storage required by the various types of files discussed above.

Interactive Links

An integral part of multimedia is its interactive nature. This means that the user can point with a mouse and click on certain screen "objects" such as a button or highlighted text and cause the program to respond in a certain way. For instance, a paragraph of text explaining how to serve a tennis ball may have certain words or phrases, such as "ad court" (see the blue text in Color Plate 1), that are unfamiliar to the user. By pointing and clicking on these words, the user may bring up a window with additional information explaining the words (see Color Plate 2). A "button" is a screen object with a label that indicates what action it activates. For example, the user may click on a "Pause" or "Replay" button to control the animation display. Or there may be a button indicating "Sound" that when clicked on causes the program to play a recording of a lion's roar or a musical tune. Some software uses what is often called "balloon help." With this feature, if you move the mouse pointer over a word or illustration that has additional information, an explanatory window automatically opens up without the need to click on the mouse button.

These interactive links, together with the information they connect, are often referred to collectively as *hypermedia*. More specific terms, such as *hypertext* (sometimes called a *hotword*), *hypergraphics*, and *hypersound*, indicate what type of information is linked. For instance, hypertext allows the user to bring up explanatory text (as we saw in the tennis example), whereas hypergraphics displays a graphic image. It is this interactive nature of multimedia that makes it extremely useful in providing information to the user. Unlike a book (see Figure 1.1a), which is designed to be read from the top of the page down and from cover to cover (sometimes called "linear" information), multimedia allows users to access information any way they choose (sometimes called "nonlinear" information access), and different users will want different information at different times. In Figure 1.1b on the next page, we see an example of this in which the user may jump from highlighted words (hotwords) or phrases to other sections of text or diagrams on any page. It is as though all the pages of a book were loose and could be accessed in any order the user chooses. Because of this, multimedia is one of the most flexible and effective ways to learn.

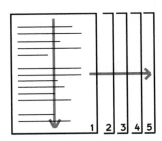

Figure 1.1a

Linear information access.

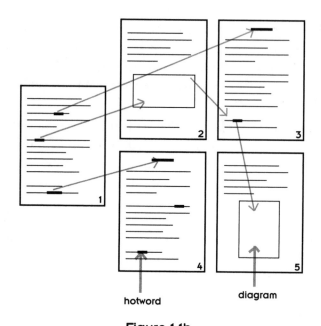

hotword

diagram

Figure 1.1b

Non-linear information access.

Putting Multimedia to Work

There are many areas that can benefit from the use of multimedia, and they tend to overlap in terms of what they provide. The following are just a few.

Education and Training

One of the hottest areas for multimedia is education. Because multimedia presents information in a variety of forms, it is extremely effective in getting across new ideas and concepts. And it has the inevitable effect of grabbing and holding a person's attention. Many users find that multimedia provides a more natural learning environment. Instead of waiting to get to a chapter or section that explains some information in more detail (as with the traditional learning process), the user can immediately access more information (perhaps in the form of a picture) on the computer.

Since the user is not forced to read through information in a rigid format, more advanced users can avoid the more rudimentary information available and skip to more advanced concepts. Beginning users, on the other hand, may continue to get more help and explanations before going on, ensuring that they understand the basic concepts necessary to build on. Because of this, a multimedia program is helpful to users of varying levels of knowledge, and allows them to proceed at their own pace. In fact, teachers find multimedia applications actually motivate students to learn—students take a more active part in learning and the spontaneous interaction can be fun.

Multimedia can greatly facilitate the learning of a foreign language, especially by those doing so on their own. Learning a language using a book has the disadvantage that one is not sure how to pronounce the words presented in the lessons. Language tapes with accompanying text solve this problem, but it is inconvenient for the listener to keep rewinding the tape to find specific information. And the user can't quickly hear the pronunciation for a particular word. Using a multimedia program incorporating both text and sound, the user may see words and phrases on the screen as they are pronounced by the computer program. If the user doesn't understand the meaning of a word, she may point to it and bring up a translation in her native language. Or the user may request that the computer pronounce any word displayed on the screen.

Just as multimedia is useful in education, it is also useful in training. For example, many companies have developed interactive multimedia programs to train new personnel about company policies, manufacturing procedures, or other operations within the company. Computer-based training has many advantages. It circumvents the need for rigid training schedules, allowing workers on a night shift to learn as conveniently as those working during the day. For this same reason, the learning process is not as disruptive of work schedules because the employee can stop training when other work must be done, and resume training when their schedule allows. The same program also can effectively train employees ranging from novice to experienced. And high-quality training can be provided even in remote offices and plants.

Marketing and Sales

Because multimedia is so effective at communicating information, many companies have found it to be a powerful marketing tool. For instance, many real estate firms use multimedia to show prospective buyers information about available houses. Such programs can search quickly through a database of listings to locate possible matches, and then display high-quality graphic images of each house, with room photographs, layouts, and maps. Although the same information can be provided on paper, the computer program has the added capabilities of rapid searches to locate houses that meet the needs of the buyer. Multimedia programs are also highly effective for making general presentations, and may be used instead of slides or overheads.

Another area in which multimedia has been successfully used is in providing information in an unattended location or kiosk, such as an airport, store, exhibit hall, or sales counter. For example, a computer in an airport might provide the traveler with information on tourist attractions, restaurants, and hotels, along with graphic images and maps showing how to get there. A cosmetic counter may provide customers with information on makeup for particular skin types and colors. Although all multimedia applications should be easy and intuitive to use, this should be particularly true in situations where the user wants very specific information and will only spend a few minutes searching for it.

Information Access

It is often said that this is the age of information. We are literally being inundated with so much information that it has become difficult to access it quickly and conveniently. Multimedia provides a very effective way of distributing masses of information and of searching for specific facts in a variety of ways. Interactive references such as encyclopedias, dictionaries, and zip code directories are now available on CD-ROMs for the PC and allow users to access the information they need quickly. Other programs provide large databases of facts and graphic images for a particular subject such as plant and animal life.

Entertainment

Home computer users are especially interested in entertainment software (generally games), which has always been very interactive in nature. Sound and animation have been particularly important in these applications to enhance the "action" of the game. Because the sequence of events in such games depends on the actions of the player, these programs offer an ever-changing contest to the user.

Examples of Multimedia Programs

There are a number of good examples of multimedia products on the market. I've selected a few to give you an idea of what is available. Some sample screen displays from multimedia programs are illustrated in the color plate section.

Bodyworks

Bodyworks is a medical reference that provides information on the body's main systems with animation of such things as a heart beating or muscles flexing. There is also extensive information on illnesses, general fitness, and first aid. The program contains numerous color graphics. A sample screen is shown in Color Plate 3.

Columbus: Encounter, Discovery, and Beyond

This educational multimedia program can be used at grades ranging from elementary school through college. Using this program, the user can look at life around the world during Columbus's time, and travel through time from 1492 to 1776 (when the United States was founded) to see what effects Columbus's discovery had on the world.

Compton's Multimedia Encyclopedia

This is an interactive encyclopedia useful in researching a variety of information from all 26 volumes of its 1991 printed version. Included in this comprehensive program (besides text, of course) are 15,000 graphic images and maps, music, narration, and animation.

Living Books

These interactive stories are entertaining and help children learn to read and pronounce words. Characters are brought to life with animation, sound, and music.

Mammals

Mammals was developed by IBM in cooperation with the National Geographic Society and provides information on over 200 mammal species. It includes color photographs, maps of habitat locations, videos of animal movements, and animal sounds. Color Plate 4 shows a sample screen display.

Microsoft Multimedia Bookshelf

This program contains several standard references, including an encyclopedia and dictionary (which provides sound with pronunciations of its entries). Using this, it's quite easy to look up a variety of information.

Multimedia Beethoven: The Ninth Symphony

With this program, not only can you listen to the entire Ninth Symphony, but you can also learn about Beethoven himself and access detailed explanations of the musical score.

Orbits

This is an educational package (with some entertainment, too) that teaches you about the solar system—from the structure of Earth to nuclear fusion of the Sun. A sample screen is shown in Color Plate 5.

Sherlock Holmes: Consulting Detective

Full-motion video, sound, and graphics enliven this entertaining program in which the user tries to solve several murder mysteries using various clues and Sherlock Holmes's private files.

U.S. Presidents

Delivered on a CD-ROM, this program provides biographical information and pictures of the presidents of the United States. Information includes, for example, their education, family background, major achievements, and cabinet members.

The Future

In the not-too-distant future, we will see multimedia with even greater capabilities—better graphics, improved sound, and faster performance. And, of course, even greater interactivity. We are already seeing prototypes of such interaction, called *virtual reality*. Using this technology, the user can put on a pair of goggles and a glove and tour a three-dimensional world that exists only in the computer, but is eerily realistic to the user.

Summary

Multimedia is a highly effective way to present information. Its incorporation of several forms of communication makes it an ideal teaching and marketing tool. Here's what we've covered so far:

- Multimedia incorporates the following types of information:
  - text
  - still graphics
  - animation
  - sound
  - interactive links
- Several areas have benefited significantly from the use of multimedia applications, especially:
  - education and training
  - marketing and sales
  - information access
  - entertainment

Glossary

animation   Refers to moving graphic images; usually involves the simulation of movement by sequentially displaying several frames showing a progression of movement.

balloon help   Feature of some software that causes explanatory information to be displayed when the mouse pointer is moved over certain words, without the need to click on the mouse button.

button   A screen object with a label indicating what action it activates.

graphics   The display of images on a computer monitor; images may be still or full-motion video.

hypermedia | Integration of text, graphics, animation, and sound into a multimedia program using interactive links.

interactive links | Connections that allow user to jump from one topic to another in a nonlinear way.

multimedia | Any form of communication that uses more than one medium to present information; computer program integrating text, graphics, animation, and sound.

virtual reality | Computer technology involving a glove and goggles that allows the user to experience three-dimensional interaction with the computer.

Hardware and Software Basics

Before a discussion of the hardware and software needed to run and develop multimedia programs, it's important to review some basics about personal computers. The information in this chapter will help you understand how the type of computer hardware you own or purchase will determine the type of multimedia software you can use. Similarly, if you expect to use certain types of multimedia programs, you'll need to know what hardware can run these programs. We refer to this hardware and software interdependence as *compatibility*.

A crucial factor that determines hardware and software compatibility is the computer's *platform*. A platform is defined by two main things: the computer's *architecture* and its *operating system*. Let's look at each of these in a little more detail.

Architecture

Architecture is simply the overall structure and design of the computer system. Obvious examples of computers having different architectures are the IBM-PC/XT and the Macintosh. Among IBM-based personal computers, there are different architectures. The most common one is EISA (which stands for Extended Industry Standard Architecture). This is used by most major brands of PC-compatible computers, such as Compaq, AST, Tandy, Epson, Zenith, NEC, Hewlett-Packard, and other manufacturers of PC "clones" (or copies). The EISA architecture uses the Intel 80386 and 80486 (referred to simply as 386 and 486) microprocessors and is an extension of, and compatible with, the earlier ISA (or Industry Standard Architecture) used in the older IBM-PC and -XT computers (with 8086 or 80286 microprocessors). Because of this, EISA is sometimes referred to as the IBM-PC/XT architecture. It can be confusing that this is not compatible with the newer IBM architecture, called MCA or Micro Channel Architecture, a proprietary design used by high-end models of IBM PS/2 computers.

Operating System

The computer's platform is also defined by the operating system being used, such as MS-DOS (or simply DOS) and OS/2. The computer's operating system is the basic software that controls how the computer operates, such as storing and managing information on a disk, and controls the computer's use of hardware devices. It also allows the user to run other software such as word processors, spreadsheets, and Windows. The user controls the operating system by inputting commands that tell it what to do, such as print out a file or copy a file from one disk to another.

When a company develops a software package, it must comply with certain standards that are determined by the platform the software will be run on. This means that a word processing package developed for a PC using the DOS operating system will not work on a Macintosh with its "Macintosh System

Software" (sometimes called "System 7") operating system. The package would have to be rewritten specifically for the Macintosh platform.

Let's look at one more aspect of PC platforms that is important to understand, namely Windows.

Windows

Although DOS is currently the most popular operating system used for PCs, it has several limitations. One of the most crucial is that you can only run one program at a time (this is called "single tasking"). This may not be a problem if you only use one software package, but if you use several and need to switch back and forth from one to another, this can be annoying and time-consuming. Another common complaint is that different software packages written for DOS each have a different "look and feel," causing many users to claim that they must learn how to use each package as if they were starting all over. In addition, many users find DOS itself to be unfriendly because the commands required to control it are difficult to remember and error messages are often cryptic.

Windows is a software program running under DOS that addresses the limitations of DOS. Its "multitasking" capabilities allow you to load more than one program into memory at one time and quickly switch back and forth from one program to another. It also has what is called a Graphical User Interface, or GUI (pronounced "goo-ee"), which displays easy-to-understand menus and symbols (or "icons") to control DOS and other software program operations. These operations function the same way from one software package to the next, so the user is generally familiar with the basic use of any Windows package. In addition, the Windows environment subdivides the screen into windows that can overlap and display graphic images, text, and animation at the same time. This capability in particular has made Windows an especially attractive environment for running multimedia software. In DOS, it is more difficult to build a program with multiple windows that can display different information.

The Windows environment is so different from DOS that it requires special software that can take advantage of its graphical and multitasking capabilities.

This means that a program written for DOS needs to be rewritten for Windows in order to use Windows's special features. This is why most popular software packages such as WordPerfect and Lotus have a separate version to run under Windows. Because of this, many refer to Windows running on a PC as a different platform than DOS running on a PC.

Popular Multimedia Platforms

Like any other software, multimedia is developed for a specific platform, and must be run on that platform in order to be compatible. There are several platforms that support multimedia programs. One of the earliest was the Macintosh, which has built-in multimedia capabilities. Another common platform is the Amiga computer. IBM has its own multimedia platform, which it calls "Ultimedia." PC-compatible computers commonly run multimedia programs under either DOS or Windows, and it is these two platforms that are the focus of this book.

In spite of the limitations of DOS, it does offer some advantages if you don't want to spend a lot of money on your computer system. For example, programs running under DOS require less memory. Most DOS-based multimedia programs require a computer with only 640 KB of memory or less. They also don't need the speed that Windows-based programs do, and so you may find that you don't require a 386 processor. And you may not need VGA (video graphics array) graphics capabilities. This all means that if you stick to multimedia running under DOS, you'll be able to spend less on hardware.

On the other hand, DOS-based multimedia programs do not provide the highly effective graphical interface provided by Windows-based multimedia. If you opt for running (and developing) multimedia under Windows, you'll need a lot of memory and a fast machine (at least a 386), and will have to spend more on hardware.

In the next chapter, you'll learn just what hardware you'll need for multimedia running under DOS and multimedia running under Windows.

Summary

The purpose of this chapter was to provide you with the background necessary to understand what hardware and software you'll need to run and develop multimedia programs. You learned the following:

- Hardware and software compatibility are determined by the computer's platform.

- The computer's platform is defined by two main things:

  architecture—this is the overall structure and design of the computer; the most common PC architectures are EISA and MCA.

  operating system—this is the basic software that controls the computer's operations; DOS is the most common operating system for the PC.

- DOS has several limitations, including:

    - it is single-tasking

    - different software packages operate differently from one another

    - it can be difficult to learn the DOS commands

- Windows is a software package that overcomes the limitations of DOS. Some appealing characteristics of Windows are:

    - it is multitasking

    - it has a Graphical User Interface (GUI)

    - all Windows software packages have the same "look and feel," making them easier to learn

    - it provides easy-to-use menu-driven commands

    - its overlapping windows can simultaneously display text, graphics, and animation, making it a good multimedia environment

- Popular platforms for running multimedia include:

  Macintosh
  Amiga
  IBM's "Ultimedia"

PC running DOS

PC running Windows

- DOS-based multimedia programs require less hardware capabilities than Windows-based multimedia

Glossary

architecture	The overall structure and design of a computer system.
clone	A computer system that is a copy of another's architecture.
compatibility	The ability of hardware and software to work together; compatibility is dependent on the computer's architecture and operating system.
DOS	Disk Operating System; the operating system most commonly used on personal computers.
EISA	Extended Industry Standard Architecture; the architecture used by most major brands of PC-compatible computers with 386 and 486 microprocessors; this is the same architecture as the IBM-PC/XT computer.
Graphical User Interface (GUI)	The graphic environment used by some software such as Windows, and which displays easy-to understand menus and symbols (or icons).
icon	A small symbol displayed on the screen that, when clicked on with a mouse, carries out some action.
ISA	Industry Standard Architecture; the architecture used in earlier IBM-PC and -XT computers with 8086 or 286 microprocessors.
MCA	Micro Channel Architecture; the architecture used by most newer models of IBM PS/2 computers.

multitasking   The ability of a computer to run multiple software packages at one time.

operating system   The basic software that controls how the computer operates.

platform   A crucial factor determining hardware and software compatibility, it is defined by the computer's architecture and operating system.

single-tasking   The ability of a computer to run only one program at a time.

Windows   A software package that provides a Graphical User Interface and overcomes many of the limitations of DOS.

Chapter 3

Hardware Requirements

I n the first chapter, you learned about the main components that make up a multimedia application. Putting all of these elements together requires that the computer system running the application have certain capabilities. In this chapter, we'll examine the hardware your computer system will need to run multimedia programs. We'll also take a look at some of the additional hardware you should consider if you want to develop your own applications. This chapter will give you some understanding of the most common hardware components you will encounter when building your multimedia computer system. There are other less commonly used hardware components that can be included in a multimedia system, but we will not be concerned with them in this book.

General Considerations

You learned in Chapter 1 that files containing graphics, animation, and sound are much larger than text files. Because of this, multimedia applications incorporating all of these features require a fairly fast computer (that can more quickly process these files) with a large hard drive or CD-ROM (for storing these files) and lots of memory to run the program. The computer must also have good graphics capabilities (to display the graphics and animation), and the means to play any sound associated with the program.

If your multimedia program does not have sound or animation, you can get away with less in the way of hardware. However, if you want to be sure your computer can run multimedia programs with all of the features discussed in Chapter 1, you'll want to have all of the necessary hardware to do so. And you'll need to be certain that the various hardware components you purchase are compatible with each other, with your computer's platform, and with the software you will be running. Because it can be confusing for inexperienced computer users to determine not only what hardware they need but also its compatibility, some standards have been set up so that the user can easily purchase a "multimedia" computer having all of the components to run full multimedia programs. Let's look at one of these standards in more detail.

The Multimedia PC (or "MPC") Standard

One very popular standard that has been developed to ensure that a computer system has all the necessary capabilities to run multimedia software is called the "MPC" standard, which stands for Multimedia PC. Only new computers that meet or exceed this standard may carry the MPC trademark. This standard, developed by Microsoft Corporation in cooperation with various hardware manufacturers, refers specifically to PCs running multimedia under Windows (with multimedia capabilities; see Chapter 4 for more information). This standard also ensures that any separately sold hardware or software carrying the MPC logo will be compatible with each other and with the MPC computer system.

Table 3.1 lists the minimum hardware requirements for a computer to meet the MPC standard. Although these basic components will allow you to run multimedia programs, you may find that some programs are sluggish, particularly when showing animation. Because of this, you may want to purchase a computer running at 33 MHZ or more, with 8 MB of memory (vs. the minimum requirement of 2 MB), and extra memory for your graphics adapter. These additional upgrades will considerably improve the performance of your multimedia application.

Table 3.1.

Minimum hardware requirements to meet the MPC standard for running multimedia under Windows.

Hardware	MPC Standard
CPU	386SX running at 16 MHz
Memory	2 MB RAM
Storage	3.5 inch high-density floppy disk drive (1.44 MB) 30 MB hard disk drive CD-ROM drive with data transfer rate of 150 KB/sec
Graphics	Standard VGA (640 x 480 with 16 colors)
Sound	8-bit 11 KHz ADC (analog-digital converter) 8-bit 11 KHz and 22 KHz DAC (digital-analog converter) Speakers or headphones MIDI I/O port
Mouse	2-button mouse
Other	Joystick Joystick port Parallel port Serial port 101-key enhanced keyboard

Although the MPC standard is not the only one for multimedia systems, it is currently the most popular one for computers running multimedia under Windows. Note that not all multimedia programs run under Windows. Some run under DOS, and the MPC standard does not apply to these applications. However, if you have an MPC computer system, you will have all of the necessary hardware to run DOS-based multimedia programs. Chapter 4 has more information on DOS- and Windows-based multimedia programs.

Hardware Required to Run Multimedia Programs

It is not necessary for you to have all of the components of an MPC computer to enjoy multimedia. If you don't care about high-quality sound, a lesser sound board will do, or you might choose to forego a sound board completely. If you don't plan to play games, you don't need a joystick. And if animation is not a part of the multimedia programs you want to run, you don't need to worry as much about storage and graphics speed. If you run DOS-based multimedia, you won't require the speed, memory, and graphics capabilities required by Windows-based programs. Table 3.2 contrasts the typical hardware requirements of DOS-based multimedia and the minimum MPC requirements. It also includes recommendations to increase performance of an MPC computer.

Whatever you decide to purchase, it's a good idea to understand the various components that are included in the MPC standard because some (or all) of them may apply to you. Figure 3.1 on page 32 illustrates the various components useful in *running* multimedia (on the right side of the diagram) and additional components that can help you *develop* multimedia (on the left side of the diagram). Many of the hardware components discussed below require a special board (sometimes called an *interface card*) that must be installed inside your computer's *system unit* (which is the main body of the computer) so that your computer can communicate with the hardware. Each board is plugged into a separate *expansion slot* (see Figure 3.2a on page 32) which has an opening in the back of your computer called an *expansion port* (see Figure 3.2b on page 33). Your

Table 3.2.

Comparison of hardware requirements for multimedia running under DOS and Windows with the MPC standard. The minimum MPC requirements are listed along with additional recommendations to improve performance.

Component	Typical for DOS	Minimum for MPC	Recommended for MPC
CPU	286	386-16	386-33 or 486
Memory	640K	2MB	8MB
Graphics	EGA or VGA	Standard VGA	Extended graphics
Storage	5.25" or 3.5" 2-3 MB/program No CD-ROM	3.5" high density 30 MB CD-ROM	3.5" high density 80 MB CD-ROM
Sound	Optional	Required	Required
Mouse	Optional	Required	Required
Joystick	Optional	Required	Required
MIDI	Not required	Required	Required
101-keyboard	Not required	Required	Required
Parallel/Serial	Optional	Required	Required

computer has a limited number of slots available. You can generally tell how many by looking at the back of your computer. The number of slots available can affect how many hardware components you can add to your existing computer, as will be discussed a little later.

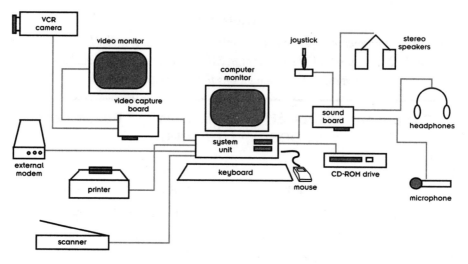

Figure 3.1

*Hardware components useful for running multimedia software (on right side),
and for developing multimedia programs (on left side).*

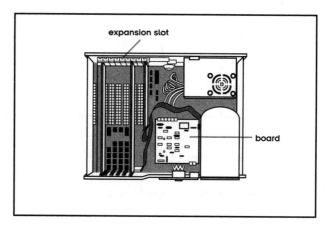

Figure 3.2a

Open system unit showing expansion slots.

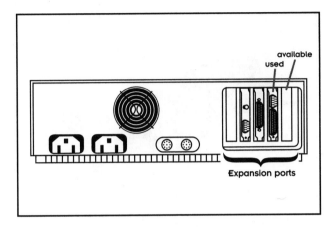

Figure 3.2b

*View of expansion ports which open to the
back of the computer.*

Let's take a more detailed look at the various hardware components you should consider.

CPU or Microprocessor

The *CPU*, or *central processing unit*, is the "brain" of the computer. It is what controls the processing of the computer, and allows it to perform instructions. The CPU is sometimes called a *microprocessor*. The speed at which a computer can process information is determined by two things: bus size and clock speed. A *bus* is simply a set of wires that can transfer information. There may be 8, 16, or 32 wires in the computer's bus (see Figure 3.3 on the next page), depending on the type of microprocessor it has. A bus with 16 wires (sometimes called 16-bit) can transfer twice as much information in the same amount of time as a bus with 8 wires (8-bit), and a 32-bit microprocessor can transfer twice as much information as a 16-bit CPU.

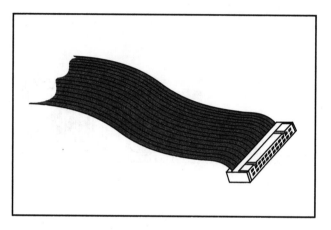

Figure 3.3

Illustration of a bus.

The CPU's *clock speed* controls the timing sequence (or clock ticks per second) at which information is sent through the bus. Because the computer transfers information so quickly, we measure its clock speed in terms of millions of clock ticks per second (called megahertz, abbreviated MHz). A computer running at 8 MHz is pulsing information through the bus at a rate of 8 million times per second, while a 33 MHz computer is transferring this information over four times faster (33 million times per second). Obviously, the faster the clock speed, the faster the machine.

In general, you should remember that the higher the microprocessor number and the higher the MHz value, the greater the computer's speed. Thus, a 486 CPU is faster than a 386, and a 386 is faster than a 286. A 386 CPU running at 33 MHZ is faster than one running at 25 MHz, and so on. Figure 3.4 provides some typical comparisons of computer speed based on CPU and clock speed.

Although the minimum MPC standard for running multimedia under Windows requires a 386SX running at 16 MHZ, you'd be well advised to buy a faster machine if you can afford it. Even a 386 running at 25 MHz can be sluggish when running multimedia.

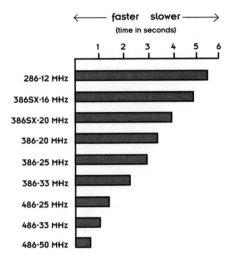

Figure 3.4

*Estimated time (in seconds) for various microprocessors to
process the same set of instructions.*

Typical DOS-based multimedia programs require only a 286 processor (or less)
running at 4 or 8 MHz, although a faster computer will provide much better
performance.

Memory (RAM)

Before your computer runs a program, it loads that program into memory
(sometimes called *RAM*, or *Random Access Memory*) by reading certain necessary
files from a disk (such as a hard disk or a CD-ROM). This loaded information is
temporary, meaning that information that is in memory is not saved when your
computer is turned off. The more memory your computer has, the more
information it can load from the disk. Most multimedia programs are large and
require lots of memory in order to run. In addition, a computer can pro-cess
information in memory much more quickly than it can read files stored on a disk.
Because of this, an increase in memory size can greatly speed up programs that
can access this extra memory (such as programs running under Windows).

The minimum MPC standard requires 2 MB of memory, but you should get more if you can afford it. Memory is pretty cheap these days, and you shouldn't have to spend too much to get as much as 8 MB of memory, and you will really notice a difference in the way your multimedia programs perform.

If you plan to run multimedia programs under DOS, you should only need 640 KB of RAM.

Storage

Storage generally refers to the means whereby information is saved when the computer is turned off. This storage may mean magnetic disks (either floppy or hard) that allow you to add your own information to them, or optical disks (such as CD-ROM) that don't allow you to write files to them.

Floppy Disk Drive

A floppy drive allows you to copy programs from floppy disks onto your hard drive. While many DOS-based multimedia programs are sold on either 5.25 or 3.5 inch floppy disks, most Windows-based multimedia programs are sold on either high-density 3.5 inch floppies or CD-ROMs. The MPC standard requires a 3.5 inch (1.44 MB) floppy drive (see Figure 3.5).

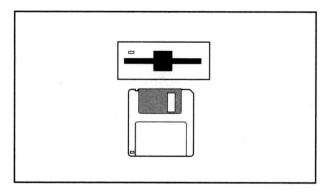

Figure 3.5

A 3.5 inch floppy disk drive and disk.

Hard Disk Drive

Because multimedia programs contain very large files with graphics, animation, and sound, the amount of hard disk storage your computer has is very important, especially if you are using Windows. This is why the MPC standard calls for a minimum storage capacity of 30 MB. That means that this space should be *available* for using multimedia programs. You may have a computer with a 40 MB hard drive, but if you have used up 30 MB to store other software, you only have 10 MB available, and will either need to remove enough files to make 30 MB available, or you will have to upgrade to a larger hard drive.

Although the MPC standard requires only a 30 MB hard drive, I'd recommend an 80-100 MB drive, especially if you plan to develop any applications of your own (see the next section, "Hardware Useful in Developing Multimedia Programs"). Any software package these days takes up a tremendous amount of disk space, especially those running under Windows.

If you are using DOS-based multimedia, a 30 MB hard drive should be adequate unless you plan to load a lot of other software programs onto your drive.

CD-ROM Drive

CD-ROM stands for *Compact Disk-Read Only Memory*. Unlike floppies and hard disks which are magnetic, a CD-ROM is an "optical" storage device that uses a laser beam to read information from the disk (see Figure 3.6 on the next page). A CD-ROM disk looks just like a musical CD and, as its name implies, you can only read data from it; you cannot save information on a CD-ROM disk. Very large multimedia programs come on a CD-ROM, which can hold up to 600 MB of information. This is equivalent to 20 hard drives, each holding 30 MB of information!

Table 3.3 on page 39 shows some examples of file types used in multimedia and compares the amount of storage various files can typically require. A color graphic image can require from 2,000 to 310,000 bytes of storage or more (depending on the size of the image, the number of colors, and the format), a 10-second animation file with about 14 frames per second may require from 8,600 to 46,000 bytes, and a 1-minute motion video file will need about 10 MB of storage (compressed from about 200 MB). Depending on the quality of sound, a 1-minute recording may take anywhere from 0.5 to 10 MB of storage. You can see that a multimedia program with 100 color images with 5 minutes of sound and animation could require from 80 to 100 MB of storage. From this you can see that the storage requirements of multimedia add up fast. This is why most Windows-based multimedia packages require a CD-ROM drive.

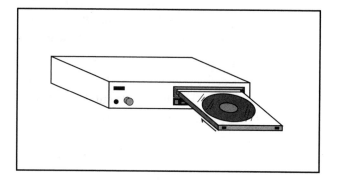

Figure 3.6
CD-ROM drive and disk.

When selecting a CD-ROM drive, you should pay close attention to two things: access (or seek) time, and transfer rate. *Access time* is the amount of time (measured in thousandths of a second, or milliseconds) it takes for the CD-ROM drive to locate information on the CD-ROM disk, and *transfer rate* is the rate at which the located information is transferred to the computer (measured in kilobytes or K per second). The MPC standard requires a transfer rate of at least 150 K per second, but higher transfer rates will improve the performance of your multimedia program. Opinions vary widely about access time. Some say that an access time of 400 ms (milliseconds) is adequate. Others stress that you should not purchase a CD-ROM drive unless its access time is 333 ms or less. In general, be sure to get a CD-ROM drive with a *low access time* and a *high transfer rate*.

Table 3.3

Examples of sizes of various file types used in multimedia.
These may vary with different formats and images.

TEXT:	No. Pages	Format	File Size (bytes)	
	1	WordPerfect	4,000	
	1	ASCII	3,000	

GRAPHICS:	Dimensions (pixels)	Colors	Format	File Size (bytes)
	250 x 250	16	.PCX	2,000
	250 x 250	16	.BMP	32,000
	250 x 250	256	.PCX	4,000
	250 x 250	256	.BMP	64,000
	640 x 480	256	.PCX	12,000
	640 x 480	256	.BMP	308,000

ANIMATION:	No. Frames per sec	Total Frames	Format	File Size (bytes)
	14	20	.FLC	8,600
	14	20	.FLI	46,000
	6	56	.FLI	108,000

(table continued)

SOUND:	Channel	Sample Size	Sample Rate	Time (sec)	File Size (bytes)
	Mono	8 bits	11 KHz	10	110,000
	Stereo	8 bits	11 KHz	10	220,000
	Mono	8 bits	22 KHz	10	220,000
	Stereo	8 bits	22 KHz	10	440,000
	Mono	16 bits	44.1 KHz	10	882,000
	Stereo	16 bits	44.1 KHz	10	1,764,000

Graphics Components

In Chapter 1, two main types of images were discussed—still and animated. Good-quality images and animation result from three main things: good resolution, lots of colors, and quick display rate. The hardware that controls these features are the graphics board and monitor (which determine the resolution), the memory attached to the graphics board (which determines the number of colors you can display, and to some extent the resolution), and a special board called a graphics accelerator board (which determines speed). Let's look at each of these in more detail.

Graphics Board and Monitor

Standard VGA (Video Graphics Array) graphics is capable of displaying 640 pixels (or "picture elements," which are units of measurement) across your monitor and 480 pixels down (see Figure 3.7), usually referred to as "640 x 480," with 16 colors (or gray scales, if displays are in monochrome). Although there are higher resolutions available, Standard VGA displays very good images (if you are not displaying photographs with many more colors) and comes with most new computers. In order to display Standard VGA images, you'll need a VGA board and a monitor capable of displaying VGA graphics. Although you can get a monochrome monitor that will display VGA graphics without colors (this is common on laptop computers, for example), a color monitor is not much more expensive and is well worth the money, particularly when running multimedia programs, which typically provide colorful displays. Another option you might consider is a multisync monitor which allows you to view images displayed using various graphics adapters such as EGA (Enhanced Graphics Adapter, which has a resolution of 640 x 350), Standard VGA, and Super VGA (which has a resolution of 800 x 600). A multisync monitor is especially useful for multimedia running under DOS which can require various graphics adapters.

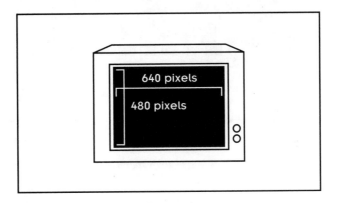

Figure 3.7

Monitor with VGA graphics display of 640 pixels across and 480 pixels down.

Graphics Memory

A Standard VGA board comes with 256 K of memory (attached to the board; see Figure 3.8 on the next page). This limits 640 x 480 VGA displays to 16 colors. You can increase not only the number of colors your computer can display to 256, but also the resolution, by increasing the memory on your graphics board to 512 K (these graphics are often called "extended graphics"; see Table 3.4 on the next page). Displays of photographs with a resolution of 640 x 480 and 256 colors are striking (see Color Plate 3). By adding more memory (for a total of 1 MB), you can display even better images with resolutions of 800 x 600 or 1024 x 768 (also referred to as extended graphics) with 256 colors, but you'll need a monitor capable of displaying these images. It costs very little to increase the memory on your graphics board, and your images will be noticeably better.

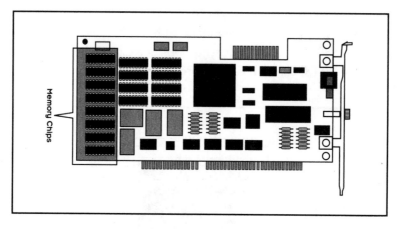

Figure 3.8

Graphics board with memory chips.

Table 3.4.

Comparison of some common graphics resolutions.

Graphics Type	Resolution	Maximum Colors	Memory
EGA	640 x 350	16	
Standard VGA	640 x 480	16	256 K
Super VGA	800 x 600	16	256 K
Extended graphics	640 x 480	256	512 K
	1024 x 768	16	512 K
	1024 x 768	256	1 MB

The MPC standard requires Standard VGA, but extended graphics will provide much better color images. Most multimedia programs running under DOS require either EGA or Standard VGA graphics.

Graphics Accelerator Board

A graphics accelerator board is a special board that not only controls the resolution and number of colors your computer can display, but also speeds up the *refresh rate*. This is the time it takes for your computer to "paint" a new image on the screen. A graphics accelerator board costs a little more than a standard graphics board, but is well worth the money if you are working in Windows or are displaying lots of animation. Without the extra speed, animated sequences can flicker. Increased speed smooths out the movements because subsequent frames that make up the animation can be displayed more quickly.

Sound Components

In order to take full advantage of multimedia, you'll want to be sure you have a sound board. Although computers have a built-in sound chip, its sound is limited to a scale of poor-quality notes (enough to beep at you when you make a mistake, or to play "Twinkle, Twinkle, Little Star"). This certainly isn't adequate for playing Beethoven's Ninth Symphony! The rich sound requirements of multimedia necessitate the inclusion of a sound board, and there is a range of boards to choose from, depending on the quality of sound you want to hear. Before a discussion of sound boards and other components, it's important to understand computerized sound.

In order for the computer to be able to understand sound, sound waves (which are analog in nature) must be converted to digital information. A sound card is equipped with an analog-to-digital converter (ADC) to do this. When the computer plays back the sound, it converts this digital information back into analog, using the sound board's digital-to-analog converter (DAC).

Just as graphic images involve resolution, so do audio recordings. You're probably already familiar with the terms *mono*, which is sound recorded on a single channel, and *stereo*, which is sound recorded on two channels (left and right). Obviously, stereo produces better sound, but it requires twice as much storage space as mono sound (see Table 3.3 on pages 39-40 for a comparison of sound file size). We must also consider two other elements of sound: sampling size and sampling rate, both of which affect sound quality. In general sound recordings are made using 8-, 12-, or 16-bit sampling sizes. The *sampling size* determines the range of sound adjustment; larger sampling sizes provide more information (and hence require more storage space). So, 16-bit recordings have better resolution and are preferable for quality music, while 8-bit recordings are noisier but require less storage space. *Sampling rate* is the number of sound "samples" the sound board takes per second. The higher the sampling rate, the truer the sound. We measure sampling rates in kilohertz (KHz) (examples are 11, 22, and 44.1 KHz). A musical CD is recorded using 16-bit stereo with a 44.1 KHz sampling rate. Obviously, this is high-quality sound—higher than is required by a multimedia computer, but available on fairly inexpensive sound boards. You may also want a CD-ROM drive because high-quality sound recordings require a tremendous amount of storage and are delivered on a CD-ROM disk. It is worth mentioning here that CD-ROM drives that have audio capabilities can play a normal musical compact disk. The drive has volume control and a jack for headphones or speakers, allowing you to listen to a CD as you would with a normal CD player.

Another term you will encounter with multimedia sound is *MIDI*, or Musical Instrument Digital Interface, which refers to an international standard developed for digital music. The MIDI standard determines the cabling, hardware, and communications protocol needed to connect a computer with electronic musical instruments and recording equipment. The MPC standard requires that the sound board have a MIDI in port, a MIDI out port and a MIDI synthesizer to translate the information transferred between the computer and the musical instrument. This means that you can connect an electronic instrument such as a keyboard or drums and the MIDI interface will allow you to record and play back music. (This is a very high-tech equivalent of the old player piano that used a punched paper roll to play the keyboard automatically.)

Now that you know more about computerized sound, let's take a look at the various sound components you should consider.

Sound Board

Any multimedia program that uses sound will require a sound board. The MPC standard requires that the board be capable of recording sound using at least an 8-bit sampling size with a sampling rate of at least 11 KHz. It should also be able to output 8-bit sound at both 11 and 22 KHz.

Not only does a sound board make ADC and DAC conversions of sound, it also has some other important features (see Figure 3.9). One of these is a connector for speakers or headphones for you to listen to sound recordings. It also has a MIDI I/O (input/output) port to input sound from an external MIDI device (such as an electronic keyboard), and to output recorded sound to the MIDI device, as well as an internal synthesizer to translate the recorded sound. Most sound cards also have a volume control dial.

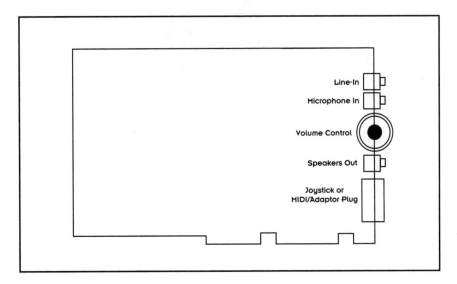

Figure 3.9

Sound board with typical features.

Speakers and Headphones

You may attach any speakers or headphones to your sound board. However, you'll want to be sure that your speakers are shielded so they don't interfere with your computer, and also amplified so that they can boost the amount of sound coming from your sound board. It is helpful to have speakers with controls for bass, treble, and volume (see Figure 3.10).

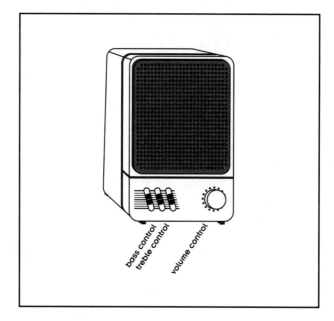

Figure 3.10

Stereo speakers with typical features.

Mouse

If you are running multimedia programs in Windows, a mouse is an essential component of a complete multimedia computer system. The MPC standard calls for a two-button mouse (see Figure 3.11), although there are one-button and three-button mice available. You should not get a one-button mouse, but you could get a three-button mouse if you prefer. Most software not use the third button.

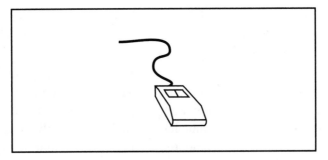

Figure 3.11
A *two-button mouse*.

You will also need to choose between a *bus* mouse and a *serial* mouse. A bus mouse runs off of a separate card that you must install in your computer. A serial mouse connects to the serial port of your computer. Your decision should be based on whether or not you need the serial port for other external devices such as an external modem or a serial printer. If you don't need to connect anything else to the serial port, you might want to select a serial mouse so that you don't devote a slot in your computer to a mouse.

One word of caution: Be sure to get a mouse that is 100% Microsoft compatible. Otherwise, your programs may get hung up or you may run into other annoying problems. Also keep in mind that some multimedia programs running in DOS do not require mouse support, but a mouse can greatly facilitate using many of these programs.

Joystick and Joystick Port

A joystick is used by many multimedia games (in both DOS and Windows)—for example, to maneuver an aircraft or dodge enemy fire. If you don't plan to play games, you probably won't need a joystick. However, if you want to conform to the MPC standard, you'll need to have one, and there is a wide range to choose from. The less expensive joysticks are not as responsive as those that cost more money. On most sound boards, the joystick port doubles as the MIDI port, but you can also purchase a joystick with a separate board. If you plan to purchase a sound board anyway and you don't need to use the MIDI port simultaneously, you might as well use the joystick port on it, because you don't want to unnecessarily use another slot in your computer just to support a joystick. One of the things you'll find in "building" a multimedia computer system is that you will soon run out of available slots in your computer. I'll discuss this in more detail later in this chapter.

Parallel and Serial Ports

A parallel and a serial port are essential parts of any computer system, whether running multimedia programs or not, and are required by the MPC standard. The parallel port (see Figure 3.12a) is generally used to connect the computer to a printer. The serial port (see Figure 3.12b) is used to connect a variety of external devices, such as a mouse, external modem, or serial printer. You will most likely use the serial port on your multimedia computer for a mouse.

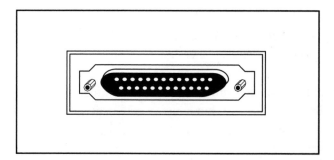

Figure 3.12a

Parallel port.

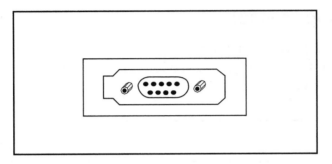

Figure 3.12b

Serial port.

101-key Enhanced Keyboard

The MPC standard calls for an enhanced keyboard (see Figure 3.13), which differs from the original IBM 83-key keyboard by having extra function keys, and a separate set of keys to support cursor movement. This can be convenient because you don't have to turn off the "Num Lock" feature to use the cursor movement keys (such as the up, down, left, and right arrow keys). You may not require this if you aren't concerned about the MPC standard.

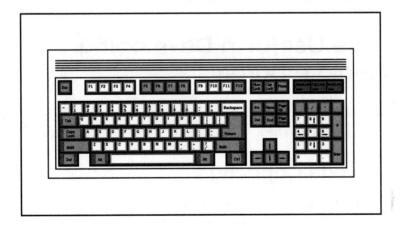

Figure 3.13

101-key enhanced keyboard.

Surge Suppressor

Be sure to protect your computer by plugging any equipment into a surge suppressor (see Figure 3.14) to prevent electrical surges from damaging your hardware investment.

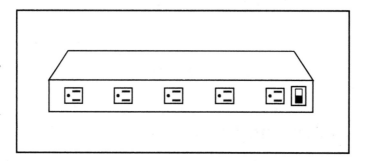

Figure 3.14

A *surge suppressor*.

So far we have been concerned with hardware to help you *run* multimedia programs. Next we'll take a look at some hardware you might want to consider if you plan to *develop* your own multimedia applications.

Hardware Useful in Developing Multimedia Programs

If you develop your own multimedia programs, you'll probably need some additional hardware. The following are a few components that will be helpful.

Extra Storage Capacity

You learned from the discussion above that multimedia files require lots of space. If you develop your own programs, you will build up multiple test files of graphics, animation, and sound, and will require a lot of disk storage to save those files.

Remember that you cannot save files on CD-ROM disks—you can only read information from them. So when developing your own applications, you will find that you quickly use up hard disk space. I recommend that you have at least 200 MB of hard disk space, but the more, the better. You might want to invest in some form of external storage device that uses a "cartridge," such as a Bernoulli drive (see Figure 3.15). This device allows you to save data on a cartridge with 40-90 or more MB of space. These cartridges are removable and thus provide you with essentially infinite storage.

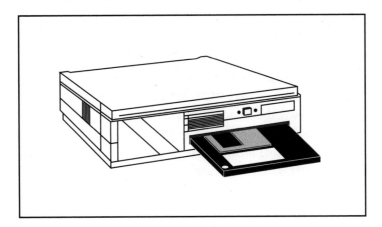

Figure 3.15

Bernoulli drive and cartridge.

Video Capture Board

A video capture board (see Figure 3.16 on page 53) allows you to capture a graphic image and save it as a file. Basically, there are two types of video capture boards. The first type captures only a single frame and as such does not involve any moving images. However, you may capture several subsequent frames and display them in rapid sequence to simulate movement. This type of movement is the basis for most animation used in multimedia. The source for the image may be a VCR or other video camera that is connected to the video capture board in your computer. Assisting in this procedure is a video monitor (attached to the video card) which permits you to view live video images as you capture them (see Figure 3.16). Generally, the capturing process involves pressing a key (or combination of keys) on your keyboard, causing the board to capture the image as it appeared the moment you pressed the key(s). The captured image is then saved as a file. A variation on this type of capturing procedure involves a special camera and video card that are not connected to each other. The camera holds a small floppy disk. You may use the camera as you would any other camera, but instead of the images being captured on film, the images are saved on the camera's floppy disk. You then insert this disk into a device connected to the special video card in your computer which can then copy this image file to the computer. The camera's floppy disk may be reused any number of times.

Another type of video capture board allows you to capture full-motion video (using a video camera such as a VCR and a video monitor to view the image during capture), and save the video clip as a file. Obviously, this involves a great deal of storage—10 MB or so (in compressed format) for 1 minute of video display. This displays images that are more impressive than standard animation because the images are real and quite striking to see displayed on the computer's monitor.

Camera

A video camera is useful for capturing video images—either still or moving. The most common video formats are *RGB* (which stands for Red, Green and Blue), *NTSC* (which stands for National Television Standards Committee, the signal output by televisions in North America and Japan), and *PAL* (which stands for Phase Alternate Line, the standard signal output by televisions in most countries outside of North America and Japan). The most common type of camera used to capture images for the computer is the standard VCR (see Figure 3.16), and this uses the NTSC format. Whatever camera you decide to connect to your computer, you'll need a compatible video board to read the signals output by your camera. A video board also compresses the video image for more efficient storage.

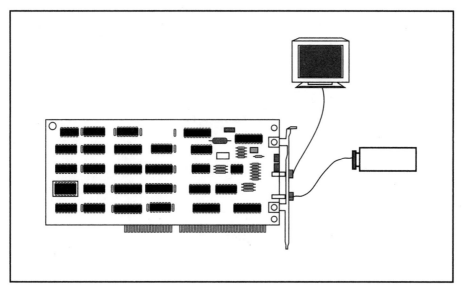

Figure 3.16

Video board with VCR camera and video monitor.

Video Monitor

This is used to help you capture video images, and attaches to the video board (see Figure 3.16). The video monitor may recognize RGB, NTSC, or PAL signals, but must be compatible with your camera and video board. The monitor allows you to observe the video images live as you are capturing them on the computer.

Scanner

Another way to get graphic images into your computer is by scanning photographs or drawings. This produces a digitized image of the original which can be saved in a variety of graphic formats. You don't need to purchase a full-size "flatbed" scanner (see Figure 3.17 on the next page) if you don't need to scan large images. Small hand scanners (see Figure 3.18, also on the next page) do quite nicely for smaller images such as clip art and small photographs.

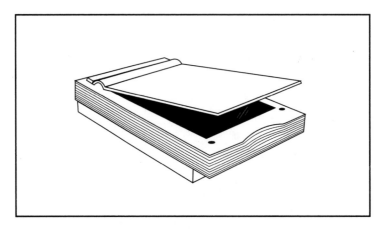

Figure 3.17

A *flatbed* scanner.

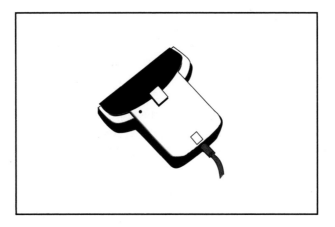

Figure 3.18

A *hand* scanner.

A scanner is also useful if you plan to input large sections of text and don't want to retype the text. In order to use a scanner to interpret text, though, you'll also need special software called Optical Character Recognition, or OCR, software. This software allows you to scan a page (or multiple pages) of text; it then recognizes this text as words instead of meaningless "squiggles." This is discussed in more detail in Chapter 4.

> **Caution:** Before scanning art work, photographs, or text, be sure you read the warning about copyright infringements in Chapter 6 to be sure you are not breaking any laws.

Microphone

If you want to incorporate your own sound into your multimedia program, you might want to purchase a microphone. Any standard microphone will suffice, although one that records higher quality sound in stereo will, of course, cost more money. You can purchase a microphone at any electronics store.

Touch Screens and Pens

A touch screen allows the user to touch the screen instead of using a mouse or keyboard to input their responses or requests. Touch screens are especially popular with computers that are to be used in areas without much counter or desk space, such as a restaurant or kiosk. They are easy to use and have an advantage over a keyboard because users do not need to take their eyes off the monitor to make a selection. Many find a touch screen easier to use than a mouse and pointer. However, others object to a touch screen because the screen becomes dirty and difficult to read from being touched. Some computers permit you to use a pen to touch the screen, or to touch a keypad. Many systems even use special character recognition software to interpret handwriting or printing that was input using a pen. You might have already used something similar when signing for a package from UPS. If your application could benefit from a touch screen or pen-based input, you might want to look into this technology.

SCSI Interface

Nearly every hardware component discussed in this chapter comes with an accompanying board that needs to be installed in your computer. Your computer has only a limited number to accommodate these boards. With all of the hardware you may be getting for your multimedia computer, you may find that you are running out of available slots. If this is the case, you might want to consider getting at least one hardware component that has a SCSI interface (which stands for Small Computer System Interface and is pronounced "scuzzy"). Using a SCSI interface, several hardware devices can be connected to your computer in a "daisy chain" configuration—sort of like chaining several sets of Christmas tree lights together. This can really save you slot space in your computer. If none of your hardware boards has a SCSI interface, you can purchase a separate SCSI interface (see Figure 3.19) to plug into your parallel port to which you can connect additional devices.

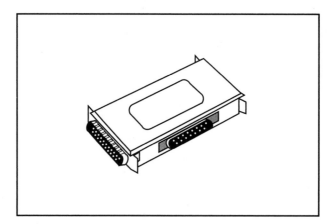

Figure 3.19

SCSI interface.

Printer

A printer is useful for both running and developing multimedia programs. Most multimedia software provides an option to print out information (text or graphic images) that is displayed on the screen. This is especially useful with educational and training multimedia because you can easily refer to specific information later on when you don't have access to the computer.

A printer is also useful in developing multimedia, because some software uses a special programming language (often called a "scripting" language) to control the program's operations. When you build your own program, you may want to enter your own commands using this language. It is very helpful to get a printed copy of any set of commands you enter so you can more easily modify your multimedia program.

Modem

A modem is a piece of hardware that, along with special "communications software" (see Chapter 4) and a phone line, allows your computer to communicate with another computer. This is especially useful if you want to "download" (or transfer) files from a bulletin board service (or BBS) to your computer. These files may be text, graphics, animation, sound, or even "public-domain" programs that are useful for multimedia application development. Public-domain software may be used legally by the public, without a fee having to be paid to the owner or developer.

When purchasing a modem, you'll need to choose between an internal modem (which is a board that is installed into one of your computer's slots) and an external modem (which is a hardware unit that sits outside your computer and connects to the computer's serial port; see Figure 3.20 on the next page). When deciding, you should take into consideration whether you can better afford to give up a slot or a serial port.

Modems transfer information at different speeds that are measured in bits per second (or bps). Be sure to get at least a 2400-bps modem. If you plan to download graphics, or other large files, you would be wise to get an even faster modem (such as a 9600 bps) so that you can download the files more quickly. A normal phone line can support up to 14,400 bps.

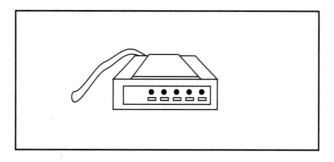

Figure 3.20

An external modem.

Caution: Before you purchase any hardware, be sure to tell the dealer what type of computer you will be using it with. Many hardware components are compatible with certain computer architectures but not others. You should be aware of which architecture your computer uses (as was discussed in Chapter 2) because some hardware components, such as video capture boards, are compatible only with the MCA architecture, whereas others are compatible with EISA. In general, if you tell your dealer what brand of computer you have, he or she will be able to determine its architecture, and provide you with the appropriate hardware.

Summary

You've probably been exposed to more hardware terms in this chapter than you care to know about, although there are many other hardware components that have not been covered here. Don't be overwhelmed. If you plan on running simple DOS-based multimedia programs, you don't need to worry about most of the hardware components discussed in this chapter. Many multimedia programs involve only text and still graphic images, and for these programs you only need to be concerned about the speed of your computer and its graphics capabilities. However, if you want to be able to run full multimedia programs under Windows with sound and animation, this chapter has given you an overview of the most common hardware components you'll need to consider for your computer. And if you plan to get really involved and create your own multimedia programs, you've also learned about some additional hardware that will help you out.

Here are the main points discussed in this chapter:

- The MPC standard indicates hardware components required to run multimedia software under Windows.

- Hardware components you should consider to *run* multimedia programs include:

  CPU or microprocessor
  Memory
  Storage (including CD-ROM drive)
  Graphics board
  Monitor
  Graphics memory
  Sound board
  Speakers or headphones
  MIDI interface
  Mouse
  Joystick and joystick port
  Parallel and serial ports
  101-key enhanced keyboard

- You should always protect your computer hardware with a surge suppressor.

- If you plan to *develop* your own multimedia programs, you should consider some additional hardware components, such as:

    Extra storage (perhaps external storage such as a Bernoulli Drive)
    Video capture board
    Camera
    Video monitor
    Scanner
    Microphone
    Touch screen and pen
    SCSI interface
    Printer
    Modem

- Be sure that any hardware component you purchase is compatible with the architecture of your computer.

Glossary

101-key enhanced keyboard	Standard keyboard having 101 keys including 12 function keys and separate cursor movement keys; requirement of MPC standard.
access time	Amount of time it takes a CD-ROM drive to locate specified information; measured in milliseconds.
ADC	Analog to Digital Converter; converts analog sound to digital information; standard feature on an MPC sound board.
Bernoulli drive	An external storage device using cartridges capable of storing large amounts of data.
board (or interface card)	A component that fits into the expansion slot of the system unit and expands the capabilities of the computer; many

allow the computer to communicate with an external hardware device such as a CD-ROM.

bps (bits per second)	A measurement of speed used with modems, such as 2400 bps or 9600 bps.
bus	Set of wires that transfers information in a computer.
bus mouse	A type of mouse that connects to a separate board in the computer.
camera	An external hardware device that, along with a video board, is used to capture video images.
cartridge	A removable, high-capacity disk used with an external storage device such as a Bernoulli drive.
CD-ROM drive	Compact Disk-Read Only Memory; a high-capacity storage device that can store up to 600 MB of data; it does not permit user to save information, but only to read stored data; required by the MPC standard to have a transfer rate of at least 150 KB per second.
clock speed	Number of clock cycles per second at which information is sent through the computer's bus; measured in millions of clock cycles per second, or megahertz (MHz).
CPU	Central Processing Unit; the computer's electronic "brain" which controls the processing of the computer and allows it to perform instructions; sometimes called the microprocessor; the MPC standard requires at least a 386SX CPU.
DAC	Digital to Analog Converter; converts digital information to analog sound; standard feature on an MPC sound board.
EGA	Enhanced Graphics Adapter; graphics adapter capable of displaying 640 x 350 pixels with 16 colors (or gray scales).
expansion port	The opening in the back of the computer that corresponds to an expansion slot.

expansion slot   A connection in the computer into which various interface boards are plugged.

extended graphics   Graphics adapters with capabilities beyond Standard VGA; examples are 640 x 480 with 256 colors, 800 x 600, and 1024 x 768.

floppy disk drive   A magnetic storage device that allows you to save data on a floppy disk; most common sizes are 5.25 inch and 3.5 inch disks; the MPC standard requires a 3.5 inch floppy disk drive with 1.44 MB capacity.

graphics accelerator board   Special graphics board that controls not only resolution and the number of colors the computer can display, but speeds up the refresh rate for displaying graphic images.

graphics board   Hardware device that allows the computer to display graphic images; the type of graphics board (EGA, VGA, and Super VGA) determines the resolution of images; the MCA standard requires a Standard VGA graphics board capable of displaying 640 x 480 pixels on a screen and 16 colors.

graphics memory   Memory attached to a video graphics card that increases the display speed and the number of colors that can be displayed.

hard disk drive   A high-capacity magnetic storage device that allows you to save data; the MCA standard requires a minimum hard disk capacity of 30 MB.

headphones   Allows you to listen to sound via a connection to the CD-ROM drive or the sound board; required by the MPC standard.

joystick   Used to control object movements, especially in games; required by the MPC standard.

joystick port   Port to accommodate the joystick; generally part of the sound board and interchangeable with the MIDI port; required by the MPC standard.

memory	RAM or Random Access Memory; the electronic storage of the computer which is temporary; information stored in the computer's memory is lost when the computer is turned off; the MPC standard requires a minimum of 2 MB of memory.
microphone	Device used to input sound into the computer's sound board.
microprocessor	The electronic "brain" of the computer; see also CPU, or Central Processing Unit.
MIDI	Musical Instrument Digital Interface; an international standard developed for digital music; the MIDI standard determines the cabling and hardware and communications protocol needed to transfer information, or music, between electronic musical instruments or recording equipment and a computer. The MPC standard requires that the sound board have a MIDI in port, a MIDI out port, and a MIDI synthesizer.
modem	Hardware device that, along with special software and a phone line, permits your computer to communicate with another computer.
monitor	A device that displays computer output; must be compatible with the graphics board.
mono	Sound recorded on a single channel.
mouse	Device used to point to and select screen options; required by the MPC standard.
MPC standard	Multimedia PC standard; popular standard developed to ensure that a computer system has all the necessary capabilities to run multimedia software; developed by Microsoft Corporation in cooperation with various hardware manufacturers, this refers specifically to PCs running under Windows with multimedia capabilities, and also ensures that any separately sold hardware or software carrying the MPC logo will be compatible.

<u>Multimedia PC</u>	A computer meeting the MPC standard.
<u>multisync monitor</u>	A monitor that can display images using various graphics adapters such as EGA, VGA, and Super VGA.
<u>NTSC</u>	National Television Standards Committee; standard signal output by televisions in North America and Japan, and by many video cameras such as VCRs.
<u>OCR software</u>	Optical Character Recognition; software used in recognizing text input using a scanner.
<u>optical storage device</u>	Storage device that uses a laser beam to read information from the disk; a CD-ROM is an optical storage device.
<u>PAL</u>	Phase Alternate Line; standard signal output by televisions in most countries outside of North America and Japan.
<u>parallel port</u>	Port commonly used to connect a computer to a printer; required by the MPC standard.
<u>pen</u>	A useful device for inputting information, by touching either a screen or a special input pad.
<u>pixel</u>	Short for "picture element," which is a unit of measurement across a computer screen.
<u>public-domain software</u>	Software that may be used legally by the public without a fee having to be paid to the owner or developer.
<u>RAM</u>	Random Access Memory; another term for memory.
<u>refresh rate</u>	The speed at which graphic images are "painted" or displayed onto the screen.
<u>RGB</u>	Red, Green, and Blue; type of output used by some cameras.
<u>sampling rate</u>	Number of sound "samples" the sound board takes per second; measured in kilohertz (KHz); the MPC standard requires a sound board with a recording sampling rate of at least 11 KHz and an output rate of 11 and 22 KHz.

sampling size	Determines the range of sound adjustment; the MPC standard requires a sound board with a sampling size of at least 8 bit for both input and output.
scanner	A hardware device used to digitize photographs and drawings so that they may displayed on the computer; may be a large "flatbed" model or a small hand scanner.
SCSI interface	Small Computer System Interface; an interface that allows several hardware devices to be connected in a "daisy chain" configuration.
serial mouse	Type of mouse that connects to the computer using the serial port.
serial port	Port that connects the computer to a variety of hardware devices such as a modem, mouse, or serial printer; required by the MPC standard.
sound board	Hardware device that records and plays sound used in multimedia applications; the MPC standard requires a sound board with a MIDI in port, a MIDI out port, and a MIDI synthesizer.
speakers	Hardware used to amplify sound from the sound board or CD-ROM drive; required by the MPC standard.
standard keyboard	Original IBM 83-key keyboard with 10 function keys and no separate cursor movement keys.
Standard VGA	Standard Video Graphics Array; graphics adapter capable of displaying 640 x 480 pixels with 16 colors (or gray scales); required by the MPC standard.
stereo	Sound recorded on two channels.
storage	Refers to the means whereby information is saved when the computer is turned off; may mean magnetic disks (either floppy or hard) that allow you to add your own information

to them, or optical disks (such as CD-ROM) that don't permit you to write files to them.

Super VGA   Super Video Graphics Array; graphic adapter with a resolution of 800 x 600.

surge suppressor   A device that prevents electrical surges from damaging electrical equipment that is plugged into it.

system unit   The main body of the computer that contains most of the electronics (such as the CPU) and internal hardware.

touch screen   Device that allows user to input information by touching the screen.

transfer rate   The rate at which the CD-ROM drive can transfer located information to the computer; measured as kilobytes per second; the MPC standard requires a transfer rate of at least 150 KB per second.

VGA   Video Graphics Array; see Standard VGA and Super VGA.

video capture board   Hardware device that captures still graphic images, animation, or live motion video and saves this information in a file.

video monitor   Monitor that allows you to observe live video images as you are capturing them on the computer.

Chapter
4

Software Requirements

I n Chapter 2, I discussed various multimedia platforms, and pointed out that
this book focuses on two of these: a PC running under DOS and a PC running
under Windows. Keep in mind that software running under DOS requires
less memory but is not as graphically oriented as software running under Windows. Windows-based software requires more memory, better graphics capabilities,
and greater computer speed, and is very well adapted for multimedia. In addition,
programs running under Windows are multitasking, which is a very convenient
feature for developing multimedia programs, as you will see a little later.

In this chapter, we'll explore the various types of software you'll need, both for
running multimedia programs and for developing them. Remember that you'll
also need to be sure that the required hardware is compatible with the software
you use.

Software Needed to Run Multimedia

You really don't need much software to run multimedia programs. If you are running DOS-based programs, you simply need the required version of DOS. Many require version 2.0 or later, but some require a more recent version. Windows-based programs require both DOS and Windows of the specified versions.

If you plan to run multimedia under Windows using the MPC standard, you'll need (in addition to DOS) a version of Windows that has multimedia capabilities. This can be either Windows 3.0 with Multimedia Extensions (an add-on product available from Microsoft) or Windows 3.1 which has built-in multimedia capabilities. These extensions allow you to configure Windows for hardware devices required by the MPC standard, such as audio and video components and a joystick.

Software Needed to Develop Multimedia

If you plan to build your own multimedia programs, you'll want to consider a variety of software packages. In most cases, multimedia programs are actually computerized books or "on-line" manuals that are much more interactive than their paper counterparts. Because of this, software used to develop multimedia is generally referred to as "authoring" software.

Most authoring software allows you to incorporate all of the features of multimedia, namely text, graphics, animation, and sound. As with any other type of software, the various multimedia software packages have their strong (and weak) points, and you'll find that certain packages are better suited for some tasks than for others. For example, some authoring software has very flexible and powerful hypertext linking and text searching capabilities, but minimal animation features. This software is a better choice for computerizing very large text-oriented manuals that don't require animated files. Other software has very powerful graphics features and is best used for multimedia incorporating lots of pictures and animation files.

The function of authoring software or "tools" is to incorporate the various components of multimedia. This is a big task and authoring tools are typically quite large, requiring a lot of hard disk space. Most authoring software provides a way for you to create the various types of components for a multimedia program, such as text or graphics. But as pointed out earlier, the software may only do an adequate job for certain tasks. Because of this, most people who develop multimedia rely on a number of additional software packages to help them create or modify specific types of files before incorporating them in the multimedia program. This supporting software may be a painting package, a word processor, or animation software.

A supporting software package is devoted to a single type of task. For example, a painting package is used exclusively to create or modify graphic images. Because of this, it is capable of producing a much better graphic image file than you can create using an authoring tool with limited drawing capabilities. An analogous example is an "integrated" software package (such as Microsoft Works) that combines word processing, spreadsheet, and database capabilities in the same program. Integrated software performs all of these tasks quite adequately, but a package devoted entirely to word processing (such as WordPerfect or Microsoft Word) has much more powerful word processing capabilities than the integrated software's word processor. Similarly, authoring software integrates the capabilities necessary to create the various features of multimedia, but separate software that is devoted to one of these features can produce much better results.

At this point, you may be wondering why one needs to use authoring software. It is important to understand that one of the key features of authoring software is its ability to integrate all of these various forms of information into a single, coherent, and highly interactive package using interactive links or hypermedia. Another key feature is that the user does not need to be an experienced programmer to build such a program. Without authoring software, this task would be very difficult to achieve and would require the use of complex programming languages. Even though most authoring software provides a specialized programming or "scripting" language, this language is much easier for nonprogrammers to understand and learn. But with most authoring software, it is not even necessary to use this scripting language to build a simple multimedia program. In the second half of this book, we will build such a program using an authoring package called *Multimedia ToolBook.*

Let's examine more closely these two categories of software, namely, authoring and supporting software.

Authoring Software

There are several authoring packages available for the PC running under DOS and Windows that range in cost from about $300 to $8,000 or more. Tools costing around $500 or less include Multimedia ToolBook (the software used in this book), Microsoft Multimedia Development Kit, Plus, HyperWriter, HyperCASE, LinkWay, HSC Interactive, and AskMe 2000. Higher-end software includes IconAuthor (about $5,000) and AuthorWare Professional (about $8,000). The more expensive authoring tools generally provide a richer programming environment and support better animation. However, some very well known and impressive multimedia products have been created using lower-end packages. Software changes so rapidly that any detailed information regarding the capabilities of specific packages can become obsolete very quickly. Recent computer magazines and periodicals are good sources for up-to-date software comparisons and reviews.

When purchasing an authoring tool, there are certain features you should look for. The features you need will depend on the nature of your multimedia project. I will discuss the most important features in terms of the five main components of multimedia: text, graphics, animation, sound, and interactive links. I will also briefly discuss some other features such as the programming environment and runtime capabilities, speed, documentation, and technical support. Table 4.1 summarizes these features.

Table 4.1

Features of an authoring system that you should consider when making your purchase.

Text

Hypertext
Auto-hypertext
Text style
Text searching
Text importing/exporting

Graphics

Integrated drawing tools
Clip art
Graphics importing
Supported resolutions

Animation

Integrated animating tools
Animation clips
Animation file importing
Recording and playback capabilities
Transition effects

Sound

Fidelity
Sound clips
Sound file importing
Recording and playback capabilities

(table continued)

Interactive links

Navigational control
Bookmark feature
Automatic linking capabilities

Programming environment

Scripting language
Debuggers
Runtime system

Speed

Documentation

Working demo version

Technical support

Throughout my discussion, "authoring tool" or "authoring package" will refer to the software that a developer (such as you) uses to *build* a multimedia program, and "multimedia program" will refer to the resulting program that is *run* by the user.

Text

Text is the basic feature of any multimedia program. There are several capabilities involving text that you should understand when purchasing authoring software. The main ones discussed here are: hypertext, auto-hypertext, text style, text searching, and text importing and exporting.

hypertext

Much of the interactive linking in multimedia depends on the use of hypertext, often called "hotwords." This means that if the user wants more information about a particular word or phrase, she can select that word (usually with a mouse pointer) and open a window with additional text (or graphics or sound) explaining that word. An example of this was shown in Color Plates 1 and 2. You, as a developer, must be able to define the text that will act as hotwords and then link this text to additional information. Generally, hotwords are distinguished from other text displayed on the screen. It may be a different color or font, or the mouse pointer may change into a special symbol (such as the hand in Color Plate 1) when it is moved over the hotword. This makes it easier for the user to identify which words have associated links with more information. Otherwise, the user can waste a lot of time clicking on words that have no other associated information.

If you will be developing a multimedia program that is strongly text-oriented (such as a reference manual), be sure to select an authoring package with good hypertext capabilities.

auto-hypertext

Some authoring software has a feature called *auto-hypertext*. With this facility, the developer does not need to define or mark specific text that has associated links. Instead, the program recognizes text that has more information associated with it and automatically displays that information if the user has selected the text. In this case, the user can't distinguish which text might provide more information, and therefore this capability is not as convenient for the user. However, the developer can save a lot of time in building a program because the program automatically creates hypertext links.

text style

One of the key elements of an effective multimedia package is screen design, as will be discussed later in this book. For now, it is only important to understand that one of the important aspects of an effective screen display is the text style. This may involve text of various colors and sizes as well as the type of font used. Be sure to purchase an authoring package that provides a variety of type styles. Windows-based authoring tools generally offer a much greater diversity of text styles.

text searching

Text searching is a handy feature that allows the user to enter a word (or select it from a list) in a multimedia program and quickly find any information associated with that word. It is equivalent to searching for a word in a book's index, and then going to the indicated page or pages for more information. However, this process is much faster in a multimedia program. Some authoring tools provide much more flexible and powerful text searching capabilities than others.

text importing and exporting

Some of the text you want to incorporate into your multimedia program may already exist as a file created by a word processor, or you may want to import data saved in a database file. If the file is large, you won't want to reenter the information into the authoring package. Be sure your authoring package allows you to import text and database files from other sources. Many can import text from word processors such as WordPerfect or Microsoft Word, and from database files such as dBASE. Nearly all can read ASCII text files. ASCII stands for American Standard Code for Information Interchange and is a standard character format that allows various computers and programs to exchange character information. Similarly, you'll want to be sure you can easily export information from the multimedia program for use by other packages.

Graphics

Graphics is another basic feature of multimedia programs. The term "graphics" is used here to mean still images such as photographs and drawings. Keep in mind that Windows-based programs are, by nature, graphically oriented, and are preferable to DOS-based programs if you plan to incorporate lots of graphics in numerous overlapping windows. Some of the more important aspects of graphics discussed are: integrated drawing tools, clip art, graphics importing, and supported resolutions.

integrated drawing tools

Most authoring software has some capability for creating graphic images such as line drawings. These graphics are drawn using a mouse and various objects such as lines, circles, and polygons with various supporting colors. Generally, the resulting graphics are fairly simple but can be useful in programs not requiring more sophisticated images.

clip art

Clip art is a collection of simple graphic images or objects, such as an airplane, typewriter, flower, or telephone, that you can use in an application either as a still image or enhance for animation. Many authoring packages provide a library of clip art. This is especially helpful if you don't have a scanner or some other means of inputting graphics into your computer.

graphics importing

As I pointed out earlier in this chapter, really good graphic images will probably come from another source. For instance, you may want to scan a photograph and incorporate this image in your multimedia program. Because of this, you'll want to be sure that your authoring package can import graphic images in at least some standard formats. Common graphic formats include .PCX, .BMP, and .GIF.

supported resolutions

You can have a beautiful, high-resolution graphic image but it is worthless if your authoring software does not support its resolution. Some software cannot display a resolution greater than 640 x 480 pixels. Others cannot display more than 16 colors. Most, however, will support Standard VGA graphic images. If very high-quality images are important to your application, be sure that you purchase an authoring tool that can support high-resolution graphics with 256 colors. If you want to be certain your program can be run using a variety of graphics adapters, be sure the authoring tool supports several resolutions.

Animation

Animation simulates movement by displaying a series of individual frames or still images in rapid succession, similar to a movie film, and may be either *frame-based* or *cast-based*. Frame-based animation is created by designing each frame individually as it will appear in the final display. Cast-based animation involves the creation and control of individual objects (sometimes called *cast members* or *actors*) that move across a background. This is a common type of animation used with games and object-oriented software written for the Windows environment.

Animation generally involves some sort of "recording" and "playback" capabilities in the authoring software. Here are some of the animation features you should be aware of when purchasing authoring software: integrated animating tools, animation clips, animation file importing, recording and playback capabilities, and transition effects.

It should also be noted here that some, but certainly not all, authoring tools support full-motion video, such as that recorded using a VCR. This can give you some very high-quality moving picture displays.

integrated animating tools

Although most authoring tools support the use of animation, not all of them have a facility that permits you to create animation files. Some require that you create animation files using another software program or even a Macintosh computer! Clearly, this is not very practical and can add to the problems of compatibility. If you plan to incorporate animation into your application, you'll probably want an authoring tool that allows you to create animation from within the program. Even if you eventually use another package to produce better animation, an integrated animating tool will be quite helpful in teaching you the basic concepts of animation.

animation clips

Animation clips are literally animated clip art. Many authoring packages provide you with a library of animation clips that you can integrate into your application.

animation file importing

As with graphics files, you may find that you want to create higher quality animation than your authoring tool permits you to create. Because of this, be sure that your software can import animation files created in a separate animation package. Common formats include .FLI and .FLC. You may also want to import still graphic images so that you can build animation around them. If this is the case, make sure your authoring software can import graphic images with the needed formats. Also pay attention to the resolution and colors supported by the authoring software to be certain that it can display the resolution and colors of your animation files.

recording and playback capabilities

No matter what the source of your animation files, your authoring tool should allow you to control how the animation is recorded and displayed on the screen. Examples of the type of control you'll want to have include the playback speed (which will also be affected by the CPU and graphics support of the user's computer) and the direction of movement. You'll also want to have the capability to provide the end user with options to "pause" and "replay" the animation sequence.

transition effects

Animation can be even more interesting if it is enhanced with transition effects such as fade-in and fade-out, layering, zooming, and rotation of objects. Not all authoring packages provide all of these transition effects.

Sound

If you plan to incorporate narration, music, or other sound effects into your application, you'll want to be sure that your authoring package provides sound capabilities and control for both recording and playback. Some software lets you select the fidelity level by capturing sound using varying sampling size and sampling rate. If you are using narration or sound effects in which sound quality is not a priority, you needn't be too worried about the software's sound capabilities. However, good musical recordings require higher sampling size and rate. Some authoring software has a conversion utility that allows you to convert the sampling rate of sound files. Most sound files use the .WAV (for Windows sound), .MID (for MIDI files), .VOC, or .INS format, and often are linked to animation sequences. You'll probably want to give the user the option to pause and replay the sound playback. Another feature to look into is a library of sound clips which provides you with pre-made sound effects, music, and narration that you can use in your application.

Interactive links

As you'll recall from Chapter 1, interactive links provide the connections that allow the user to access more information. Under the text section on page 72, I discussed the role of hypertext in connecting text with additional information. Similar links can also connect graphics, animation, or sound. Interactive links, sometimes called *hyperlinks*, are probably the most important (and distinctive) feature of authoring software because they provide the interactive nature of multimedia. The term *navigation* refers to the user's chosen path as he progresses through a multimedia application.

Most authoring packages use a "bookmark" function which permits the user to return to the previous screen or even a starting point after jumping to associated information. Some provide automatic linking such as the auto-hypertext feature discussed in the text section above.

Some other considerations

The programming environment is the part of the authoring tool that allows the developer to use the software's scripting language to control the operation of the multimedia application. Most authoring tools permit you to build a simple multimedia program without entering any program commands, and initially you may not want to use the scripting language. But eventually, you will want to control some operations using the scripting language because it provides you with greater flexibility and power. Some authoring tools provide "debuggers" which help you find any errors you may have entered using the scripting language.

A "runtime system" is another useful feature. It allows the multimedia program you've created to run on other computers that do not have the full authoring system available. This is especially important if you plan to sell your multimedia program for others to use. If you need a runtime system, find out if it comes with the basic software, or if you have to pay extra for this feature.

Unfortunately, speed is one of those important aspects of a program that you can't determine until you purchase the product and develop an application. Only then do you know for sure how it will perform for your needs. However, magazine reviews that compare products nearly always consider speed and will rate the various packages based on performance.

Another feature that you should check out is documentation. Again, you often can't determine how poor or good the documentation is until you purchase the product and begin to use the accompanying manuals. This is one aspect that is often overlooked in magazine reviews. Some vendors have a 30-day return policy, allowing you to use the software and return it if you don't like it. This can really help if you run into a program with poor documentation.

Many software packages have a working demo version that is either free or available for a very low cost. This can really help you decide if a software package will work for you—but only if the working copy has all the features you need to check out for your application. Some companies charge for the demo version, but allow you to apply that cost toward a full working version when you decide to purchase it.

Finally, you'll want to be sure the product has good technical support. Reviews can often warn you about this. You should also investigate the cost for support. Many companies charge a yearly technical support fee, while others provide support for free. Another consideration is whether the technical support number is toll-free.

Supporting Software

You may find that your authoring tool does not have the capabilities to produce the type of graphics, animation, or sound required by your multimedia application. Or you may need some very specialized software to perform tasks not even possible with authoring software, such as optical character recognition (OCR, discussed on the next page). Most multimedia developers use a variety of additional software to produce files that they incorporate into a multimedia program. Here are some types of supporting software you should consider. A summary is provided in Table 4.2 on the next page.

Table 4.2

Supportive software useful for developing multimedia programs.

Software Type	Function
Word processor	Develops text.
Scanning	Scans graphic images or text.
OCR	Interprets scanned characters as text.
Screen capture	Captures images from computer screen.
Conversion	Converts graphics formats.
Painting/drawing	Creates and modifies graphic images.
"Clip" software	Provides simple graphics, animation, and sound clips.
Animation/sound	Creates animation and sound.
Communications	Downloads public-domain graphics software; exchange information with other users.

Word Processor

If you are entering large amounts of text, you may prefer to use a separate word processor because you are more familiar with its operations for editing and inputting text. Most word processors, such as WordPerfect, Microsoft Word, and Wordstar, allow you to save files in formats other than their own, including ASCII format. This should be an important consideration so that your authoring package can read the text file.

Scanning and OCR Software

Those who have access to a scanner may want to scan in pages of text or graphic images such as photographs and drawings to save them as digitized information. Most scanners come with their own scanning software, and so you probably won't need to purchase this separately. For example, the Hewlett-Packard Scanjet IIC comes with scanning software called Deskscan. If you scan text, you will require Optical Character Recognition (OCR) software, which is capable of interpreting the scanned characters as text instead of meaningless shapes. Examples of OCR software are OmniPage, Readright, Recognize, and Perceive. Better OCR software is more accurate and can read a greater variety of text styles. Most OCR software can save the text in a variety of standard text formats.

Screen Capture and Conversion Software

You may want to incorporate images from computer displays. This will require that you have screen capture software to capture these images. There are several packages available, such as Hijaak, SnapIt!, CollagePlus, and Conversion Artist; most allow you save the graphic images in a variety of graphic formats. These programs are also useful if you have a graphic image in a particular format that cannot be used by your authoring software because you can convert the images into other formats.

If you are using Windows, you can press the **Print Screen** key to save the displayed full-screen image on Windows' clipboard. You can then paste the contents of the clipboard into a graphics painting program where you can modify the image and save it in various graphic formats.

Painting or Drawing Software

Painting or drawing software allows you to draw graphic images from scratch (using a mouse and various "objects" such as lines, circles, and polygons). It also is very useful in modifying and enhancing graphic images produced using a scanner or screen capture software. For example, you may want to crop out certain features or add labels and arrows to an illustration. Windows has a built-in painting package called "Paintbrush" that may be adequate for your needs. However, more powerful painting software is available, such as Publisher's Paintbrush (which comes with the scanning software provided by Hewlett-Packard), CorelDRAW!, and Harvard Draw.

Art, Animation, and Sound Clip Software

Even if an authoring package provides libraries of clip art, animation, and sound, they may be too limited for your purposes. Several packages are available that provide thousands of simple clip art images, animation clips, or sound clips. Most clip art focuses on a specific theme such as the office or sports (examples are ClickArt, Presentation Task Force, and Picture Pak), whereas animation or sound clip packages (for instance, Tempra Show, DigiSound, and Sound Solution) usually contain a variety of themes.

Animation and Sound Software

Most low-end authoring software provides a way to create simple animation. However, much more powerful animation facilities are available in separate software packages, such as Autodesk Multimedia Explorer, AnimationClips, and Animation Works Interactive. These packages provide more powerful and flexible control over the animation such as movement and transition effects. Be sure that the format of the animation files is compatible with your authoring software. Common animation formats are .FLI and .FLC, but many animation packages use their own special format that can't be read by other packages. Some animation software gives you a choice of output formats.

Sound software allows you to create sound effects, such as narration or music. This requires some type of input device such as a microphone. Common file formats are .WAV (the Windows format), .VOC, and .INS. Windows with multimedia capabilities (either Windows 3.0 with Multimedia Extensions or Windows 3.1) has a built-in sound recorder, allowing you to input sound and save it as a .WAV file. Be sure your authoring software can read the file format of your sound files.

Communications Software

You may want to download public-domain graphics and software from various bulletin board services (or BBSs) such as CompuServe. CompuServe has a special multimedia forum that you access by entering "Go Multimedia." This is a good source for help and a wide spectrum of information dealing with multimedia. To access CompuServe or another BBS, you'll need a modem and special software, called *communications software*, that allows your computer to communicate with the BBS computer. Some of the better-known communications software includes ProComm, Crosstalk, and Carbon Copy.

Other Software with Multimedia Capabilities

Authoring software is not the only type of software used to develop programs with multimedia capabilities. There are many software packages that provide hypertext linking and permit you to display graphic images. This software is generally used for developing other types of interactive programs. For example, if you need to develop an application that provides some decision support, you need to build some rules into the program. Knowledge Pro is an expert system development tool useful for building decision support software that requires hypertext and multimedia capabilities. Visual Basic is another package that allows you to develop programs using the Basic language, and can display graphic images.

Presentation software is used to display information in the form of graphs, charts, and diagrams (usually for business meetings and oral presentations). This software has become increasingly multimedia-oriented. Many of these packages can now incorporate animation and sound. Examples are Harvard Graphics, Aldus Persuasion, and Freelance Graphics.

Finally, many of the standard application software packages, such as spreadsheets and databases, are now incorporating multimedia capabilities. Lotus 1-2-3 now has a multimedia-based Help facility, and several database packages allow you to store a photograph or graphic image as a database field. Because so many software packages now incorporate graphics, animation, and even sound, there is no longer a clear separation between multimedia authoring packages and a variety of other software used for tasks other than computerizing books.

Multitasking and Software Development

As you can see from the discussion of supporting software, you may find that you are using several software packages to develop your multimedia application. Remember that the DOS environment is single-tasking and permits you to use only one program at a time. Because of this, you can spend a lot of time calling up and exiting each software package. For example, let's say you have just scanned a photograph using your scanning software. Next you must save this image and exit from the scanning software in order to load your painting software so you can crop and label the image. Next you want to test your multimedia program by calling up the image you've just produced. So now, you'd have to exit from the painting package and call up your authoring program to run a test program. All of this switching from one program to the next is very time-consuming.

This is one of the reasons many developers prefer the Windows environment. Using Windows-based packages, you can initially load your authoring, painting, and scanning software into memory. Each software appears as a small icon on the bottom left side of your screen. By clicking on different icons, you can quickly switch from one program to another to do your various tasks.

Summary

In this chapter, you've learned what software you need to run and develop both DOS- and Windows-based multimedia programs. Although most authoring software provides capabilities to create text, graphics, animation, and sound, you may find that you need some additional supporting software when developing your own applications.

The following are the main points covered in this chapter:

- To run DOS-based multimedia, you will need the version of DOS specified by the software; Windows-based multimedia requires the appropriate Windows version.

- To run Windows-based multimedia using the MPC standard, you will need Windows with multimedia capabilities.

- To develop multimedia applications, you will probably want to use special "authoring software."

- Features to look for in authoring software include:

    - text capabilities (such as hypertext, auto-hypertext, text styles, full-text searching, and text importing/exporting)

    - graphics capabilities (such as graphics creation and importing, clip art, and high-resolution graphics support)

    - animation capabilities (such as animation creation and importing, animation clips, recording and playback control, and transition effects)

    - sound capabilities (such as sound clips, and selection of formats and fidelity)

    - interactive links (such as "bookmark" facility)

    - debugger

    - runtime system

    - speed

- documentation

        - technical support

- ■ Supporting software may be helpful in creating some components of your application. The following are the most commonly used:

        - word processor

        - scanning and OCR software

        - screen capture software

        - painting or drawing software

        - art, animation, and sound clip software

        - animation and sound software

        - communications software

- ■ Multimedia capabilities are being incorporated into a variety of software besides authoring software.

- ■ Multitasking capabilities are especially useful for facilitating the development of Windows-based multimedia programs.

Glossary

actor
An individual object that moves in an animation sequence; also called "cast member."

animation clip software
Software that provides a library of animation sequences that can be included in a multimedia application.

animation software
Permits user to create and control animation sequences and incorporate sound to accompany the animation.

ASCII
American Standard Code for Information Interchange; standard character format that allows various computers and programs to exchange character information.

authoring software	Specialized software used to develop computerized books and multimedia applications; uses interactive links to connect associated information.
auto-hypertext	An automatic hypertext facility; using auto-hypertext, the program recognizes text that has more information associated with it and automatically displays that information.
bookmark	A facility that permits the user to return to the previous screen or starting point after jumping to associated information.
cast-based animation	Animation that involves the creation and control of individual objects ("cast members" or "actors") that move across a background.
cast member	An individual object that moves in an animation sequence; also called "actor."
clip art	Software with a collection of simple graphic images that can be incorporated into other applications.
communications software	Software that allows a computer to communicate with another computer.
debugger	A facility that helps developers locate errors in a program, and may suggest how to correct these errors.
frame-based animation	Animation that is created by designing each frame individually as it will be displayed.
hotwords	Words that have associated information that is accessible to the user; sometimes called "hypertext."
integrated software	Software that integrates several types of applications, such as word processor, spreadsheet, and database.
navigation	A term that refers to the user's progress through a multimedia application.

<u>OCR software</u>	Optical Character Recognition; software used to interpret scanned characters as text information rather than as meaningless shapes.
<u>painting/drawing software</u>	Allows you to create and modify graphic images.
<u>presentation software</u>	Software used to present information in the form of graphs, charts, and diagrams.
<u>runtime system</u>	Feature that permits an application to be run on a computer without the complete program software used to develop the application.
<u>scanning software</u>	Software that allows the user to scan graphics or text and store them as digitized information.
<u>screen capture software</u>	Captures graphic images displayed on the computer screen and saves them as graphic image files.
<u>scripting language</u>	Programming language used by authoring software that controls the application.
<u>sound clip software</u>	Software that provides a library of sound effects and/or music that can be included in a multimedia application.
<u>supporting software</u>	Software that is used in addition to an authoring tool that provides more powerful capabilities to create certain types of files or performs some other function useful in developing an application.
<u>text searching</u>	Feature that allows user to search quickly for a word and access associated information.
<u>transition effects</u>	Special effects used in animation such as fade-in and fade-out, layering, and rotation of objects.

Building a Multimedia Computer System

I n the last three chapters, you've learned what hardware you'll need to be able to run the software you intend to use. You've also learned that the software you use depends on what type of multimedia you want to run. If you want to develop your own multimedia applications, you've also learned what software you might need to create the various components of your program. In this chapter, we'll use this knowledge to build a multimedia computer system.

Deciding Whether to Upgrade or Start from Scratch

One of the things you must decide is whether you can (or should) upgrade your existing microcomputer, or whether you'd be better off purchasing a new PC with multimedia capabilities. This decision depends on the system you intend to upgrade, and whether or not you want a computer that conforms to the MPC standard. Here are some of the main things you should consider when deciding whether or not you should upgrade.

Age of Your Computer

Current estimates indicate that the value of your computer drops by 40% each year you own it. So if your computer initially cost $3,000, after the first year it is worth only $1,800, and after the second year its value drops to about $1,100. After three years, it is essentially obsolete. You can upgrade the value of your computer by adding more hard disk space, better graphics, and more memory, but you may end up spending more on these upgrades than your computer is worth.

Cost to Upgrade

Some experts estimate that it should cost no more than 20 to 25% of the cost of a new PC to upgrade an old one. For example, if you can purchase a new PC with all the components you need for $3,000, it should not cost you more than $600 to $750 to add these same components to your old computer. If it does, you should seriously question the wisdom of upgrading.

What Hardware Needs to be Added

You must also consider what needs to be added to your system. Hard disk space is one of the most common upgrades, and for a good reason. Newer versions of software consume much more hard disk space than their older counterparts. For instance, Windows 2.0 used only about 1 MB of hard disk storage, while Windows 3.1 requires from 6 to 8 MB. Lotus version 1A needed less than 1 MB, whereas the newer Lotus 2.3 needs over 5 MB of storage. Obviously, hard disk space is the fastest growing need of computer systems, and older systems just don't have enough storage to accommodate new software. Fortunately, hard disk upgrades are feasible and not too expensive.

Memory is another commonly upgraded feature that can really improve the performance of an old system, and like hard disk storage, memory upgrades are easy and inexpensive.

Other components such as sound, graphics, and video boards and CD-ROM drives are also quite easy to add to an older PC. However, keep in mind that your PC may not have enough available expansion slots (explained in Chapter 3) to accommodate all the components you'd like to add. You should also be aware that some capabilities—such as sound and video—are combined on a single card. This can really help conserve slot space when you are adding several components. You should also check to see how many slots your computer has available. Some computer systems come with more slots than others, and if your computer does not offer enough extra slots to accept the various upgrades you plan to add, you'll probably need to purchase a new computer.

Another source of obsolescence in older systems is CPU speed. With all the power available in newer software packages, older computer systems are noticeably sluggish. And the CPU is not easily upgraded. If you have an 8088 or 8086 microprocessor, plan to purchase a new computer. If you have a 286, you can run most current DOS-based multimedia programs. If you require a faster computer, you might be able to upgrade to a 386 by purchasing a 386SX CPU replacement. However, these run around $500, and unless your other upgrade requirements are minimal, this is probably not the way to go. If you have a 386SX or 386 CPU, your other upgrades might be minor and therefore worthwhile.

Upgrading Your Existing System

If you have a computer with a 286 CPU, but only plan to use DOS-based multimedia programs, you may not need to do much to upgrade your system. You'll probably need some more hard disk space, and you might want to get a VGA board (and monitor) to better enjoy the graphics in multimedia programs. You might even want a sound board. You won't be out too much money to upgrade for these needs. But this will only be a temporary solution, because programs will only grow in size, eventually necessitating a CD-ROM drive, more memory, and a faster computer.

If you have a 386SX with 2 MB RAM, VGA graphics, and a 40 MB hard drive, it is feasible for you to upgrade your computer, even to the MPC standard. The simplest way to upgrade such a system is to purchase a multimedia upgrade kit, which consists of a sound board and CD-ROM drive, both of which meet the minimum MPC requirements. There are several available which cost anywhere from $650 to $1,900, depending on their quality.

> **Caution:** If you decide to upgrade your computer, you must also decide whether you will install your additional hardware components yourself, or if you will have a dealer install them. Although installing boards and other hardware is not difficult, you should only do this if you are familiar with (or want to learn about) the "insides" of your computer. Refer to *Welcome to Personal Computers* for more information on installing hardware.

Purchasing a New Computer

If you have decided that it is more feasible to purchase a new computer system, take heart—you'll be able to get a lot more for your money than you could a few years ago. The cost of computers is continually dropping and systems that cost $6,000 a few years ago can now be purchased for about $2,000, and they have greater capabilities, too. If you don't plan to buy a system that meets the MPC standard, at least be sure that you get the following to ensure that your computer will be useful for a couple of years:

- 386 or 486 CPU (don't get a 286!)
- VGA graphics or better
- hard drive with at least 80 MB of storage
- at least 4 MB of RAM
- 3.5 inch high-density floppy drive
- 5.25 inch high-density floppy drive
- parallel and serial ports

However, if you want to purchase a new computer that meets the MPC standard, you'll need to be sure your computer has all the hardware components listed in Table 3.1 on page 29 for the MPC standard. You're probably best off buying an MPC computer so that you don't have to put all of the individual components together yourself. Retail prices for MPC computers range from about $2,000 to $5,000 depending on the CPU, hard disk storage, memory, and brand of computer. Very low-end systems will be slower and will become obsolete sooner than more expensive systems, but they can provide an inexpensive way to get involved with Windows-based multimedia applications if your budget won't allow for a more expensive system. In Chapter 3, I pointed out that a computer that meets the minimum requirements for an MPC computer is not necessarily the ideal way to go. You should get more memory, better graphics, a bigger hard drive, and, if possible, a faster CPU. If you can afford it, you should purchase a 486 computer, because many experts believe that its usable life will be three to five years longer than a new 386 computer.

Installing Your Software and Hardware Drivers

Software is pretty easy to install these days. Usually, you just follow the instructions in the "Installation," "Getting Started," or some other similar section of the manual. Once you begin installation from DOS or Windows, just follow the directions displayed on the screen.

> **Caution:** I have one warning, however, and that involves upgrades to Windows. If you add a sound board, CD-ROM, or some other hardware device to your computer after installing Windows, you will need to modify the Windows drivers so that Windows recognizes these new hardware devices you've just added. A *driver* is simply a software program that tells your computer how to control or operate a hardware device. Changing your Windows drivers is not difficult to do, but if you don't do it, you won't be able to hear sound from your sound board or play any multimedia from your CD-ROM when using Windows.

Here are some step-by-step instructions to follow to get your new devices installed in Windows. The example below pertains specifically to installing a sound board:

1. First of all, be sure you are using Windows with multimedia capabilities. This means either Windows 3.0 with Multimedia Extensions or Windows 3.1 (with multimedia capabilities built in).

2. Next, call up Windows (by entering "win" at the DOS prompt).

3. Click on the Main programs icon.

4. Click on the Control Panel icon (see Figure 5.1).

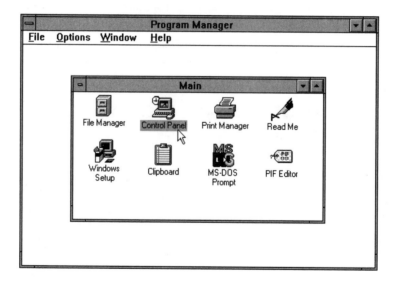

Figure 5.1

Control Panel icon.

5. Click on the Drivers icon (see Figure 5.2).

6. What you see displayed is a list of drivers that Windows automatically installed when you installed Windows (see Figure 5.3). You'll want to add another driver specific to your sound board.

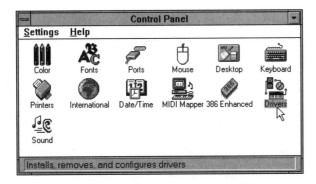

Figure 5.2

Drivers icon.

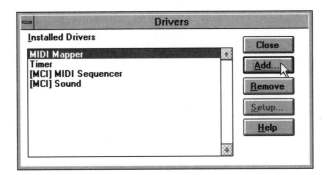

Figure 5.3

List of installed drivers. Click on "Add" to add a driver.

7. Click on the "Add" button (don't be confused that one of the installed drivers, such as MIDI Mapper, is highlighted when you click on "Add," since you will be selecting from another list of drivers).

8. Highlight the sound board you have (such as, Creative Labs Sound Blaster 1.5) and click on the OK button (see Figure 5.4 on the next page). (If your sound board is not listed, highlight "Unlisted or Updated Driver." When prompted by Windows, insert the disk from

your sound board manufacturer that contains the sound board's specific driver. When it appears in the list box, be sure it is highlighted and then click on the OK button.)

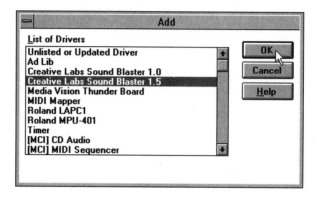

Figure 5.4

Select new driver (such as Sound Blaster 1.5).

9. After selecting your sound board, you will need to indicate the port address and the interrupt line (see Figure 5.5). You would have this information from the installation and testing of your sound board.

Figure 5.5

Indicate port address and interrupt line.

10. You'll now see your sound board driver listed along with the other installed drivers.

11. When you have added your driver(s), close Windows and restart so that your newly installed drivers are recognized by Windows.

Now when you run multimedia under Windows, you'll get the full effect of your sound board. In fact, when you start and exit Windows, you'll also hear some accompanying sound effects.

Summary

Deciding whether to upgrade an existing system or to purchase a new one is difficult, but this chapter provided some guidelines that should help you decide.

- In deciding whether to upgrade, you should consider:
  - the age of your computer
  - the cost to upgrade
  - what hardware needs to be added
- If you decide to upgrade, the hardware you'll need will depend on the type of multimedia you plan to run and develop.
- If you purchase a new computer without concern for the MPC standard, be sure you purchase one with certain components that will ensure its usefulness for several years.
- If you purchase a computer that meets the MPC standard, think about adding to its capabilities to increase its performance and to be sure it is useful for as long as possible.
- If you install new hardware devices and are using Windows, be sure to update the Windows device drivers so that Windows can recognize your new hardware.

Glossary

driver   A software program that tells the computer how to control or operate a hardware device.

Building a Multimedia Application

In Part I of this book, you learned what was needed to prepare your computer system to run and develop multimedia applications. In Part II, you will learn how to build a multimedia program of your own. We will start out with a discussion of some general guidelines for page design and general program structure. We'll also go over some basics about the authoring tool packaged with this book, Multimedia ToolBook. Finally, we'll develop text, graphics, animation, and sound, and link the information together into an interactive multimedia program.

Designing Your Application

Once you have the hardware and software you need, you're ready to start building a multimedia program (sometimes referred to as a "book"). In this chapter, you'll learn how to design your application—from the type of screen (or "page") layout you should plan to the text styles you might use. You'll also learn how to structure your interactive links so that they flow smoothly from one topic to the next.

A Warning About Copyrights: Although it is tempting to scan images or text from published works such as magazines and books, you will be violating copyright laws if you use this material in a final product unless you get permission to use it. The same is true of audio recordings such as music. This permission must come from the owner of the copyright—either the author (or artist, musician, photographer, etc.) or the publisher of the work. A good reference on this topic is *The Multimedia Producer's Legal Survival Guide*, written by Stephen Ian McIntosh. This gives valuable information on what constitutes copyright infringement and how to avoid it.

Design Considerations

Professional multimedia developers often have a team of specialists with different areas of expertise who work together to produce a final product. These specialists might include an artist, a media expert, a program designer, a project manager, and an expert in the topic that is the focus of the application. As you build your own application, you will play the role of all of these specialists because you will design your own graphics, decide on the structure of the program, manage the project, and provide the information that is at the heart of the application. The chapters that follow will guide you through the procedures for building a simple application. But when you build an application on your own, you should focus on a topic that is interesting or familiar to you because you will likely have some expertise in that area.

Although there are many considerations that a professional developer is concerned with, such as market analysis, production teams, and end-user input devices and control, we will focus our attention on the actual design of the application itself. The following are some guidelines that will help you when you develop your own application.

Topic of Your Application

Obviously, before you start, you must decide on a topic that would be appropriate for a multimedia application. The types of projects that benefit most from multimedia are those involving different types of information (such as text and illustrations) that the user can access many different ways. Perhaps you'd like to develop a travel guide or logbook with pictures and narration about particular sites. Maybe you'd like to develop a training program for work that would help others learn about company policies or manufacturing techniques. Or you might consider an educational program to teach someone how to play a sport such as tennis or golf. Perhaps you want to computerize some children's stories to include drawings and narration. The possibilities are endless.

Type of Presentation

Once you have decided on the purpose of the application you want to develop, you next need to decide on the type of presentation it should have. What multimedia components will you include? Will it include graphic images? Will there be any animation? What about sound—will you include narration, music, or sound effects such as crickets or crashing waves? One thing you don't want to do is "force" some feature into the application if that feature serves no useful purpose. Suppose you are a musician and you are creating a log to keep track of your musical recordings. You will find that including sound is useful but there may be no use in having animation. If this is the case, don't include animation just to have it in your program.

You should also give some thought to the look of the program you want to develop. Will it be colorful and have a freehand or cartoon look? This is a good choice for children's stories or entertainment such as games. If you plan to use the program for business presentations or training for work, you probably want it to look more professional and subdued (both in color and style).

Gathering Your Material

Once you decide on the type of presentation and the components to be included, you'll want to gather and organize your materials. Part of your task will be deciding where your resources will come from. If you don't have your own material (such as photographs or music), you will either have to create it or acquire it elsewhere. Some public-domain material may be downloaded from CompuServe, and this may provide you with some resources. As noted earlier in this chapter, if you want material from a published source, be sure you get the necessary permission to use it.

Maximizing the Impact of Your Application

The impact your application has on the user will be determined by many things, including its overall screen design, the type of text you use, and the way you present other information such as graphics, animation, and sound.

Screen Design

There are several important aspects of screen design or "page layout." One is to be sure that your screens are not cluttered with too much information. Because multimedia provides a unique opportunity to pack lots of different types of information onto a single screen (especially in Windows), it is sometimes tempting to overdo it. You can easily present so much information that it overwhelms the user. The unfortunate result is that the user may not pay attention to all the material presented and could ignore some essential information that you wanted to get across. A good guideline is to present no more than three windows of information on each screen. This will also ensure that your screens display at a reasonable speed. The more information there is on a screen, the longer it takes for the computer to display that screen. And, above all, don't display too much text at one time (such as a full screen of text) because chances are good that the user won't read it.

When designing your screens, be sure that they are balanced. This doesn't necessarily mean that the screens need to be completely symmetrical (as in Figure 6.1a). In fact, having too many symmetrical screens can be monotonous. You can still have a balanced screen but achieve a more interesting look by varying the display windows (see Figure 6.1b). The full version of Multimedia ToolBook provides several samples of page layouts that you can use for your application.

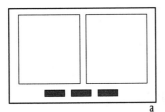 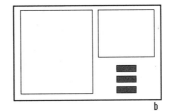

Figure 6.1

Screen displays with a balanced layout.

Another rule is to be consistent. If you put the control buttons in the bottom right of the screen at the beginning of the program, don't switch their position to the upper left later on, or the user will become confused and frustrated. Keep the buttons in the same place as much as possible, and close to each other. Wide separations between buttons require that the user move the mouse pointer greater distances, which can be annoying.

Text Style

Text style is an important feature of your screen displays because it can substantially affect readability and draw attention to certain information. Size is not the only consideration here. Different type styles, such as Helvetica, are easier to read than others, such as Roman (see Figure 6.2 on the next page), especially on a computer screen. However, type styles that are easy to read lack some of the "character" that fancier styles convey, and if your application warrants stylish text, then use it—but only if it is clearly legible on the computer screen.

You can generally control other characteristics of text. Bold and italics are useful in emphasizing certain words or phrases, as are colors. Hotwords (or hypertext) usually have a different "look" to distinguish them from words with no associated information. Again, you are cautioned to be consistent with your text. If you use bold to indicate hotwords, don't use it to also indicate something else, or the user will futilely click on bold words that are not linked to other information.

Helvetica

Times Roman

Goudy

Figure 6.2

Different fonts and type sizes.

Line Intensity

Be careful with your use of lines. Lines should be used to surround information that belongs together and to separate different types of information. Be sure your lines aren't too thick. Figure 6.3a illustrates how thick, heavy lines can distract the user from the main body of information. Figure 6.3b is much more readable.

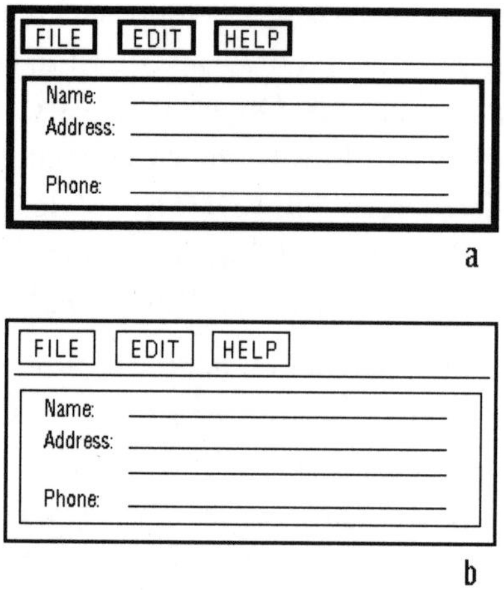

FILE	EDIT	HELP

Name:
Address:

Phone:

a

FILE	EDIT	HELP

Name:
Address:

Phone:

b

Figure 6.3

(a) Thick lines distract the eye from the main body of text, whereas (b) thin lines help to surround related information but are not distracting.

Color

In general, you want to use subdued colors such as pastels. Very bright colors can be difficult to read. Be especially careful with using colored text on a colored background. Contrasting colors such as red text on a green background are particularly difficult to look at (and read from). Select a subdued background color first and then choose foreground colors to complement the background.

Many times, it is advisable to use different intensities of the same color (such as light blue and dark blue) to accent the screen, rather than using lots of different colors (such as blue and yellow).

When using colors, be consistent with their meaning. If your background window is blue, and special information is provided in a green window, and warnings in a red window, use these same color schemes for the same functions throughout the program.

Graphics and Animation

If you plan to use graphics in your application, be sure that any illustration shows clearly what you are trying to convey. Keep line drawings as simple as possible so that the user does not get confused. Be sure to use labels where appropriate. If you plan to draw your illustrations using the computer, it will help if you have made sketches beforehand.

In general, graphics are more impressive if they are in color and have as high a resolution as possible. Photographs can make a big impact, especially if they are close-ups. Animation is most effective when it illustrates a movement that is difficult to describe in words or with a still image.

> **Caution:** Be aware that the larger the graphic image, the more time it will take to "paint" that image onto the screen. This is particularly true of animations that involve the rapid display of many images. If you can keep your illustrations small, your program will run faster, and your files will be smaller in size.

Sound

Sound effects and narration can add real impact to your application if used effectively. For example, sound effects are highly effective when they convey a noise that is difficult to describe. Music or bird calls are good examples. Sound can also have an impact if it logically enhances visual images. For instance, you might play a recording of waves crashing while illustrating an animated wave or a photo of the seashore.

Narration can enhance our understanding of an animated sequence by informing the user of what she is seeing in the animation. If you narrate some information, be sure that you are conversational and lively. Dull narration isn't any more interesting in multimedia than it is elsewhere. Be sure that the tone of your narration matches the topic of your application. Children's stories require more characterization with your voice than an educational program, and travel logs should sound as if you are enjoying yourself. Think about the tone you want to convey.

Keep your narrations short. Try to convey the essence of the information using as few words as possible. Think of narrations in terms of discrete units of information. Remember, long narration is not only boring, it also uses up more disk space.

Planning the Structure of Your Application

Before you actually begin building your program, you must first outline the structure of the program. Although the user will be able to jump around in a way that you (as the developer) can't predict, you still need to have a basic structure and flow.

One of the best ways to develop a structure is to generate a *storyboard*. A storyboard is a visual outline (with rough sketches, notes, and instructions) of the actions, sounds, and images that will appear or occur during the program. This will also help as you plan your screen displays. Figure 6.4 illustrates a page of a simple storyboard used to create the multimedia program displayed in Color Plates 1 and 2. The first sketch illustrates the opening page with its title, table of contents, and a drawing to add interest. An arrow connects the "Service" button to the next sketch, illustrating the page that will be displayed if the user

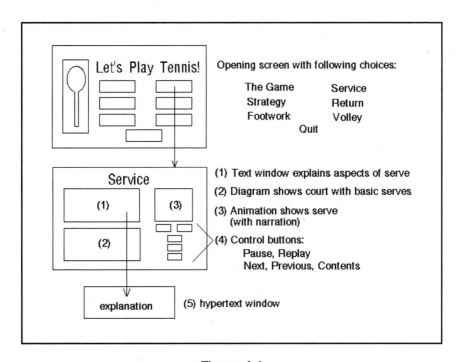

Figure 6.4

*Example of a small storyboard to plan two screens of the multimedia
program displayed in Color Plates 1 and 2.*

makes this selection. Short descriptions summarize the various components
making up the "Service" screen. Arrows from the text window indicate explanatory
windows that will be linked to hypertext.

You should also structure your program so that it has a table of contents or a
starting point. The contents should be easily accessible to the user from
anywhere in the program so that there is some reference point for orientation,
and to facilitate quickly jumping to another topic. An index of terms is also useful
so that the user can quickly look up a piece of information.

You must also structure the way that you will allow the user to navigate
through the program. To initiate certain actions, the user usually clicks on a
hotword, or a command "button" which is a screen object with a label (either a

word or an icon) indicating the resulting action. Buttons that are commonly used (see Figure 6.5) include:

- "Next" (or right-pointing arrow), which jumps the user to the next page.
- "Previous" (or left-pointing arrow), which jumps the user back to the previous page.
- Buttons that take the user to the last page or first page.

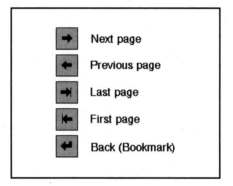

Figure 6.5

Buttons commonly used to navigate
through a ToolBook package.

- A "Bookmark" button (with various icons such as a curved arrow), which jumps the user back to the screen displayed just before the present one.
- A "Contents" button, which takes the user to the table of contents (or beginning of the program).
- A "Map" button (with various icons such as a compass), which displays a map of the program's organization.
- "Pause," which allows the user to stop action on an animation or sound.
- "Replay," which allows the user to replay an animation or sound.
- "Quit," which exits the program.

Two other things are of utmost importance when structuring your application: *be consistent* and *be intuitive*! Consistency means, for example, that page layouts are similar to each other, buttons with the same word or icon *always* mean the same thing, and all windows of information close the same way. If you are not consistent, the user will be confused and literally get lost in the application.

Intuitive means that you, as the developer, perceive beforehand how the user will interpret something presented to him. For instance, because we read books by turning the next page (which is to the right of the current page), a right-pointing arrow is an intuitive way to indicate to the user that this will turn the page, or "go forward" with the program. Similarly, a left-pointing arrow indicates "go back" or turn the page from the left. Some applications use an icon of a house on a button to indicate "home," or the beginning of the program. Intuitive controls usually involve some type of mnemonic that triggers some association of a word or icon with an action.

Being careful to use consistent and intuitive controls allows you to streamline the screen design because you don't need to clutter the screen with unnecessary explanations of what various buttons do.

Summary

This chapter has provided you with several guidelines that will help you design your application. Some of the most important points discussed include:

- Be careful about copyright infringements. Get permission if you plan to use any published material.

- The topic of your application will determine the type of presentation the application should have.

- When designing your screens, do not display too much information at any one time. Keep screen displays simple and balanced.

- Take advantage of different text styles and sizes to emphasize certain information.

- Keep colors, text styles, and button positions consistent on the screen.

- Don't use lines that are too thick because they will distract the user from the main body of information.

- Line drawings should be simple and clearly indicate what you mean to convey.

- Graphics are most impressive if they are high-resolution photographs using lots of colors.

- Narration should be short and have a tone appropriate to the type of application it is used with.

- When you structure your application, develop sample screens or a storyboard to help visualize the screen displays.

- Use a table of contents and an index to help the user find information more quickly.

- Navigational control is an important aspect of the program's structure. The user controls navigation by clicking on hotwords or command buttons.

■ It is important to be consistent and intuitive when structuring your program so the user does not get confused.

Glossary

<u>book</u>	Another name for a multimedia program that focuses on computerizing a book.
<u>page</u>	Another term for an individual screen display.
<u>page layout</u>	A term that refers to the layout of the screen in a computerized book.
<u>storyboard</u>	A visual outline (with simple sketches, notes, and instructions) of the actions, sounds, and images that will appear or occur during the course of a multimedia program.

Chapter

7

An Overview of Multimedia ToolBook

I n this chapter, we'll take our first look at Multimedia ToolBook, the authoring package we'll use to build a simple multimedia application. You'll learn what hardware and software you'll need in order to use Multimedia ToolBook, some basic terminology, and an overview of what is on the enclosed disks. And we'll go through some simple exercises to get you acquainted with some of the operations we'll use when we build our application. You'll find that there is a lot more on the enclosed disks than we'll use to build our application for this book. We'll do a little exploring in this chapter to introduce you to some of the other possibilities available using Multimedia ToolBook.

What is Multimedia ToolBook?

Multimedia ToolBook is an authoring package used to develop Windows-based multimedia software, or "computerized books." Some well-known applications have been developed using Multimedia ToolBook, including Beethoven's Ninth Symphony (by Voyager) and Hyperglot's Spanish Lessons. An "Evaluation Edition" of Multimedia ToolBook has been enclosed with this book to help you build your own applications. This version is a full working copy of the complete software package with one main limitation—it allows you to work on any single "book" (at "author" level, to be explained in more detail later) for a maximum of 6 hours. You can work on many different books—but you can only work on each book at author level for 6 hours. So if you are working on four books, you can spend 6 hours per book (or 24 hours total). That's actually a lot of time, because you can learn using several books, and then apply what you know to another, more complete book. If you decide to purchase the full version of Multimedia ToolBook, there is also a coupon enclosed that will give you a discount toward your purchase. Any books you develop using the Evaluation Edition can be used with the full version of the software without any changes. The full version also provides you with additional useful applications such as a daily calendar and personal information manager, a larger clip art library, additional animated objects to use in your applications, and full documentation.

Requirements for Using Multimedia ToolBook

Multimedia ToolBook is an MPC software package. That means that it is compatible with the MPC standard. To take full advantage of all of its capabilities (and to build all the components of the application in this book), you'll need to have certain hardware and software as follows:

- DOS version 3.1 or higher
- Windows with multimedia capabilities (either Windows 3.0 with Multimedia Extensions or Windows 3.1)

- a 386SX 16 MHz computer or better

- a minimum of 2 MB RAM (at least 3 MB is recommended)

- VGA graphics (Super VGA is recommended)

- a sound board and microphone (optional)

- a hard drive with at least 4 MB of available storage to install the basic ToolBook programs; 8 MB is required to install all the additional sample applications (which is recommended)

- a 3.5 inch high-density floppy drive

- a Windows-compatible mouse or pointing device

Although you don't need a sound board (or microphone) to use Multimedia ToolBook, you'll certainly get more out of the sample applications if your computer has sound capabilities. Music, sound effects, and sample narrations are interspersed throughout and give you a better idea of the sound you can add to your applications. Also, you'll be able to create all of the components of the sample application that we'll be developing in the chapters that follow.

Before You Install Multimedia ToolBook

Before you attempt to install the enclosed software, you should be sure that:

- You have properly installed Windows 3.0 (with Multimedia Extensions) or Windows 3.1.

- You have installed your Windows device drivers (as described in Chapter 5) for sound, and a CD-ROM drive if you have one.

- There are no other versions of ToolBook on your computer; if there are, be sure that the version supplied here is the only one specified in the PATH command of your AUTOEXEC.BAT file.

Installing Multimedia ToolBook

In order to install the Multimedia ToolBook Evaluation Edition properly, you must follow certain instructions because the files provided on the enclosed disks are compressed. Only proper installation will uncompress these files and allow Multimedia ToolBook to function correctly.

To install Multimedia ToolBook, you must first install Windows. Once you have installed Windows, do the following:

- Insert the Multimedia ToolBook Setup Disk 1 into your disk drive (probably the B: drive for 3.5 inch disks).

- From Windows Program Manager, select File, Run, and type **b:setup** in the command line (assuming the setup disk is in the B: drive) and press the **Enter** key, or click on the OK button.

- Follow the instructions displayed on the screen.

- After you have successfully installed Multimedia ToolBook, you should reboot your computer so that the new path command takes effect.

Starting, Using, and Quitting ToolBook

To call up Multimedia ToolBook (referred to as simply "ToolBook" throughout the rest of this book), type **win** at the DOS prompt. This will bring up Windows Program Manager. If the "Multimedia ToolBook Eval" window is not already open (see Figure 7.1), double-click on its icon in the Program Manager window. There are several ToolBook icons that are displayed in the Multimedia ToolBook Eval window, most of which open up tutorials explaining how to use ToolBook. The last icon that is labeled simply "ToolBook" is the actual program you will use to build your applications. To start any of these programs, point to the appropriate icon and double-click your left mouse button.

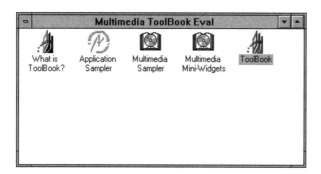

Figure 7.1

Opening window of Multimedia Toolbook Evaluation Edition.

There are several ways to use your mouse buttons. Unless otherwise indicated, you should always use the left mouse button. Throughout this book, a "click" will mean a quick single press and release of the mouse button. A "double-click" will mean two clicks in rapid succession. In some cases, you can move objects around on the screen by pointing to them with the mouse pointer, and moving the mouse while holding down the mouse button, thus moving an object to a new position. This operation is usually referred to as *dragging*.

Most of the applications have very clear instructions that guide you through them. However, you should be aware that the various screen buttons that help you navigate may look slightly different, depending on whether they are operational or not. Figure 7.2a on the next page illustrates three buttons, but only the right-arrow button (meaning "next page") is operational (its label is black). The other buttons are "dimmed," indicating that clicking on these will not produce any action. The illustration shows an example in which the table of contents page is displayed (which is also the first page of the book). Therefore, clicking on the table of contents or left-arrow (for "previous page") buttons will not take you anywhere else in the book. Once you go to another page (unless it is the last page of the book), all three buttons are active (and have black labels; see Figure 7.2b on the next page), meaning that each one will cause some action to take place.

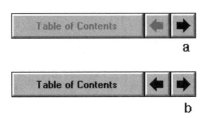

Figure 7.2

Dimmed buttons in (a) cannot be activated.
All buttons in (b) can be activated.

Figure 7.3a illustrates some of the basic features of a window that will be referred to throughout the chapters that follow. The control-menu box allows you to control the window itself, that is, close it, resize it, or move it. By double-clicking on the control-menu box, you can close the window (and exit ToolBook, if this is the window that is open). The title bar contains the title of the software you are using, and the title of the file that is open (if any). As will be explained a little later, the title bar can also be used to move a window to a new position. The menu bar contains a set of commands that helps you develop or use a program. The tool palette illustrated in Figure 7.3a is unique to ToolBook and is used to create objects on the screen. This will be explained in more detail later in this chapter.

control-menu box   title bar

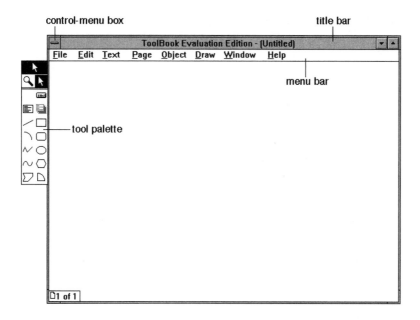

menu bar

tool palette

Figure 7.3a

*Opening window of ToolBook shown at author level. Various parts
of the window are illustrated.*

To quit any of the programs, you may click on an "exit" or "quit" button, if
available on the screen. You may also click on the File option in the menu bar
(see Figure 7.3b on the next page), and then click on Exit. Or, as mentioned
above, you may simply double-click on the control-menu box of the main display
window. This will close only the current window. If you have any other
ToolBook windows open, this operation will not close all of them. To exit from
Windows, just double-click on the control-menu box of the Program Manager
window.

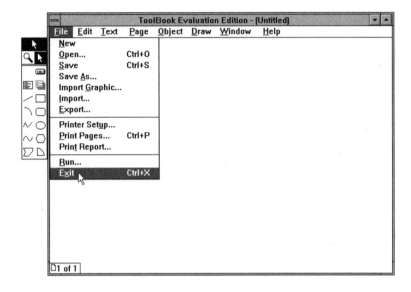

Figure 7.3b

Illustration of alternative procedure for exiting ToolBook.

Many other Windows-related operations are possible. You should consult your Windows manual to get an overview of general Windows usage. This book assumes that you are somewhat familiar with Windows.

ToolBook's Application Sampler

All of the ToolBook tutorials displayed as icons in the main Multimedia ToolBook Eval window are accessible through the "Application Sampler" icon (refer to Figure 7.1 on page 119). The Application Sampler program also provides you with many other sample programs that will help you understand how ToolBook can be used. Let's start the Application Sampler (by double-clicking on its icon), and then click on the button labeled "Using this book." This will explain the general structure of the Application Sampler book, and how to navigate your way through it. Next, click on the button labeled "Table of Contents" to see the Application Sampler's main window (see Figure 7.4).

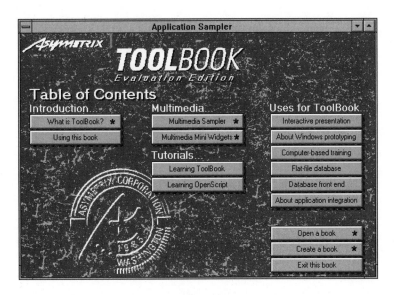

Figure 7.4

The Application Sampler's Table of Contents.

The table of contents displays a number of options for you to choose from. I have placed an asterisk (*) next to those options in Figure 7.4 that are also directly accessible from the Multimedia ToolBook Eval window by clicking on an icon with the same name (see Figure 7.1). The only icon having a different name is the "ToolBook" icon which corresponds to the options "Open a book" or "Create a book" in the Application Sampler's Table of Contents.

On the following page is a brief discussion of the choices displayed in the table of contents of ToolBook's Application Sampler. Before building your application, you should take some time to go through the various programs to better understand ToolBook. Many programs contain hypertext, which shows up as words with a surrounding box. By clicking on one of these boxes, you may bring up more information about that topic.

> **Note:** You can spend as much time in any of the tutorials and example programs as you like. This time will *not* be subtracted from your 6-hour time limit to create an application. However, you will be timed if you are creating or modifying your own book. Remember that you do this by selecting either "Create a book" or "Open a book" from the Application Sampler's Table of Contents, or by accessing your book through the "ToolBook" icon in the Multimedia ToolBook Eval window. When we create and modify the sample application for this book, we will be using some of the time allotted in the Evaluation Edition.

What is ToolBook?

This provides an overview of ToolBook, including how it can be used, some basic concepts, creating graphics, demonstrations of animation, and interfacing with other programs.

Using This Book

This explains how to use the Application Sampler book.

Multimedia Sampler

When you first open the Multimedia Sampler, you'll hear some music (if you have a sound board), and throughout, there are demonstrations of animation and sound. A map of the complete book is accessible from every page of the book.

Multimedia Mini Widgets

This book provides objects (or "widgets") that you can copy into your applications, such as buttons and controls for sound clips (see Figure 7.5a), and "sliders" (see Figure 7.5b) which can be used to control the playback of multimedia elements such as sound and animation. When you paste these objects onto your application, any scripts (or commands) associated with them are also pasted into your application. This can save a lot of time and is a good way to learn ToolBook's programming language, called OpenScript.

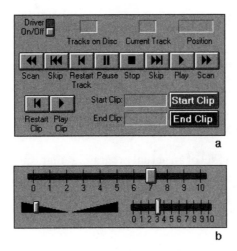

Figure 7.5

Sample "widgets" for controlling multimedia components such as sound and animation.

Learning ToolBook

This provides step-by-step instructions for building an address book that uses a *flat-file database*. A flat-file database is a simple database that is not associated with other database files. Flat-files are adequate for many database applications, such as address books and catalogs. This is a good tutorial to introduce you to such concepts as "background," "foreground," "page," "book," "author level," and "reader level." I will discuss these concepts a little later in this chapter.

Learning OpenScript

OpenScript is the programming or scripting language used by ToolBook. This tutorial is meant for those who want to go beyond simple application development and get into the actual scripting that controls certain operations. For our sample application, you will be exposed a little to OpenScript.

Interactive Presentation

This is an actual ToolBook application that helps you build interactive presentations. To get more information, click on "Help" in the menu bar displayed in this application.

About Windows Prototyping

A *prototype* is a model of an actual program. It may only illustrate sample screens that would be displayed when the program is run, and is a good way to build a mock-up of an application. This program shows you how to quickly build prototypes of Windows programs using ToolBook.

Computer-based Training

This small program shows an example of computer-based training using a manual for earthquake safety. It also demonstrates the use of hypertext (or hotwords), and other "hot objects" such as hypergraphics.

Flat-file Database

As you recall from the previous page, a flat-file database is a simple database file that is not associated with any other database files. The example provided here is a software catalog that allows you to keep an inventory of your software. With a few simple modifications, you could change this application to be a catalog of anything else you want to inventory, such as musical CDs or books.

Database Front End

This example shows how you can build a simple screen display around data stored in a dBASE file and provide your own graphical display complete with buttons and other screen objects.

About Application Integration

This demonstrates how you can integrate any ToolBook application with other Windows software such as Microsoft Word or Excel using special Windows features such as Dynamic Data Exchange (or DDE), which allows you to exchange data quickly and easily among various Windows programs, and Dynamic Link Libraries (or DLL), which can be used to control other Windows applications from within a single Windows program.

Open a Book and Create a Book

These options permit you to work on your own application. You first "create" your book and then "open" it for any changes or additions you want to make to it. You can also create and open your book through the "ToolBook" icon in the Multimedia ToolBook Eval window. You can also open any other ToolBook application and modify it for your own use (although you are cautioned about doing this until you are more familiar with ToolBook). For example, you might want to open up the software catalog book (which has a file name of "catalog.tbk") and make a few simple changes so you can use it to inventory your musical CDs. If you save your modified version under a new name, the original will remain available for other changes you might want to make later. In addition, once you are in ToolBook, you can run any of the ToolBook programs discussed by selecting "Run" from the File menu option.

Before we go on, let's exit from the Application Sampler by clicking on the button labeled "Exit this book" in the lower right-hand corner of the table of contents page. This will take you back to the Multimedia ToolBook Eval window.

Some Basic Concepts and Terminology

Now that you've taken a look at some ToolBook applications, it might be easier for you to understand some basic concepts and terminology that will be important as we begin to build an application.

We refer to any "thing" displayed on the screen as an "object." This includes the buttons to control actions, the fields in which you enter or display information, and graphic images. Figure 7.6 shows some common objects that are included in screen displays. We refer to any software that uses such objects as being *object-oriented software*. In addition, the user can control program actions or "events" by clicking on menu items, objects, or hypertext. This is the reason we refer to such interactive software as being *event-driven software*. When you create your own application, you will be using objects and events to control what the program does when certain objects are activated.

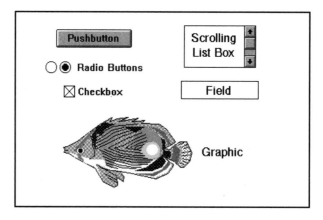

Figure 7.6

Common objects included in screen displays.

In the various ToolBook applications discussed, you were exposed to individual *books*. A book is another name for a ToolBook program or application, and each is stored as a separate file on your computer. By convention, each ToolBook file name has a file extension of .tbk.

Each book is made up of *pages*. If you simply went through any of the ToolBook examples by clicking the right-arrow button, you paged through the book sequentially, as you might read a paper book. However, if you clicked on any hotwords or buttons for more information, you skipped to pages out of order and were reading the book more interactively. This spontaneous interaction is the real advantage to multimedia software.

The various pages in a book that share common screen objects, such as the same control buttons and page layout, are using the same template or *background* (see Figure 7.7). On top of this background, you may create several pages that each have a slightly different layout or *foreground*. Note that all of the six pages illustrated in Figure 7.7 share the same background objects (such as a title and a command button which are always in the same place), but each foreground differs slightly in its layout. A page, then, is made up of a background and a foreground. A book may have several backgrounds, and the pages that follow those backgrounds all share the objects and properties of those backgrounds.

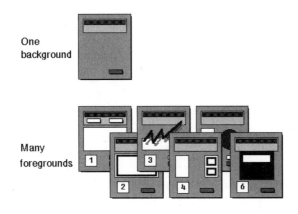

Figure 7.7

Illustration of a background shared by many foregrounds.

Each object you create is placed on its own *layer*, and the layers together form either a foreground or a background. The layers are numbered in relation to the order in which they were created. For instance, the first object you create has a layer number of "1," the second one a layer number of "2," and so on. In Figure 7.8 on the next page, you see that a single background may be composed of many layers, each with its own object. In the example shown, there are four layers of objects that together form the complete background.

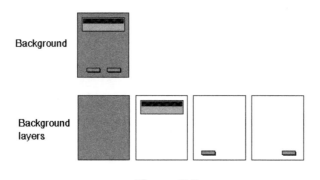

Background

Background
layers

Figure 7.8

*Illustration of the various layers (each with its own object)
making up a background.*

ToolBook allows you to interact with a book in one of two ways—either as a
reader (in which you simply read the book or add datalike information to the
book) or as an author (in which you create or modify the structure of the book).
These two levels of interaction are appropriately named *reader level* and *author
level*. The author level has many more commands available than the reader level,
and displays the screen shown in Figure 7.3a. Note the *tool palette* that is displayed
at author level. This allows you to create screen objects such as buttons, fields,
and graphics. When you are at reader level, the tool palette is not displayed, nor
are many of the author-level commands in the menu bar. To switch to reader
level, simply press the **F3** key, and the tool palette will disappear. You can test
your application at the reader level to see how it will run for the user. Pressing
the **F3** key again will return you to the author level.

There are two major types of books you could create using ToolBook. One is
a book made up of pages of data or information entered by the user, such as the
address book you learn to develop in the "Learning ToolBook" tutorial, or the
software catalog that is provided as an example of a flat-file database. The other
type of book is one in which the developer provides all of the information, and
the user reads through this book, interacting only to the extent of flipping to
various pages in the book. The application you will develop in the chapters that
follow is an example of this latter type of book. Obviously, these represent two

extremes of the types of books you can develop; you could just as easily develop a book that is a combination of the two.

Some Simple Exercises in ToolBook

Let's reinforce some of what we've learned so far by doing a few simple exercises. Initially, you will be helped with many detailed figures of screen displays to ensure that you understand the procedures described in the text. As you become more familiar with various operations, I'll provide fewer detailed figures.

First, get into ToolBook by double-clicking on the ToolBook icon in the Multimedia ToolBook Eval window. You will now be in a new book at author level, and your screen should look like Figure 7.3a. The tool palette is illustrated in more detail in Figure 7.9. This consists of a set of icons indicating the various tools available. The title bar of the tool palette indicates which tool is active. The selection arrow is used to select specific objects on the page. This is important when you want to move or resize an object, or define its properties. The button tool is used to create buttons that initiate certain actions. The record field tool

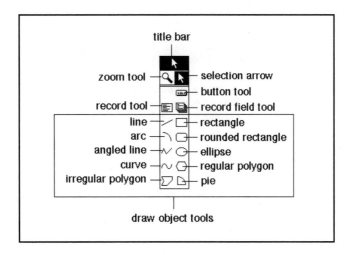

Figure 7.9

Detail of the tool palette.

is used to create special background fields in which the developer or reader can enter different text on every page of the book. The draw object tools create objects of various shapes such as lines, ellipses, and rectangles. The field tool creates fields, which are objects that generally hold text specific to each page. If you create a field on the background, the text entered on the background shows up on every page. Finally, the zoom tool is used to magnify portions of your page to help you design fine details.

> **Note:** Holding down the **Control** key while using the zoom tool demagnifies the page.

You may find as you use ToolBook (or any other Windows program) that some of the opened windows may get in your way, such as various palettes you will use when setting up your pages. You can move any window around the screen as long as it has a "title bar" (see Figure 7.10). To move a window, place the mouse pointer on the title bar, and while holding down your left mouse button, simply drag the window to another spot on the screen. Release the mouse button when you are satisfied with the window's new position. You can try this now with the main ToolBook window or with the tool palette window.

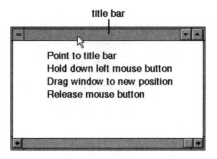

Figure 7.10

Procedure for moving a window using the title bar

Many of the windows that open as you use ToolBook are called *dialog boxes*. These may either communicate a message or request that you supply specific information. You generally close a dialog box by clicking on the OK button (but be sure you first supply any required information).

> **Note:** To get help with any ToolBook operation, you may select Help from the menu bar or press the **F1** key.

Exercise #1: Setting Up a Background

Let's start by creating a background with a record field and two buttons. Figure 7.11 illustrates the background objects we will create in this exercise, as well as their layout on a grid.

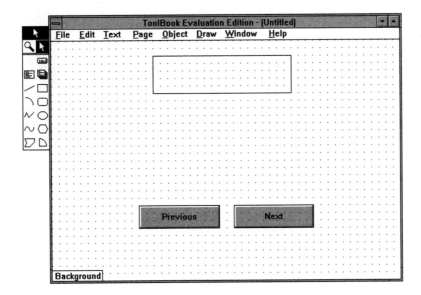

Figure 7.11

Layout of background objects created in Exercise #1.

Step 1. Switching Between Foreground and Background

When you first open up ToolBook, you'll notice a small "status box" in the lower left-hand corner of the screen that should look like Figure 7.12a. This indicates what page you're on (page 1 of 1 when you open a new file). Any page other than "Background" is a foreground page. Let's go to the background by pressing the **F4** key. Now the status box should look like Figure 7.12b. To switch back to foreground, press **F4** and the status box will indicate that you're on page 1 again (the foreground). Now switch to the background. Any objects you create on the background, such as buttons, will show up on every page in the book.

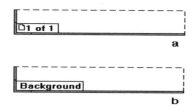

Figure 7.12
Status box indicating the (a) current page or (b) background.

Step 2. Setting Up a Grid

Let's set up a grid to help us align our objects on the background. Click on Window to open its menu, and select "Grid" (see Figure 7.13). Click on both "Show grid" and "Snap to grid" in the Grid dialog box (see Figure 7.14). We'll keep the grid spacing of 0.125 inch. Then click OK to close the dialog box. A dotted grid now appears in the window. The "Snap to grid" feature forces any object lines to form along the grid lines.

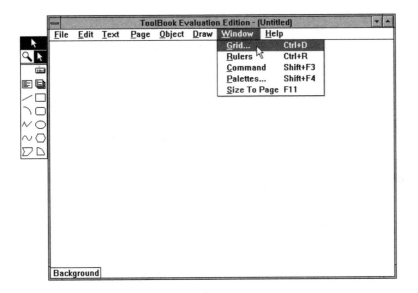

Figure 7.13

Procedure for setting up a grid.

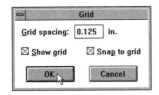

Figure 7.14

Grid dialog box.

Step 3. Creating a Record Field

Let's create our first object—a record field. Click on the record field tool in the tool palette (refer to Figure 7.9 on page 131 to see which icon this is). Notice that the record field tool is highlighted and that a cross shows up in the title bar of the tool palette (see Figure 7.15). Note also that after you select the record field tool, your cursor changes into cross-hairs. Place the cross-hairs near the upper left of the screen (see Figure 7.11 on page 133 for the position of this field), and draw a rectangle by pressing the left mouse button and dragging the cross-hairs down and to the right while still pressing the mouse button. Figure 7.15 illustrates the procedure of drawing a rectangular object from starting point to ending point. You'll see a record field appear on the screen, and its size will depend on how far you drag the cross-hairs. When you release the mouse button, you will complete the operation and paste the record field to the page. Notice that the object's outline snapped to the grid lines because you selected the "Snap to grid" option.

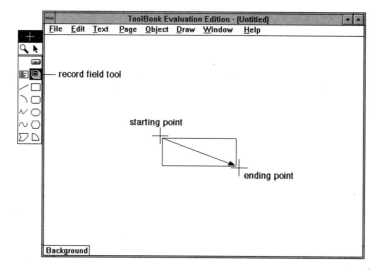

Figure 7.15

Procedure for drawing a rectangular object, such as a record field.

Step 4. Moving and Resizing an Object

Click on the selection arrow from the tool palette, point to the object you just drew, and click on it.

> **Shortcut:** You can also select the object you just drew by pressing the space bar.

In either case, you will see some small squares surrounding the rectangle (see Figure 7.16). These are the objects's "handles", and indicate that this object is selected. Using the selection arrow, you can point inside the object and drag the object to a new position. Or you can change the object's size by dragging one of the handles up or down, or to the side. A corner handle changes both the height and width of the object. If you want to change both its height and width proportionally, press and hold the **Control** key on the keyboard as you drag a corner handle. When you are pleased with the object's size and position, release the mouse button to paste it to the background.

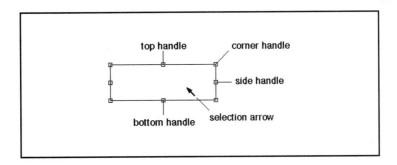

Figure 7.16

Detail of selection handles surrounding a rectangular object.

Step 5. Assigning Properties to the Record Field

Once you have created the record field, you need to assign certain properties to it so that it responds the way we want it to in the sample book. To assign properties to the record field, select Object in the menu bar, and Recordfield Properties. A dialog box will open up (see Figure 7.17 for the features you should select). Select the following options:

- Single line text
- Activate scripts

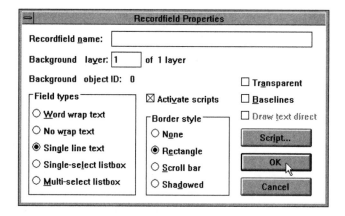

Figure 7.17

Dialog box for assigning record field properties.

Leave the other options as they are. Click OK to save these properties. The "Activate scripts" property causes any scripts (or program commands) associated with this object to be activated. It also prevents the reader from changing any text in this field when it is displayed.

Step 6. Creating a Button

Let's now create our first button. Select the button tool from the tool palette. Place the cross-hairs near the bottom quarter of the screen, and draw a button by pressing the left mouse button and dragging the cross-hairs down and to the right while still pressing the mouse button. Figure 7.11 shows the location of this button (labeled "Previous"). You'll see a button object appear on the screen, and its size will depend on how far you drag the cross-hairs. When you release the mouse button, you will complete the operation and paste the button to the page. You can move or resize the button by selecting it and either drag it to a new position or use the handles to modify its shape.

Step 7. Copying a Button

Now we want to copy that button to make a second one. To copy a selected object (it must have handles around it to be selected), click on Edit and Copy (see Figure 7.18a), and then Edit and Paste (see Figure 7.18b). Although no change will be visible, an exact copy of the button has been pasted on top of the original button. You can point to this button with the selection arrow and drag the copy to the right until it is positioned where you want it (see Figure 7.18c). When you release the mouse button, you will paste the object to the page. You can reposition your buttons if you want.

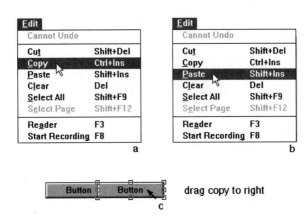

Figure 7.18

Procedure for copying and pasting a button object.

Step 8. Assigning Button Properties

Now we need to name the buttons, change their labels, and give them a "script" so that they perform some action when pressed. First, select the button on the left using the selection arrow. Be sure the button has handles around it. Now click on Object (from the menu bar) and Button Properties (see Figure 7.19). You will now see a dialog box where you can define that button's properties (see Figure 7.20). Note that this is background layer two of three layers. That is because this is the second object we created on the background (the first was the record field), and so far we've created three background objects (and therefore have a total of three layers).

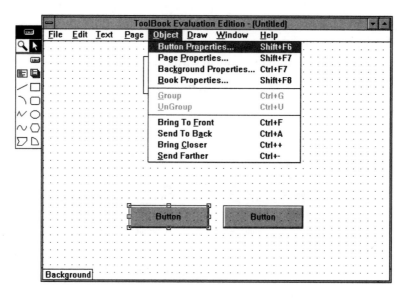

Figure 7.19

Procedure for accessing button properties.

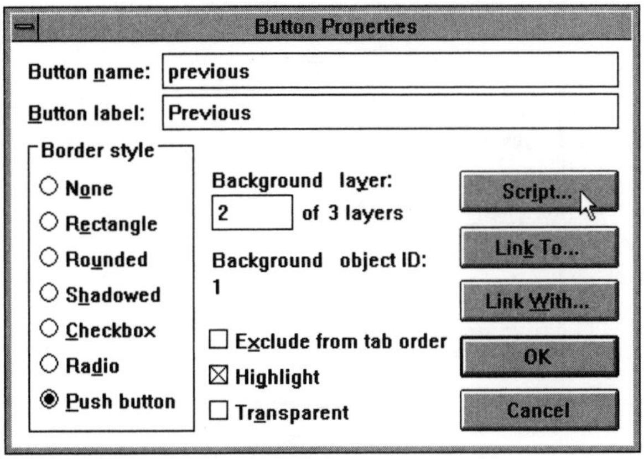

Button Properties

Button name: previous

Button label: Previous

Border style
- ○ None
- ○ Rectangle
- ○ Rounded
- ○ Shadowed
- ○ Checkbox
- ○ Radio
- ● Push button

Background layer: 2 of 3 layers

Background object ID: 1

☐ Exclude from tab order
☒ Highlight
☐ Transparent

Script...

Link To...

Link With...

OK

Cancel

Figure 7.20

Dialog box for assigning button properties.

First change the button's label to "Previous," and its name to "previous." (Use **Tab** and **Shift+Tab** to move from field to field in a dialog window.) Then click on the Script button. A script window opens with a vertical cursor waiting for you to enter some text. Enter the following three lines exactly as they appear below:

to handle buttonUp

     go to previous page

end buttonUp

Save this "script" by clicking on Script and Exit/Update (see Figure 7.21 on the next page). The script window closes and you are back to the button properties window. Click OK to save your work. (If you get a syntax error when you try to save your script, it probably means that you have a typographic error. Be sure that your three lines of script match those above *exactly*.)

Now we will set up the second button. Select the button on the right (be sure it has handles around it), then click on Object and Button Properties. (Note that this is background layer three of three layers because it was the third object we created.) Give the button a label of "Next" and a name of "next," then click on

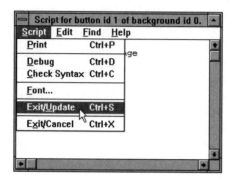

Figure 7.21

Procedure for saving a script.

the Script button. When you enter the script for this button, the only thing that will change is the specified page:

to handle buttonUp

go to next page

end buttonUp

Save the script (click on Script and Exit/Update), and then click OK in the Button Properties window.

You have just created your first background. Before we can test it, though, we need to create a few pages, or foregrounds. But just to be on the safe side, let's save our work so we don't lose anything.

Exercise #2: Saving a ToolBook File

Let's save our first exercise by clicking on File, and Save As from the menu options (see Figure 7.22). You now need to enter a name for this file. Let's name it "book1.tbk" (don't enter the quotes) (see Figure 7.23), and click OK. You don't need to enter the file extension of .tbk—ToolBook automatically adds this to your file name. Although you could use a different extension, you are cautioned to conform to the .tbk extension because this will help you identify ToolBook files.

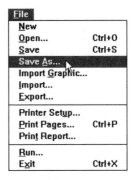

Figure 7.22

Procedure for saving a new file.

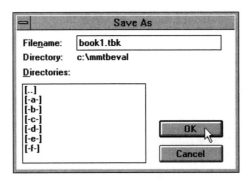

Figure 7.23

Dialog box for naming a file.

> **Caution:** When you name a file, be sure you limit its name to eight characters (not including the ".tbk"). Otherwise, you will get an error message.

Each time you save your file, the time you've spent on that "book" will be subtracted from the time remaining (initially 360 minutes, or 6 hours), and a dialog box appears that tells you how much time you have left to work on this particular book (see Figure 7.24 on the next page). Don't worry if you don't have much time left. You can begin as many new books as you want, and once you practice these exercises, you'll find that you can build your books faster as you go along. Any time you spend practicing these exercises will not shortchange you when building the final application in the chapters that follow.

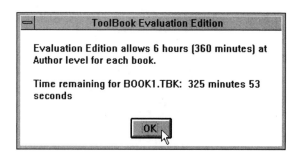

Figure 7.24

Dialog box indicating the time remaining to work on a book.

Exercise #3: Exiting from ToolBook

Now that you've saved your file, you can exit from ToolBook. You don't have to follow this exercise right now if you want to continue working. To exit from ToolBook, click on File and Exit. You now see the Multimedia ToolBook Eval window displayed. You may now exit from Windows by double-clicking on the control-menu box in the Program Manager window.

Exercise #4: Opening a ToolBook File

You learned earlier how to get into ToolBook by double-clicking on the ToolBook icon in the Multimedia ToolBook Eval window. Now you should open up the file we worked on for the first exercise (assuming you exited from ToolBook in the last exercise). To do this, click on File and Open (see Figure 7.25). A list of ToolBook files will appear (see Figure 7.26). Select "book1.tbk" (you may either double-click on the file name or single-click to highlight the name and then click OK). Again, the dialog box displays how much time you have remaining to work on this book.

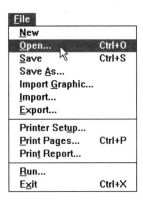

Figure 7.25

Procedure for opening a file.

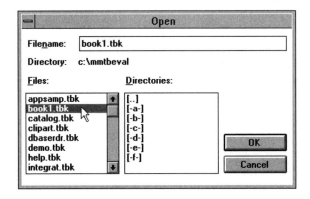

Figure 7.26

Dialog box for selecting a file to open.

Exercise #5: Creating Pages

If you exited from ToolBook and then reopened the exercise file, you will probably notice that your grid lines are gone. To get them back, click on Window and Grid, select "Show grid" and "Snap to grid," and click OK. Recall that we created the record field and buttons on the background. Notice that we are on page 1, and these objects are displayed here as well. This is because any objects you create on the background will be displayed on every page of the book until you change the background. However, the objects you create for the foreground of each page are unique to that page and do not show up on other pages unless you copy the objects to those pages.

Let's create a title for this first page.

Step 1. Entering Text in a Record Field

We must first select the text style that we want to use. To select the text that will be used for any field, you must first select that field using the selection arrow. Notice that you can't select the record field while you are on page 1 of 1. This is because this is a background object, and you must be on the background to select it. Press **F4** to get to the background (check the status box in the lower left-hand corner of the screen to verify that you are on the background).

Now select the record field. It will be surrounded by handles. Click on Text from the menu bar, and Character. The default font is "System" (which is the font used for the words you see displayed in the menu bar). To select a different font, click on the down arrow next to the font box (see Figure 7.27a). This opens up a scrolling list box (see Figure 7.27b). You can scroll up and down in this box using the up and down arrows in the scroll bar. Select "Times New Roman." This now appears in the font box. Now select a different point size using the same method. We want a point size of "40." Once you have done this, click OK. Because of our changes, any text entered in the record field will have this type style on every page of the book.

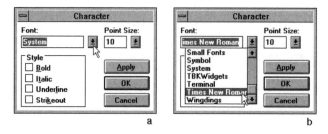

Figure 7.27

Character dialog box indicating the procedure for selecting a different font.

Press **F4** to return to page 1 of 1. To enter text in the record field, double-click inside the field with the selection arrow. The cursor now appears as a vertical bar. Type "Chapter 1" and then click on the selection arrow in the tool palette. This will let you exit from text input mode. Your page should look similar to the one in Figure 7.28. If the field is excessively large, you may return to the background and resize it using the handles. Don't worry if the field is just a little large. We will later go back and change the properties of the record field so that its border doesn't show.

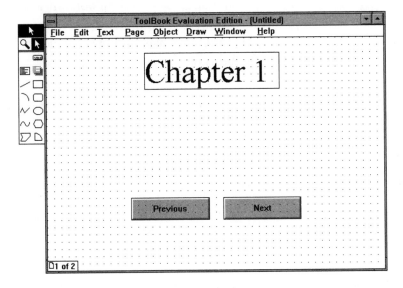

Figure 7.28

Layout of the background and foreground for the first page of the sample book created in the exercises.

Step 2. Creating a New Page

Now we're ready to create a second page. It will look identical to the first page, except that it will have a heading of "Chapter 2." Choose Page from the menu bar, and New Page. Note that the status box now indicates that this is page 2 of 2. This means we are on the second page of the book (which has a total of 2 pages). Note also that the background objects are displayed on this page. Now, double-click inside the record field, and enter the text "Chapter 2" (without the quotes). Now create a third page following the same procedures, and enter the text "Chapter 3" to the record field.

Congratulations! You've just completed your first book. I know it's small (only three pages) and simple (only a few objects), but you've already learned the basics for creating books using ToolBook. Before we test what we've done so far, let's save our work. This time you can just click on File and Save (rather than Save As) because you have already named this file. Your work will automatically be saved with the same file name. (If you want to save it as a different file, click on File and Save As; then enter a new file name.) Again, a dialog box notifies you of the time remaining for this book.

Exercise #6: Switching to Reader Level to Test Your Book

Now you are about to see your book as a reader would see it. Before you do this, you might want to center the book on the computer screen. To do this, click on Window and Size To Page. You could do the same thing by pressing **F11** (as indicated on the Window menu next to the Size To Page option). Recall that **F4** toggles you between background and foreground. (A toggle is any option that is selected or unselected using the same key press, mouse click, or function key.) The **F3** key toggles you between author level and reader level. To go to reader level, press **F3**. Notice that at reader level, the grid and tool palette disappear, and the menu bar at the top of the screen provides fewer options.

Now click on the Previous and Next buttons to see how these turn the pages of your book. You'll notice that these buttons will cycle you completely through the book. For example, if you are on Chapter 1 and click Next, Chapter 2 is displayed. If you click Next again, Chapter 3 is displayed. If you click Next one more time, you are back to Chapter 1. This is because the book has reached its last page and is cycling back to the beginning. In the next exercise, we'll fix this problem.

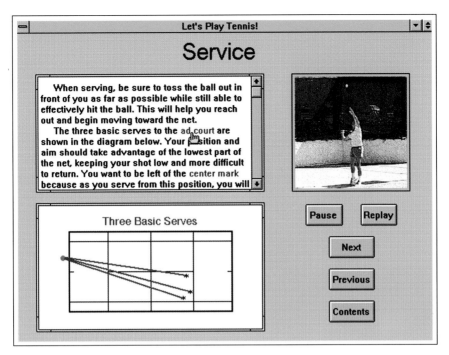

Color Plate 1

Screen display of a multimedia program to teach the user to play tennis. Windows simultaneously display text, graphics (a line drawing), and animation, while a narration describes what the animation is illustrating. Note the yellow "hand" cursor pointing to the hotwords "ad court." By clicking on these words, a window opens explaining this phrase (see Color Plate 2).

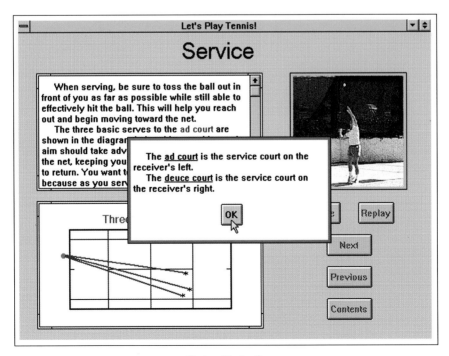

Color Plate 2

Screen display illustrating a window with explanatory text resulting from the user clicking on the hotwords "ad court" (shown in Color Plate 1).

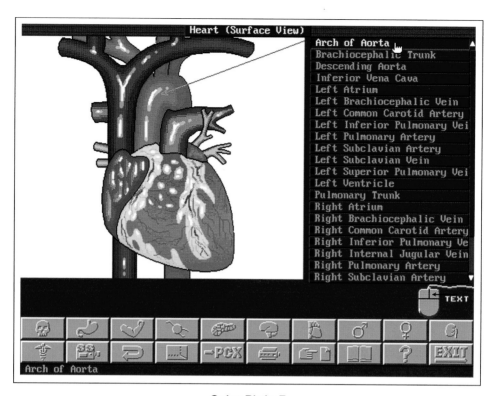

Color Plate 3

Sample screen display from the multimedia program Bodyworks.

Color Plate 4

Sample screen display from the multimedia program Mammals,
developed by the National Geographic Society and IBM.

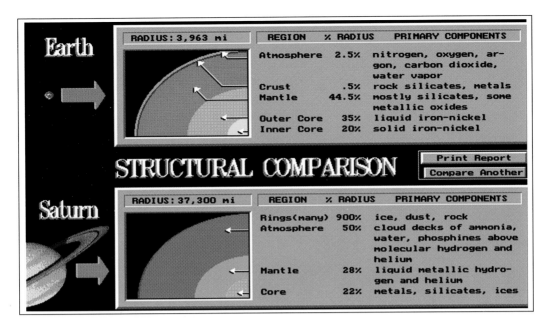

Color Plate 5

Sample screen display from the multimedia program Orbits.

Color Plate 6

Illustration of a graphic file with a resolution of 640 x 480 pixels with 256 colors.

Color Plate 7

Page one of The Color Book.

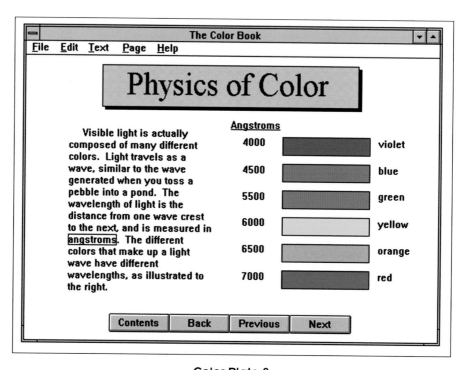

Color Plate 8

Page two of The Color Book.

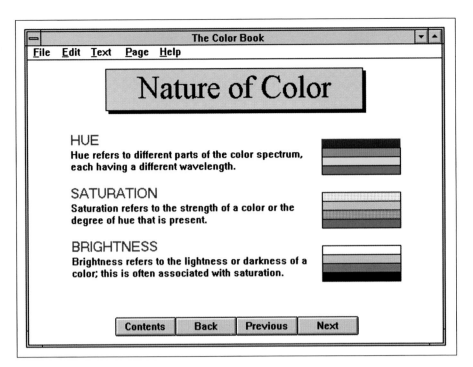

Color Plate 9

Page three of The Color Book.

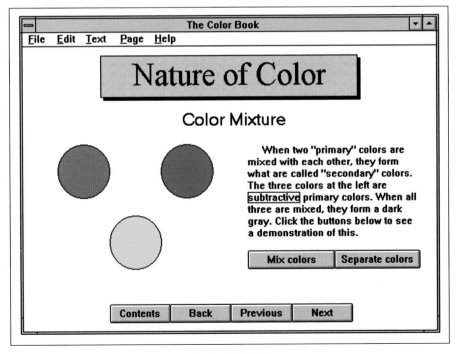

Color Plate 10

Page four of The Color Book.

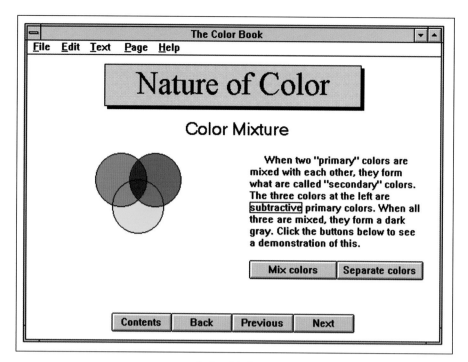

Color Plate 11

Page four of The Color Book, *after the animation to "Mix colors."*

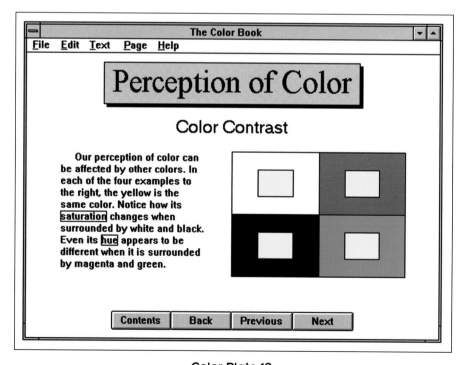

Color Plate 12

Page five of The Color Book.

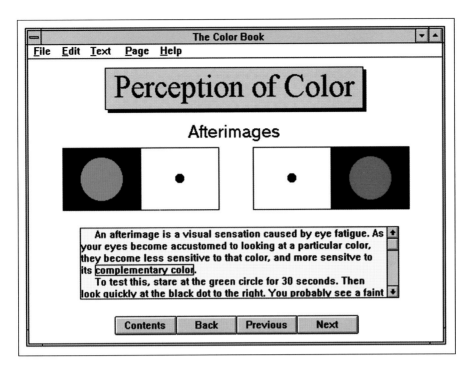

Color Plate 13

Page six of The Color Book.

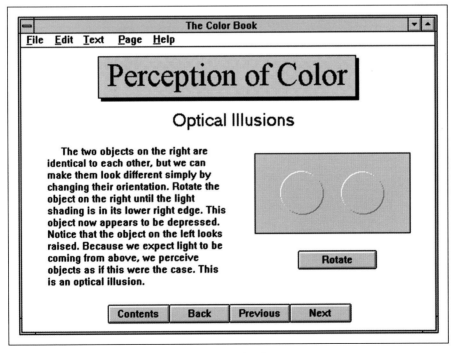

Color Plate 14

Page seven of The Color Book.

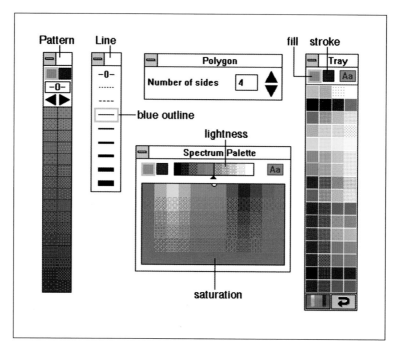

Color Plate 15

Palettes available in Multimedia ToolBook. Note that the fill and stroke colors selected in the color tray affect the colors displayed in the spectrum and pattern palettes.

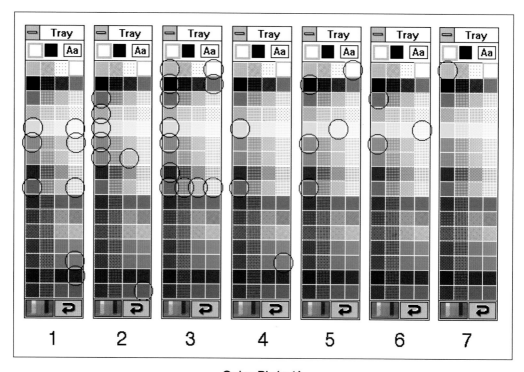

Color Plate 16

Color trays illustrating the colors used for the seven pages of The Color Book. *The corresponding page number is indicated by the number under each color tray.*

Exercise #7: Controlling Page Cycling

In this exercise, you'll learn how to stop page cycling so that if you are on the last page of the book, a dialog box will inform you of this, and prevent page cycling from taking place.

Step 1. Switching Back to Author Level

Switch back to author level by pressing the **F3** key. A dialog box will notify you of the time you have remaining to work on your book.

Step 2. Modifying the Button Scripts

Once you are at author level, click on the selection tool in the tool palette. Remember that we created the buttons on the background. If you try to select one of the buttons on a foreground page, you won't be able to. You must be on the background to select objects created on the background. Press **F4** to go to the background.

Now select the "Previous" button. When it has handles around it, click on Object and Button Properties. Click on Script. We want to modify the button's script to prevent cycling. The vertical cursor should be in front of "to..." in the first line. Using standard word processing operations, modify the script to add the following lines that appear in boldface:

to handle buttonUp

    if this page is first page of this book

        request "You are on the first page of the book."

    else

        go to previous page

    end

end buttonUp

Although it is not necessary, you might want to add a tab to the front of the line "go to previous page." Structured indentations are helpful when reading scripts. To save your new script, click on Script and Exit/Update. Then click OK in the

Button Properties window to save your changes. The "request" command you entered causes a dialog box to open up and display the message you entered in quotes.

Now click on the "Next" button, and change its script to match the following (with additions indicated in boldface):

to handle buttonUp

if this page is last page of this book

request "You are on the last page of the book."

else

go to next page

end

end buttonUp

To save your script, click on Script and Exit/Update, and then click OK in the Button Properties window to save your changes.

Exercise #8: Hiding Borders

While we're still on the background, let's change the field record's border style. Select Object and Recordfield Properties. Select a border style of "None" (see Figure 7.29) and click OK.

Exercise #9: Testing Your Changes

To test your changes, press **F3** to access reader level. Notice that the record field has no borders (because you set this property to "None"). Test your other changes by pressing the "Previous" and "Next" buttons. When you get to the end or beginning of the book, you will see a dialog box indicating where you are in the book, and the book will no longer cycle you through as it did before.

Exercise #10: Exploring on Your Own

Now that you have gone through some exercises, you should try to make some changes on your own. For instance, you might want to change the message that

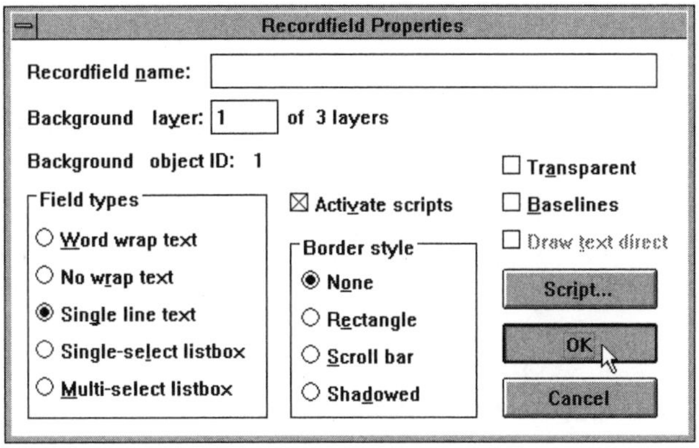

Figure 7.29

Dialog box of record field properties illustrating the change of border style to "None."

is displayed if you click one of the buttons while on the first or last page of the book. Or you might want to change the headings of your pages to something else. You could also change some of the objects' properties. For example, select one of your buttons, and change its border style.

In the chapters that follow, we will experiment with drawing and importing graphics, creating animation, and incorporating sound. But try to modify your first book using some of the suggestions above to be sure that you understand the basic elements of a book. This will help you build later applications.

Summary

This chapter provided you with an overview of Multimedia ToolBook. You learned how to install ToolBook, and you also learned some basic concepts and terminology. By going through some basic exercises in which you created a small book, you were able to apply some of the concepts you learned. Here are the main points discussed in this chapter:

- The Evaluation Edition (enclosed with this book) allows you to work on each book for a maximum of 6 hours.

- ToolBook uses the same basic operations used by any other Windows program; in particular, it is object-oriented and event-driven.

- A book is made up of pages, and each page consists of a foreground and background, each with its own unique set of objects.

- Objects on the background are displayed on every page of the book (until a new background is created).

- Objects on the foreground are unique to that foreground and do not appear on other foregrounds.

- Each object has its own layer which is numbered relative to the order in which it was created.

- You may interact with a book at either reader level or author level.

- The tool palette allows you to create and modify objects.

- Each object has a unique set of properties that determines how it appears and behaves in the program.

Glossary

author level   The mode in ToolBook in which the user develops a program or "book" by creating objects, foregrounds, and backgrounds.

background   A template consisting of objects and properties that are shared by pages in the book.

book	Another name for a ToolBook program or application consisting of a group of pages with which the user interacts.
click	Term for the rapid press and release of the mouse button.
dialog box	A window that either communicates a message or requests specific information.
double-click	Term for two rapid clicks of the mouse button.
dragging	A mouse operation that involves pointing to an object and moving the mouse while holding down the mouse button, thus moving the object to another position.
Dynamic Data Exchange (DDE)	Feature that allows user to exchange data quickly and easily among various Windows programs.
Dynamic Link Libraries (DLL)	Feature that permits user to control other Windows applications from within a single Windows program.
event-driven software	Software that is driven by events or program actions as a result of clicking on menu options or buttons, or other objects.
field	An object that generally holds text entered by either the author or the reader.
flat-file database	Simple database that is not associated with any other database.
foreground	Element of a page that consists of objects specific to that page.
hot objects	Any object that when clicked on initiates some action; examples are hypertext (or hotwords) and hypergraphics.
layer	The relative order of objects on a background or foreground. Each object has its own layer, with the most recently created object having the highest layer number.
object	Any "thing" that is displayed on the screen, including buttons, fields, text, or graphics.

object-oriented software	Software that is based on the creation and manipulation of objects.
OpenScript	The programming or scripting language of ToolBook.
page	The basic unit of a book that is made up of objects on a background and a foreground.
properties	Unique attributes of an object that control how it appears on the screen, and how it behaves in the program.
prototype	A model or mock-up of an actual program that often is used to illustrate sample screen displays.
reader level	The mode in ToolBook in which the user reads a program or "book" and interacts with it using hot objects; the user may also enter text in specified fields to be stored with the book.
record field	A special field that is associated with the background and allows the developer or reader to enter different text in the same field on every page of the book.
selection arrow	A tool that is used to select specific objects for some operation.
sliders	Objects that control the playback of multimedia elements such as sound and animation.
title bar	The wide bar along the top of a window that displays a title such as a file name or name of the window; the title bar is used to drag the window to a new position on the screen.
tool palette	The set of icons displayed at author level that allows the developer to create and work with objects.

Beginning the Application — Text and Graphics

T he exercises in the last chapter gave you some experience in working with ToolBook. In this chapter, you will begin to build an actual application. The various exercises in this chapter will teach you how to draw some simple objects, enter text, and add color to objects and pages. You'll also learn how to create hotwords.

> **Note:** In the last chapter and those that follow, there are some useful shortcuts, tips, and commonly used scripts for buttons, hypertext, and other hot objects. These are compiled in Appendix B so that you can more readily find this information when you develop your own application.

An Overview of "The Color Book"

For our application, we will write a small book about color, called simply "The Color Book." All seven pages of "The Color Book" are shown in Color Plates 7 through 14, with an extra plate (Color Plate 11) showing the result of an animated sequence. This book contains all the components of multimedia discussed in earlier chapters—namely, text, graphics, animation, and sound. "The Color Book" is subdivided into three sections, "Physics of Color," "Nature of Color," and "Perception of Color," with a table of contents page that serves also as a title page (see Color Plate 7). In this chapter, we will build the contents page and the first section of the book, "Physics of Color."

Sample Exercises

Before you learn how to create the various sections of the book in this chapter and those that follow, you will be given some sample exercises to teach you how to perform the operations needed to build the application. This will give you a feel for the techniques you'll be using without draining the limited time available for building "The Color Book."

Exercise #1: Drawing and Copying Simple Graphics

For this exercise, you'll learn how to draw and copy simple rectangles. In addition to using grids (as you did in the last chapter), you'll also use a ruler to help you center the objects on the page.

Begin by opening up ToolBook. You are now working on a new file that is "Untitled" (as shown in the title bar of the main window). Select Window from the menu bar, and Grid. Accept the default spacing of 0.125 inch, and check "Show grid" and "Snap to grid," then click OK. Now select Window again, and click on Rulers. You'll now see rulers along the vertical and horizontal of your page, which have small lines every 1/8 inch. Notice that as you move the mouse cursor, faint lines on the horizontal and vertical rulers indicate the cursor position.

In order to see the entire page, you should click the "maximize" button in the upper right corner of the main window (see Figure 8.1a). To shrink the window to the original size, click the "restore" button, which now appears as an up-down arrow in the upper right corner of the window (see Figure 8.1b). The down-arrow button to the left is a "minimize" button which shrinks the window to an icon. If you click on this button by accident, you can restore the window to its previous size by double-clicking on the ToolBook icon (which appears in the lower left-hand corner of the screen if the window was minimized).

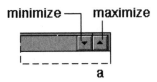

a

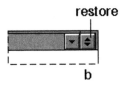

b

Figure 8.1

(a) Minimize and maximize buttons; (b) restore button.

With the rulers showing and the page maximized, you will probably want to move the tool palette to the far right side of the screen. Recall that you drag a window by pointing to its title bar, and while holding down the left mouse button, simply drag the window to a new position, and then release the mouse button to paste it to the screen.

The default page size is 6 inches by 4 inches. You can change the page size by clicking Object from the menu bar, Book Properties, and Page Size, but we'll keep the default page size of 6 x 4 inches.

We will start by creating the two large rectangles shown in Figure 8.2. Click on the rectangle tool in the tool palette (see Figure 7.9 on page 131 if you need a reminder about the icon for this tool). Now position the cross-hair cursor at 1 inch on the horizontal ruler and 1/2 inch on the vertical ruler. Draw a rectangle that extends to 2-1/2 inches horizontally and 2-1/2 inches vertically. Now, click the selection arrow to select the graphic object you've just drawn.

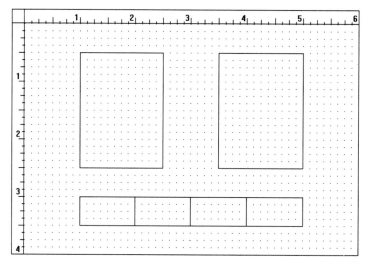

Figure 8.2

Layout of objects for sample exercises.

Shortcut: Recall from the last chapter that you can also select the object you've just drawn by pressing the space bar. The space bar toggles you from the last tool you've used to the selection of the last object you've drawn.

We're going to make a copy of the rectangle and position it next to the original. Be sure it is selected (it will have handles around it if it is selected). Click on Edit and Copy. This copies the object to the Windows clipboard. Now click on Edit and Paste to paste a copy of the rectangle on top of the original. Now point to the rectangle and drag the copy to the right, positioning its upper left-hand corner at 3-1/2 inches on the horizontal and 1/2 inch on the vertical. You should now have two rectangular objects placed symmetrically on the page. Next, you'll learn how to fill them with color.

Exercise #2: Applying Color to Objects

Now that you have two rectangles, you'll learn how to color them using ToolBook's color tray. To display the color tray, click on Window in the menu bar, and Palettes. Check the color tray, then click OK. The color tray window is now displayed on the screen. Drag it to a new position so it doesn't cover the tool palette.

> **Shortcut:** You can also call up the color tray by pressing the **Control** key (on the keyboard), positioning the mouse arrow on any tool in the tool palette *except* the selection arrow and the zoom tool, and double-clicking the left mouse button.

For your own exploring, you might want to open the spectrum palette, which allows you to fine-tune your colors. The various palettes you may open up are illustrated in Color Plate 15. At the top of the color tray (at the far right of Color Plate 15) are two icons that will help you assign colors to objects. The "fill icon" on the left of the color tray controls the color that fills the inside of a closed object, and the "stroke icon" in the middle controls the color of its outline and text. The third icon on the right in the color tray illustrates how text will appear with the stroke and fill selected. The color tray illustrated in Color Plate 15 has a fill color of light blue and a stroke color of dark blue. Notice that the third icon (with text) has a fill color of light blue and text (and outline) of dark blue, corresponding to the fill and stroke colors selected.

Let's take a brief look at the other palettes in Color Plate 15. The pattern palette determines the pattern of the inside of an object and the pattern of its outline. Note that its fill and stroke icons have the same colors as those selected in the color tray, and that these colors are used in the various patterns. The line palette determines the width of the line used in the outline or any lines that you draw. The blue outline surrounds the line width selected. It is somewhat difficult to see the blue outline in the other palettes, but it surrounds selected colors and patterns in the various palettes. The polygon palette is used to select the number of sides of a polygon drawn with the polygon tool (in the tool palette). Finally, the spectrum palette is used to alter the lightness and saturation of the color selected in the color tray.

To select a fill color, first click on the fill icon (it will be surrounded by a blue outline to indicate that it is selected). Now click on a color from the tray (which is also outlined now in blue to indicate its selection). Note how the fill color of your object changes. Try a few colors to get the feel of coloring the fill of objects.

To select a stroke color, first click on the stroke icon (which is now surrounded by a blue border), and then click on a color from the tray (again, surrounded in blue when selected). Notice how the outline of the object changes with the stroke color. It may be difficult to see the outline color with a thin outline. To widen the outline, select Window, Palettes, and Line Palette. With an object selected, change the thickness of the outline by selecting a different line width in the Line Palette. Notice that the outline thickness corresponds to the selected line thickness. Now try to change the stroke color. With a thick outline, the stroke color is much more detectable.

Experiment until you feel comfortable painting your objects. You can close the color tray (and other palettes) at any time by double-clicking on the control-menu box in the upper left-hand corner of the palette window. You may also want to experiment with the pattern palette, which changes the fill and stroke patterns of the object.

Exercise #3: Selecting and Moving Multiple Objects

Let's create four more rectangles. These will be much smaller than the first ones (see bottom of Figure 8.2). Begin by selecting the rectangle tool. Now, draw a rectangle starting at 1 inch on the horizontal and 3 inches on the vertical, and extending it to 2 inches on the horizontal and 3-1/2 inches on the vertical. Let's make three copies of this rectangle. Begin by selecting the rectangle (you may just press the space bar to select it, since it is the last object you've drawn). Select Edit and Copy to paste the rectangle to the clipboard. Now select Edit and Paste, three times. There is no need to make another copy each time, since the same object remains on the clipboard until you paste another object there. Although you can't immediately see the three copies, they are stacked on top of the original rectangle.

Now drag each copy to the right until they are aligned as in Figure 8.2. Notice that as you select each one, a set of handles surrounds that rectangle (see Figure 8.3a). Sometimes it is convenient to select multiple objects so that you can move them simultaneously to a new position, or copy them to another page. The following are two ways to select several objects using the selection arrow tool:

- While pressing the **Shift** key on the keyboard, successively point to and select several objects. Note that if the objects are touching each other, the selection handles grow to enclose each new object (see Figure 8.3b). Otherwise, each selected object will have a set of handles around it.

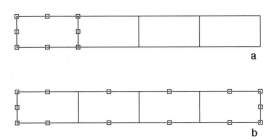

Figure 8.3

*Selection handles surrounding (a) a single object, and
(b) multiple objects that are touching each other.*

- While pointing the selection arrow outside the boundary of an object, click and drag a rectangular "net" around the objects you want to sel-ect. Notice that selection handles surround all the objects you enclosed.

In either case, you will cancel a multiple selection as soon as you point and click anywhere on the page that is outside the selection handles. You can keep the objects together as a group if you plan to work with them this way for several operations by clicking on Object in the menu bar, and Group. The Group option is only selectable (it will appear black vs. gray) once you have selected multiple objects on the page. Now the grouped objects will remain together until you Ungroup them (by selecting Object, and Ungroup).

Once you have selected multiple objects, you may drag them as a single object to another position, or you may copy and paste them in a single operation. Let's try this with the four small rectangles you just drew. Using the selection arrow, press the **Shift** key, and click on each rectangle until selection handles surround all of them (see Figure 8.3b). You can now move these rectangles as a single unit by pointing to any one of the selected objects and moving it. All other selected objects will move along with it.

Exercise #4: Creating a Field with Wrapping Text and a Hotword

For this exercise, let's begin by creating a new page. Select Page in the menu bar, and New Page. Notice that the status box indicates that this is page 2 of 2. Select the field tool (*not* the rectangle tool) from the tool palette. Position the crosshairs at 2 inches from the left and 1 inch from the top. Draw a field that extends to 4 inches from the left and 3 inches from the top. Select this field, and click Object and Field Properties. In the dialog box, check "Activate scripts" and click OK. Double-click inside the field and enter the following text (with five leading spaces):

> In Southern California, many people enjoy water sports such as swimming, windsurfing, and sailing.

Don't enter a carriage return at the end of each line. Instead, let the text automatically wrap inside the field. When you have entered the text, place your cursor just in front of the word "windsurfing." Press the left mouse button while you drag the cursor across the word. Release the mouse button when the entire word is highlighted (be sure nothing is highlighted other than the letters in the word; see Figure 8.4).

> **In Southern California, many people enjoy water sports such as swimming,** ▓windsurfing▓ **and sailing.**

Figure 8.4

Illustration of highlighted word which will be defined as a hotword.

We will now define this word as a hotword. Select Text, and Create Hotword. Next select Object and Hotword Properties. In the Hotword Properties dialog box, enter a hotword name of "windsurfing" (without the quotes). Click on Script and enter the following lines of script:

to handle buttonUp

request "Windsurfing involves a modified surfboard and a sail."

end buttonUp

Save the script by clicking on Script and Exit/Update, and then click OK in the dialog box. The request statement will cause the program to open a dialog box with the message that follows in quotes when the reader clicks on the word "windsurfing" at reader level. In order to surround this hotword with a rectangle, select Text and Show hotwords.

> **Shortcut:** You may also enter the command to show hotwords by pressing the **F9** key on your keyboard.

Exercise #5: Testing the Hotword

To test the hotword, get into reader level by pressing the **F3** on your keyboard. Move the cursor over the word "windsurfing." The cursor should change into a small rectangle. Click on the word, and check to see if the dialog box with the explanation of windsurfing is displayed in the screen.

> **Note:** If the hotword is not surrounded by a rectangle, press **F9** on the keyboard. If the dialog box is not displayed, be sure the script for this hotword looks exactly like the one given above. Any typographic errors will cause problems.

Completing the Sample Exercises

Once you feel comfortable performing the various operations covered in the sample exercises, you're ready to begin the exercises to build the application. Before starting, you may want to save your sample work. Be sure that you give each of the sample files a different name if you want to refer back to them individually at a later date. And be sure you don't give them the same name as "The Color Book" file.

Application Exercises

Now that you've done some sample exercises, you should be well prepared to create the first two pages of "The Color Book."

> **Note:** "The Color Book" application that we will begin building has a total of seven pages. Remember that you have a total of 6 hours to build a single book, which should be plenty of time for this application. However, I realize that users of varying levels of computer experience will be working on these exercises. If you are a beginner with little experience (particularly with Windows operations) you may want to practice building various

parts of your book (such as the exercises to follow) in different practice files until you feel comfortable with the operations. When you feel ready to work on your actual application file, simply repeat those steps. This can save you some time in your application file. Also, you may work on your actual application file and choose *not* to save your work. The time spent will *not* be subtracted from your total time unless you save your work. By the time you work through the first two pages in the exercises below, you'll be better able to gauge the amount of time it takes you to build each page (because you'll be notified about the time remaining each time you save your file). Remember that as you become more familiar with the various operations, you will get faster, so don't worry too much if these initial exercises take longer than you'd like.

Exercise #1: Building the Contents Page

In the steps that follow, you will develop the contents page shown in Color Plate 7. The only object on this page that you will not create in this chapter is the button labeled "Click for Sound." Color Plate 16 contains a set of color trays used for each page of the book, with circles surrounding the colors used for that page. The numbers below the trays indicate which page those colors were used for. Refer to the color tray for page 1 to be sure you are selecting the same colors as those shown in Color Plate 7. To further help you, Figure 8.5 on the next page shows the layout of the foreground (without the sound button) with rulers and a grid. Unlike the next section of the book, we'll make the background after we've developed most of the foreground because the background color is a dark blue and will make the grid difficult to see.

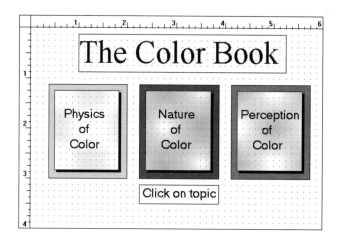

Figure 8.5

Layout of contents page (without the sound button).

Step 1. Setting Up a Grid and Rulers

Let's begin by opening a new book. Click on File and New. Next click on Window and Grid and check "Show grid" and "Snap to grid" in the dialog box. Leave the spacing at 0.125 inch, then click OK. Select Window again, and Rulers. Now maximize the window by clicking on the maximize box in the upper-right corner of the main window. Move the tool palette to the far right so you can see the entire page. Now we're ready to start drawing some objects.

Step 2. Entering the Book's Title

Be sure you are on page 1 of 1 and not the background, because we want the title to show up only on the first page of the book. To enter the title, we'll need to use the field tool (*not* the record field because we want this title to be displayed only on this page). Select the field tool from the tool palette. Keep in mind that the ruler is divided into 1/8-inch segments, each of which corresponds to a segment of the grid. Place the cross-hairs at 1/8 inch from the top and 1 inch from the left side. Now draw a field that extends to 5-1/4 inches on the horizontal ruler, and 7/8 inch on the vertical ruler.

Once you have drawn the field, select it using either the space bar or the selection arrow (be sure it is surrounded by handles). Then select Object in the menu bar, and Field Properties. We want to select the following options for this field in the dialog box:

- Single line text

- Activate scripts

- Transparent

Then click OK to return to the main window. We'll change the border style a little later. The "Transparent" property causes the color of the background to show through the field.

Now click on Text in the menu bar, and Character. When the dialog box appears, select a font of Times New Roman, and a point size of 46. Click OK. To enter text in the field, double-click inside the field with the selection arrow. A large vertical cursor appears. Enter the following text:

The Color Book

It should just fit inside the field. (If it doesn't, be sure you have *not* entered a space at the beginning or end of the text, and that you have selected the proper font and point size.) To exit from text input mode, click on the selection arrow in the tool palette, and the handles to the field will be displayed.

Step 3. Drawing and Copying the Rectangular Graphic

The titles of the three sections of the book are each displayed in a shadowed field on top of a rectangular graphic. Let's first create a rectangular object, and then copy it twice.

Select the rectangle tool (*not* the field tool) from the tool palette. With the cross-hairs at 3/8 inch from the left margin, and 1-1/8 inches from the top, draw a rectangle that extends to 2 inches on the horizontal, and 3 inches on the vertical. If you draw an object that is not the right size, you can either resize it, or you can delete it by clicking Edit and Cut, and then redraw the object.

Select the rectangle, and click on Edit and Copy. Now click on Edit and Paste, and Edit and Paste again to paste two copies of the rectangle on top of the original. Drag the two copies to the right until they are aligned as shown in Figure 8.5 on page 166. Each should be separated by 1/4 inch.

Step 4. Creating and Copying the Shadowed Field

Now let's draw a field on top of the first rectangle. Select the field tool (*not* the rectangle tool) from the tool palette. Draw a field on top of the left-hand rectangle that is 1/8 inch smaller on all four sides. Refer to Figure 8.5 for an illustration of this. Once you have drawn the field, select it, and then click on Object in the menu bar, and Field Properties. Select the following properties in the dialog box:

- Activate scripts
- Border style—shadowed

Keep the field type of "word-wrap text." Click OK. Let's also specify the type style for this field. Click on Text in the menu bar, then Character. In the dialog box, select a font of MS Sans Serif (you'll probably have to scroll up to locate this font) with a point size of 18. Then click OK.

Next, we'll copy this field (and all the properties we've given it) to positions on top of the other rectangles. Be sure the field is selected. Now copy the field to the clipboard and paste two copies of it on top of the original field. Drag the two copies until they are centered in the other rectangles, as shown in Figure 8.5.

Step 5. Entering the Section Titles

Next, we need to add the titles of the three sections of the books. First select the far left field. Double-click inside the object to begin entering text. When the vertical cursor appears, you'll need to do the following in order to be sure the text is centered in the field:

- Enter one carriage return to bring the cursor down one line.
- Enter three spaces and the word "Physics" and another carriage return (the three leading spaces ensure that the word is centered horizontally).

- Enter eight spaces and the word "of" followed by a carriage return.
- Enter five spaces and the word "Color."

Your text should look centered in the field. If it doesn't, experiment with the spacing until it looks close to the layout in Figure 8.5. Now select the center field, and double-click inside to enter the text as follows:

- Enter one carriage return.
- Enter four spaces and the word "Nature" followed by a carriage return.
- Enter the next two lines (that is, "of" and "Color") exactly as you did for the previous field.

Select the far right field, and enter the text as follows:

- Enter one carriage return.
- Enter one space and the word "Perception" followed by a carriage return.
- Enter the next two lines exactly as you did for the other fields.

The section titles with their surrounding fields and rectangles should look like those in Figure 8.5. If yours look a little different, you might want to modify them to match as closely as possible.

Step 6. Assigning Scripts to the Fields

These shadowed fields that contain the titles of each book section will be used as "hot objects" that will take the reader to those sections if clicked on with the mouse pointer. In order for this to work, we need to enter some script for each of these fields (just as we did in the last chapter for buttons).

Select the field with the text "Physics of Color." Click on Object, Field Properties, and Script. In the Script dialog box, enter the following lines:

```
to handle buttonUp
    go to page "physics"
end buttonUp
```

Be sure to enclose the word "physics" in quotes. Then click on Script and Exit/Update to save your script, and click OK in the Field Properties dialog box. This short script will cause the program to jump to the page with the name of "physics" when the reader clicks anywhere in this field.

Let's enter similar scripts for the other section fields. Select the one for "Nature of Color." Enter the following lines of script:

> to handle buttonUp
>
> > go to page "nature"
>
> end buttonUp

Save the script. Then select the field for "Perception of Color" and enter the same lines of script, substituting "perception" for "nature" when indicating the page to go to. Save your script. As we develop the three sections, we will name the first page of each section either "physics," "nature," or "perception," so that when the user clicks on these fields on the contents page, the program will take them to the appropriate pages in the book.

Step 7. Creating the Final Field and Text

At the bottom of the page is a short instruction, "Click on topic," that tells the user how to begin the program. To create this, we must first create a field. Select the field tool from the tool palette. Position the cross-hairs at 2-1/4 inches from the left (directly underneath the center rectangle's left edge) and 1/8 inch below the center rectangle. Draw a field that extends to the right edge of the center rectangle and 3-1/2 inches from the top (refer to Figure 8.5).

Now select this field, click on Object, and Field Properties. In the dialog box, select the following:

- Single line text
- Activate scripts
- Transparent

Then click OK. We'll change the border style a little later. Now select a text style (click on Text, Character) of MS Sans Serif and a point size of 18, and click OK. Double-click on the field to enter the following:

- A single space followed by the words "Click on topic" (the leading space will center the text in the field).

Click on the selection arrow (in the tool palette) to exit text input mode.

> **Note:** If you don't plan to add sound to your application, you should move the field you just created down 1/8 inch to 1/4 inch. If you plan to add sound, keep the field where it is because you will need the space below it to create a sound button.

Step 8. Coloring the Objects

Select Window and Palettes to check the color tray, then click OK (or use the shortcut method of double-clicking on the lower part of the tool palette while pressing the **Control** key). You may want to move the color tray around the screen to reposition it as you color various objects. To select the colors used in Color Plate 7, refer to the color tray labeled "1" in Color Plate 16. Let's begin by coloring the rectangles and fields that surround the section titles. Select the far left rectangle (the handles should surround the *outer* border). This should be bright yellow. Click on the fill icon in the color tray, then select the bright yellow indicated in the first color tray in Color Plate 16. Now select the inner field (with the text "Physics of Color") and select a fill color of very pale yellow. Do the same to color the other rectangles and fields, referring to the first color tray in Color Plate 16 and to Color Plate 7 for the colors used.

Next, we want to change the color of the book's title. Select the field containing the text "The Color Book." Next select the stroke icon in the color tray, and click on the light blue indicated in the first color tray in Color Plate 16. We still need to change the text of "Click on topic" to white, but first we must create the blue background so this text does not disappear.

Step 9. Completing the Coloring

We don't need to be on the background to color the background. While still on page 1 of 1, select Object in the menu bar, and Background Properties. When the dialog box appears, click on Colors. If your color tray were not already open, this operation would automatically open it. It also opens the spectrum palette, which is now displayed. You may have to move one or more windows to select the color needed from the color palette. Referring to the first color tray in Color Plate 16, select a fill color of dark blue for the background (the stroke color should be white, but it does not matter in this particular case, since there will be no other objects on the background), then click OK in the Background Properties dialog box.

Finally, we need to change the field containing the text "Click on topic." Select this object, and then click on Object and Field Properties... Now select a border style of None. With the field still selected, select a stroke color of white. This will change the enclosed text to white. Then click OK.

Your page should now look like the one in Color Plate 7 except that yours will not have the "Click for Sound" button. We will add this button in a later chapter when we add sound to "The Color Book."

Step 10. Assigning Book and Page Properties

We're almost finished with the contents page of the book. Let's first assign a title to the book that will be displayed in the main title window. Select Object and Book Properties and enter a caption of "The Color Book" (without the quotes). Then check "Show caption in title bar" and click OK. You'll now see this caption displayed in the title bar of the window.

Next, select Object and Page Properties... and enter a page name of "contents" (without the quotes). Then click OK. This contents page will also serve as the title page of the book.

Step 11. Saving the Book

Congratulations! You've just completed the first page of the book. Be sure to save your work by clicking File and Save As. Enter any file name you wish, such as COLORBK.TBK, and click OK. No matter what name you give to the file, that file will have a timer associated with it, and the time you've spent building this first page will be subtracted from a total of 6 hours for the book. As the exercises go on, you'll get faster at creating and positioning objects.

In order to conserve the time allotted to your book, you should switch to reader level right after saving your file if you don't plan to work on it. ToolBook does not subtract any time you spend at reader level. You should look at your book at reader level anyway to see how it will look in its finished form. After switching to reader level, you can press **F11** on the keyboard to size the page to fit the screen. Clicking on the restore button (with the up-down icon) in the upper right corner of the window will serve the same purpose.

Exercise #2: Creating the Second Background for the Book

In this exercise, we will create the background for the rest of the book. Its layout is shown in Figure 8.6. Before you begin this exercise, be sure "The Color Book" file is open and displayed on the screen (you may have to open that file if you exited from ToolBook after creating the first page). Also be sure that a grid (with 0.125 inch spacing) and rulers are displayed, and that you are at author level.

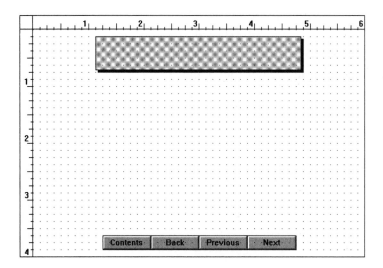

Figure 8.6

Layout of background for remaining pages of the book.

Step 1. Creating a New Background

The background color will be white and the objects we will create are a record field for the title of each section and four buttons for navigation. To create a new background, be sure you are on page 1 of 1 (the contents page you just created). Now select Page and New Background. You will now see a blank page displayed on the screen; the status box indicates that this is page 2 of 2. Because it does not have a blue background, you know that this page has a different background than the previous page. To access its background, press the **F4** key. The status box now displays "Background."

Step 2. Creating the Record Field

The title that will be on each page will have the same properties. We will therefore create a record field on the background that will be displayed on every remaining page of the book. The title of each page will be entered in this record field.

Select the record field tool in the tool palette. Position the cross-hairs at 1-1/8 inches on the horizontal and 1/8 inch on the vertical. Draw a record field to 4-7/8 inches on the horizontal and 3/4 inch on the vertical (refer to Figure 8.6). Select the object, click on Object and Recordfield Properties, and select the following options:

- Single line text
- Activate scripts
- Border style of shadowed

Click OK. Now we want to fill this record field with color. While it is still selected, open the color tray. When this is displayed, click on the fill icon and select the pale blue color indicated in the second color tray in Color Plate 16. Be sure the stroke is set to black. Close the color tray, since we won't need it for a while (double-click on the small bar in the upper left-hand corner of the color tray).

Next, we need to assign a text style to the record field. Be sure this object is selected. Now click on Text and Character and choose a font of Times New Roman with a point size of 32. Click OK. Any text entered in this record field on subsequent pages will have this text style.

Step 3. Creating the Background Buttons

Let's start out by creating the first button. Select the button tool from the tool palette. Position the cross-hairs 1-1/4 inches from the left, and 3-5/8 inches from the top. Draw the button until it extends to 2-1/8 inches from the left and 3-7/8 inches from the top (see Figure 8.6). Now select this button, and copy it to the clipboard (by pressing Edit and Copy). Now paste three copies onto the original, and drag each one until they are aligned as shown in Figure 8.6.

Now we need to assign properties and scripts to these buttons. Select the first button on the left. Click on Object and Button Properties. Enter a label name of "Contents" and a button name of "contents."

> **Shortcut:** To move from one entry field to another in a dialog box, you can use the **Tab** and **Shift+Tab** keys instead of clicking on each field with the mouse pointer. This can be faster when you are entering information using the keyboard and don't want to switch back to the mouse to get to another field.

Once you have labeled and named the button, click on Script and enter the following lines of script:

```
to handle buttonUp

    go to page "contents"

end buttonUp
```

Be sure to enclose the word "contents" in quotes. Click on Script and Exit/Update to save your script, and click OK in the dialog box. The meaning of this script is that when the button is pressed and released, the program will go to the page with the name of "contents." You'll recall that this is the name we gave the first page of the book. When the reader clicks this button, it will take him to that page.

Now select the button to the right of this. In the Button Properties dialog box, give this button a label of "Back," a name of "back," and enter the following lines of script:

```
to handle buttonUp
```

>   send back

>   end buttonUp

The second line of script tells the program to go to the last page that was displayed before the current one. This is the "bookmark" discussed in Chapter 6. Save your script and click OK in the dialog box.

> **Shortcut**: You can press **Control+S** to save a script quickly. Try this procedure next time.

Select the next button to the right. Give this button a label of "Previous" and a name of "previous," and enter the following lines of script:

>   to handle buttonUp

>   go to previous page

>   end buttonUp

Save this script and click OK in the dialog box.

For the last button on the right, label it "Next," name it "next," and enter the following script lines:

>   to handle buttonUp

>   if this page is the last page of this book

>   request "This is the last page of the book."

>   else

>   go to next page

>   end

>   end buttonUp

Save the script and click OK in the dialog box. Notice that we added some script to stop page cycling from occurring. We don't need a similar script for the "Previous" button (as we did in an earlier example) because the "Previous" button doesn't appear on the first page of the book (that is, the contents page) and therefore it can't be clicked on the first page. You have just completed the background for page 2 of the book.

Exercise #3: Creating the Foreground for the "Physics of Color" Section

The "Physics of Color" consists of only a single page. The foreground of this page has a title, several fields containing text, and some rectangular graphics. This page is illustrated in Color Plate 8, and its layout is shown in Figure 8.7. Before you begin working on the foreground, be sure you press **F4** to go to the foreground. The status box will indicate that this is page 2 of 2. Note that the blue record field and the buttons from the background are displayed on the page.

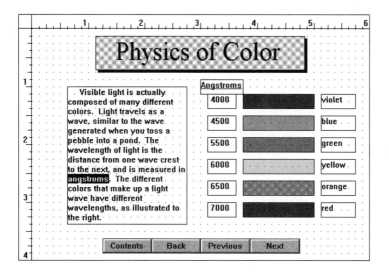

Figure 8.7

Layout of second page of the book (including background and foreground objects).

Step 1. Entering the Title in the Record Field

To enter a title in the record field, double-click on the record field. A large vertical cursor will appear. (If you are still on the background, you will not be able to enter text in the record field.) Now enter three leading spaces followed by **Physics of Color**.

It should appear centered in the field. If it doesn't, be sure you have entered three spaces before the text. Now click on the selection arrow in the tool palette to stop inputting text.

Step 2. Creating the Large Field of Text

In the next few steps, we will create the various fields that hold the remaining foreground text. Figure 8.7 shows the layout of the objects we will be creating. Although the field borders are visible in this figure, we will change the border style to "None" after creating this page. Color Plate 8 shows the finished page.

Select the field tool from the tool palette. Let's begin with the large field on the left side of the screen. Position the cross-hairs at 5/8 inch from the left side and 1 inch from the top. Draw a field to 2-3/4 inches horizontally and 3-3/8 inches vertically. Select this object and check the "Activate scripts" box. We'll later change its border style to None, but for now, it will be helpful to see the outline of the field. Click OK to return to the main window.

Select Text and Character. Notice that the default font is "System" and the point size is 10. These are ideal for the type of text we will enter, so accept these defaults by clicking OK. Double-click on the field and enter the following text (with five leading spaces):

Visible light is actually composed of many different colors. Light travels as a wave, similar to the wave generated when you toss a pebble into a pond. The wavelength of light is the distance from one wave crest to the next, and is measured in angstroms. The different colors that make up a light wave have different wavelengths, as illustrated to the right.

Don't enter carriage returns at the end of each line. Because the field type is "word-wrap text," the text will automatically wrap inside the field as you type it. When you have finished entering the text, it should look like that in Figure 8.7.

Don't worry that the word "angstroms" is not highlighted in your text. We'll next define this word as a hotword.

Step 3. Defining "angstroms" as a Hotword

Now we'll define "angstroms" as a hotword in the field of text that we just entered. Position the cursor just in front of the word "angstroms" and highlight this word by pressing the mouse button and dragging the cursor over the word. When it is highlighted, select Text and Create Hotword. Now you must set its properties. Select Object and Hotword Properties. In the Hotword Properties dialog box, enter a hotword name of "angstroms" (without the quotes). Click on Script and enter the following lines of script:

    to handle buttonUp

        request "1 angstrom = 4 billionths of an inch"

    end buttonUp

Save the script, and then click OK in the dialog box. The "request" statement will cause the program to open a dialog box with the message that follows it when the reader clicks on the word "angstroms" at reader level. In order to surround this hotword with a rectangle, select Text and Show Hotwords.

Step 4. Creating the Small Fields of Text

Let's next draw the field that holds the underlined word "<u>Angstroms</u>" that heads up the column of numbers. Position the cross-hairs at 3 inches horizontally and 7/8 inch vertically. Draw a field that extends to 3-3/4 inches horizontally and 1-1/8 inches vertically. Select the field and set its properties to:

- Single line text
- Activate scripts
- Border style of None (the border is displayed in Figure 8.7 to show you where to position it on the page).

Click OK to save these properties. We don't need to specify the text style, since we'll use the default font and point size (as we did with the last field). However, you should select "Underline" by clicking on Text and check "Underline" (be sure the field was selected first). Now double-click on the field and enter the word **Angstroms**. Notice that it is underlined.

Click on the field tool again. We will create several more to hold the other text. Position the cross-hairs at 3-1/8 inches horizontally and 1-1/8 inches vertically. Draw a field to 3-5/8 inches horizontally and 1-3/8 inches vertically. Select the field and set its properties as follows:

■ Single line text

■ Activate scripts

Click OK to save the properties. Later, we'll change the border style to None, but to do that now would make it difficult to align the copies we're about to make. Copy this field to the clipboard and paste five copies onto the original.

> **Shortcut:** You can paste an object not only by using the Edit, Paste command from the menu, but also by pressing **Shift+Insert** on the keyboard. This can sometimes be faster. You might want to try that here.

Now drag each copy down, and separate them by 1/8 inch. Figure 8.7 shows the layout of these fields. We'll use the default text style, so now you simply double-click on each field and enter the numbers (with a leading space to center it in the field) as shown in Figure 8.7 (that is, 4000, 4500, 5500, 6000, 6500, and 7000). Let's keep the borders until we are through entering the other objects. This will help us position all the objects on the page.

The last fields on the page are those containing the names of the various colors. (The colored rectangles are not fields but rectangular graphics, which we will draw in the next step.) Draw the first field with starting coordinates of 5-1/8 inches and 1-1/8 inches, and ending coordinates of 5-3/4 inches and 1-3/8 inches (refer to Figure 8.7). Select the field, then click on Object and Field Properties, and set its properties to:

■ Single line text

- Activate scripts

We'll change its border style to None a little later. Click OK to save these properties. Now copy the field to the clipboard and paste five copies onto the original. Drag the copies to position them 1/8 inch below each other. They should be aligned exactly across from the fields containing the numbers. Enter the text shown in the corresponding fields in Figure 8.7 (that is, violet, blue, green, yellow, orange, and red). There is no need to enter a leading space before each word.

Step 5. Drawing and Coloring the Rectangular Graphics

Now we'll draw the rectangles and fill them with color. Select the rectangle tool (*not* field tool) in the tool palette. Position the cross-hairs at 3-3/4 inches horizontally and 1-1/8 inches vertically. Draw a rectangle that extends to 5 inches horizontally and 1-3/8 inches vertically. Copy the rectangle and paste five copies onto the original. Then position them as shown in Figure 8.7.

Now open the color tray, and select the fill icon. (You may have to move the color tray to the left of the screen to access the tool palette.) Select each rectangle and fill it with the appropriate color as shown in the second color tray in Color Plate 16. You might also want to refer to Color Plate 8 to see the colors on the final page. These are the brighter colors in the tray—the pale blue was used for the record field in the background. After you have filled the rectangles with color, close the color tray.

Step 6. Changing the Border Styles

Once you have positioned the objects, filled the fields with text, colored the rectangles, and are generally satisfied that the page layout looks like that shown in Figure 8.7, you're ready to change the border styles of the fields. You may change all the borders at one time using the shortcut on the next page, or you will need to select each field individually, click on Object and Field Properties, and select the border style of None. Then click OK.

> **Shortcut**: You can avoid performing this operation for every individual field by selecting all of the fields (using the multiple select operation). When you have all of the fields surrounded with handles, click on Window and Command. A window will open with a vertical cursor. Enter the following command:
>
> set borderstyle of selection to none
>
> Then press the **Enter** key. This will change the border style of every selected field to None. Close this window by double-clicking on its control-menu box.

Once you have completed this operation, your page (at reader level) should look like the one in Color Plate 8.

Step 7. Naming the Page

We need to name this page so that when the reader selects the "Physics of Color" section from the contents page, the program will know where to go. Be sure you are at author level. Select Object and Page Properties, and enter a page name of "physics" (without the quotes). Then click OK.

Step 9. Saving and Testing the Book

Now save your book before testing it at reader level. The dialog box will tell you how much time you have remaining for this book. Now switch to reader level, and press **F11** to size the page to fit the display. If the hotword is not surrounded with a rectangle, press the **F9** key. Your display probably shows the "Physics of Color" page. Test the two pages you created in this chapter by trying these operations:

- Move the mouse cursor over the word "angstroms" (which should be surrounded by a rectangle) in the large field of text. The cursor should change into a small rectangle.
- Click on the word "angstroms." Be sure that a message window explaining this term opens up (see Figure 8.8).

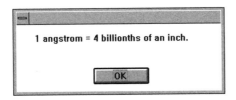

Figure 8.8

Dialog box for the hotword "angstrom."

- Click on the "Contents" button. It should take you to the first page.

- On the contents page, click on the rectangular section titled "Physics of Color." This should take you to that page.

- On the "Physics..." page, click on the "Back" button to be sure you go back to the contents page.

- On the "Physics..." page, click on the "Next" button to be sure that a dialog box warns you that this is the last page (because it is right now) and that you are not cycled back to the contents page.

- On the "Physics..." page, click on the "Previous" button to be sure you go to the contents page.

Note: If any of the buttons you've tested so far does not work as indicated above, check the following:

- You have properly labeled the contents page "contents" (without the quotes).

- You have properly labeled the "Physics of Color" page "physics" (without the quotes).

- You have entered the script for the yellow field containing the text "Physics of Color" (on the first page) exactly as indicated in this chapter.

- You have properly entered the scripts for the buttons exactly as indicated in this chapter.

- You have properly entered the scripts for the hotword "angstroms."

- You have selected Text and Show Hotwords (or pressed **F9**) to surround the hotword with a rectangle.

Be sure that you don't have any typographic errors in the scripts or they will not function properly.

Summary

In this chapter, you were presented with an overview of the application you will create, "The Color Book." You went through some sample exercises to teach you some of the operations used to create the first two pages of the book. These pages consisted of two backgrounds (the first background contained only a blue color), and two foregrounds with a variety of objects. You also learned how to create hot objects, color a background, and create graphic objects such as rectangles.

Glossary

color tray	One of the color palettes (the other is the spectrum palette) used to color objects.
fill icon	Used to assign color to the inside of an object.
line palette	Palette used to select width of lines and outlines.
maximize button	Button used to expand a window to its maximum dimensions.
minimize button	Button used to shrink a window to an icon.
multiple selection	Procedure for selecting more than one object for some operation, such as moving.
pattern palette	Palette used to select the pattern of objects.
polygon palette	Palette used to select the number of sides of a polygon.
restore button	Button used to shrink a window to its original size.
spectrum palette	One of the color palettes (the other is the color tray) used to color objects.
stroke icon	Used to assign color to the outline and text of an object.

Expanding the Application and Adding Animation

In the last chapter, you learned several operations that will be useful in building the next section of the book, "Nature of Color." We'll learn some additional operations in this chapter, such as copying and pasting multiple objects, drawing simple circles, and creating animation. We'll also learn about transparent color. We'll begin with some sample exercises to give you a feel for these new techniques, and then we'll go through the actual exercises used to develop the second section of "The Color Book."

An Overview of the "Nature of Color" Section

This section of the book consists of two pages that use the same background you created for the "Physics of Color" in the last chapter. These pages are shown in

Color Plates 9 and 10. The second page will have an animated sequence in which the three colored circles will converge to show color mixing, shown in Color Plate 11. Let's begin by running through a few sample exercises to learn some new techniques.

Sample Exercises

Exercise #1: Copying and Pasting Multiple Objects

Let's begin this exercise by creating four rectangles and copying them as a single object. Begin by opening a new file (File and New). Click on Window and Grid and check "Show grid" and "Snap to grid," keeping the grid spacing of 0.125 inch. Next click on Window and Rulers to display horizontal and vertical rulers, and maximize the window. Move the tool palette to the far right side of the screen.

Now, select the rectangle tool (*not* the field tool) in the tool palette. We want to create the rectangles shown in Figure 9.1. Place the cross-hairs at 2 inches on the horizontal and 1 inch on the vertical. Create a thin rectangle that extends to 3 inches on the horizontal and 1-1/8 inches on the vertical. Next, select this rectangle, copy it to the clipboard, and paste three copies to the original. Recall that to do this, you click Edit and Copy. To paste three copies, you may either press **Shift+Insert** three times (this means that you press the **Shift** and **Insert** keys at the same time), or you may click Edit and Paste three times. Now drag each copy down and position it just at the lower boundary of the rectangle above it (see the upper set of rectangles in Figure 9.1).

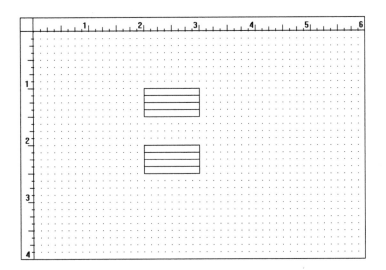

Figure 9.1

Layout of rectangles for sample exercise.

Now, we want to select all four rectangles so that we can copy this set. Recall from the last chapter that you can either click on each rectangle while holding down the **Shift** key on the keyboard, or you can use the selection arrow and draw a rectangular "net" to surround the four rectangles. In either case, your rectangles should look like those in Figure 9.2 when all are selected. Note that a single set of selection handles surrounds all four rectangles.

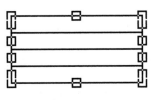

Figure 9.2

When all four rectangles are selected, the selection handles surround all objects, as shown here.

While all four rectangles are selected, let's make a copy of them and paste it to the same page. Select Edit and Copy to copy the rectangles to the clipboard. Now select Edit and Paste to paste a copy on top of the original set. Drag the second set of rectangles down to 2 inches on the vertical. Your page should now look like the one in Figure 9.1.

Exercise #2: Drawing Squares

Although we won't actually be drawing squares in our application, this is a good place to point out that you can control the dimensions of rectangles and constrain them to form squares of equal sides. First start a new page by clicking on Page, and New Page. Now select the rectangle tool from the tool palette, and position the cross-hairs anywhere on the screen. Now begin to draw a rectangle, but at the same time, hold down the **Control** key on the keyboard. Notice that the sides snap to form a square with sides of the same dimension as the largest side of the rectangle you are drawing. Continue to press the **Control** key until you have extended the sides as far as you want. Then release the mouse button and the **Control** key.

> **Note:** The **Control** key is useful to constrain several types of drawing tools so that, for example, rectangles have sides of equal dimensions, ellipses form circles, and lines are perfectly horizontal or vertical.

Exercise #3: Drawing Ellipses and Circles

Let's draw some simple ellipses and circles now. Either select a new page (Page, New Page) or begin a new file (File, New). Click on the ellipse icon in the tool palette. Then bring your mouse pointer to the middle of the page. Press the left mouse button, and while holding down the button, begin to drag the cross-hairs across the screen. This is the same operation as that used to draw a rectangle. When you release the mouse button, you will complete the drawing process and "paste" the ellipse to the page. Make a couple of ellipses until you feel comfortable with this operation.

Now, we want to make a circle (instead of an ellipse). To do this, press the **Control** key (on your keyboard) as you drag the ellipse's outline. This will force the ellipse to be circular. Try drawing a few circles, and then try to make several of the same size.

Exercise #4: Creating Transparent Objects

In the last chapter, and in the previous exercises, we have drawn opaque objects. This means that as you draw one object over the other, it covers the other object to the extent that you overlap the two. Try this now by dragging some of the ellipses and circles over each other. The one that covers the other is a more recently created object (see Figure 9.3a) and has a higher "layer" number.

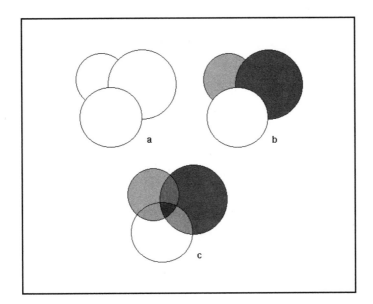

Figure 9.3

*(a) Opaque objects cover other objects and (b) hide any colors
of those objects; (c) transparent objects allow other objects
and their colors to be seen from behind.*

> **Note:** You can determine an object's layer number by selecting the object and clicking on Object and Graphic Properties (or Field Properties or Button Properties, etc.). The layer number of the object is displayed in the dialog box.

Now apply different fill colors to these opaque objects. Notice that the color of the most recently created object (with a higher layer number) covers the colors of the older objects (see Figure 9.3b). What we will do in this exercise is to create transparent objects so that the colors of the various objects can be seen through each other.

Either start a new page or a new file. Before drawing any objects, select Draw in the menu bar, and Transparent. This will cause any objects to be drawn as transparent rather than opaque objects. Now select the ellipse tool in the tool palette. Draw three or four circles. Fill the circles with yellow, cyan (light blue-green) and magenta (lavender) (see the colors of the circles in Color Plates 10 and 11 and the colors circled in the fourth color tray in Color Plate 16). Now, drag the circles to overlap each other slightly. Note that the objects are now transparent, and that the overlapped portions of the circles produce different colors (see Figure 9.3c).

> **Caution:** The colors used with computer graphics are "subtractive," meaning that they absorb certain wavelengths of light. Because of this, only certain colors can be used to produce different colors with overlapped objects on a computer. Yellow, cyan, and magenta are the best colors to work with to illustrate mixing of colors, and these are the colors we will use in our application.

Exercise #5: Creating Animation

So far, you have learned how to create text and graphics. Well, we're finally to the point where you will learn to create some animation. Let's begin a new file. First click on Draw and Draw Direct, and be sure to *uncheck* this option (that is, if there is a checkmark next to this option, click on the option to remove the checkmark). This is important to prevent some of the flickering of the animated object. Now draw a circle (about 1/2 inch in diameter) in the lower left-hand side of the screen. Fill the circle with a red color. (It doesn't matter in this exercise whether the circle is drawn opaque or transparent.) We will think of this as a red ball, and we will create some animation to make the ball bounce. Click on Object and Graphic Properties. Name this draw object "red ball" (without the quotes), and click OK.

Step 1. An Example of Jerky Animation

Before you understand what constitutes smooth animation, it's useful to create some jerky animation so you can see the difference.

Creating animation is really quite simple. You simply start ToolBook's recorder and then drag the object around the screen. Each time you release the mouse button, you record the object's position on the screen. When you are through, you stop the recorder. Obviously, if you only record four or five positions across the entire screen, while the object is drastically changing positions, the resulting animation will show only a few positions of the object. It will be too fast and jerky to produce good results.

To illustrate this, let's animate the ball to make it look like it's bouncing, but we'll only record five positions for it across the screen (see Figure 9.4 on the next page for an illustration). Start the recorder by clicking on Edit and Start Recording. Now single-click on the ball (this selects this object for the recording and records its first position). Next, depress the left mouse button and drag the ball up a couple of inches and a little to the right (see position 2 in Figure 9.4). Release the mouse button. Now depress the mouse button again while you drag the ball down and to the right. Again release the mouse button. Keep doing this until you have "bounced" the ball up and down a couple of times. When the ball is in the lower right-hand corner of the screen, stop recording by clicking on Edit and Stop Recording. Now click on Object, Graphic Properties, and Script. When the Script dialog box is open, click on Edit (in the Script window's menu bar) and Paste Recording. Look at the lines of script that have been automatically added to the script window. These lines tell the program to what positions (x and

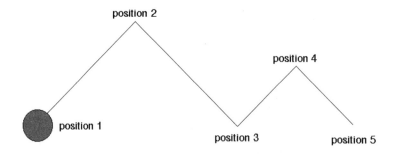

Figure 9.4

Recorded positions for jerky animation.

y coordinates on the screen) to move the object. Save the script using **Control+S** or by clicking on Script and Exit/Update. Click OK in the dialog box.

Now you're ready to test your animation. Press **F3** to access reader level. Click on the red ball. Notice that it bounces across the screen according to the positions in your script. (You can bounce it multiple times simply by clicking on the object.) Also note that the bounces are quick and jerky; this is because you only recorded a few positions as it moved across the screen.

Step 2. An Example of Smoother Animation

In order to smooth out your animation, you must record your positions more frequently. Instead of releasing the mouse button only when the ball is about to change directions (either to bounce up or to go down), we'll next try to record several positions of the ball each time it moves up, and several positions each time it moves down (see Figure 9.5 for an illustration). First, let's erase the previous animation script. Be sure you are at author level. Next, select the ball, click on Object, Graphic Properties, and Script. The dialog box shows the last script you pasted from the recording. Click on Edit (in the Script window's menu bar), and Select All. This will highlight all of your script. Then click Edit again and Clear. This will erase your old script. Then click on Script and Exit/Update (or **Control+S**) to save these script changes, namely an empty script.

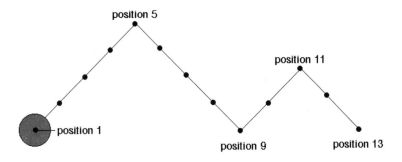

Figure 9.5

*Increasing the number of recorded positions results in
smoother animation.*

Now, drag the ball back to the lower left-hand corner of the screen. Begin recording by clicking on Edit and Start Recording. This time, as you move the ball
up and to the right, record several positions by releasing and pressing the mouse
button several times (see Figure 9.5).

> **Caution:** A position is recorded when you release the mouse
> button. After releasing the mouse button, you should not move the
> object until after you have pressed the mouse button again. Then
> hold the button down while dragging the object to a new position.

As you drag the object down and to the right, record its positions several times
by again releasing and pressing the mouse button. After you have recorded
several bounces of the ball, you can stop recording (Edit, Stop Recording). Now
select Object, Graphic Properties, and Script. Select Edit and Paste Recording
to paste your script to the screen. Notice that there are many more positions
recorded in this script. Save your script. Then go to reader level and test your
bouncing ball again. Note how much smoother its animation is this time.

Step 3. An Example of Very Smooth Animation

In this example, we'll actually move the ball in measured increments across the screen. Its movement won't be as interesting but it will be very smooth and controlled.

First, go to author level and select the red ball. Move it to the lower left-hand corner of the screen. Now erase your old script by selecting Object, Graphic Properties, and Script. With the script displayed in the dialog box, select Edit, Select All, and then Edit and Clear. Save your script changes (**Control+S**).

Now, be sure the red ball is selected. Also be sure that your window is set to Grid (both "Show grid" and "Snap to grid") with a spacing of 0.125 inch. This will help to calibrate your movements. Figure 9.6 illustrates successive positions of the ball as you move it 1/8 inch to the right and then record its position by releasing the mouse button. Begin recording (Edit, Start Recording). Select the red ball, and with the left mouse button depressed, drag it to the right 1/8 inch (the distance of one grid segment). Release the mouse button to record its position. Without moving the ball, depress the mouse button again, and drag it to the right another 1/8 inch. Release the mouse button to record its position. Repeat this procedure until you have moved the ball to the right several inches (see Figure 9.6). Stop recording (Edit, Stop Recording) and paste this new script to the red ball (Object, Graphic Properties, Script, Edit, Paste Recording), and save this new script.

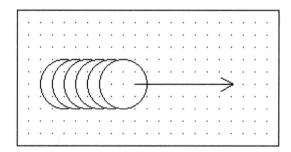

Figure 9.6

*Illustration of the incremental movement of a circle to the right
to produce very smooth animation.*

Now test your smooth animation by going to reader level and clicking the red ball. Notice how smoothly the ball moves. This may be more appropriate for some animation (and in fact we'll use it in our application), but other animation may be best with the rapid examples shown before.

Exercise #6: Assigning an Animated Script to a Button

In the examples we've created so far, the animation was triggered by clicking on the object that moves. This is because when we saved the recorded script, we assigned it to the object's properties. In this exercise, we'll record an animation and assign the script to a different object—a button.

Start a new file (File, New). Refer to Figure 9.7 on the next page for the four objects (two circles and two buttons) that we'll draw for this exercise. Be sure the rulers and grid are showing, and that the "Show grid" and "Snap to grid" features are checked. Select Draw in the menu bar, and be sure that the Transparent option is checked and that Draw Direct is *not* checked. Now select the ellipse tool, and with the cross-hairs at 1-1/2 inches on the horizontal and 1 inch on the vertical, draw a circle (using the **Control** key to keep the object symmetrical) that extends to 2-1/2 inches on the horizontal and 2 inches on the vertical. Copy the circle and paste it so that its left margin is at 3-1/2 inches on the horizontal and its upper margin is at 1 inch on the vertical. Open the color tray and color the left object magenta and the right object bright yellow (refer to the magenta and yellow in the color tray labeled "4" in Color Plate 16). Next select the magenta circle and select Object and Graphic Properties, and give it a name of "magenta circle" (without the quotes), then click OK. Select the yellow circle and name it "yellow circle" and click OK.

Next, create two buttons in the positions shown in Figure 9.7 on the next page. Label the top button "Mix" and the bottom one "Separate." Now we will begin recording some animation in which both circles will move toward each other, causing their colors to mix. We will then paste that recording to the script associated with the Mix button. Then we will reverse the movement and paste this animation to the Separate button.

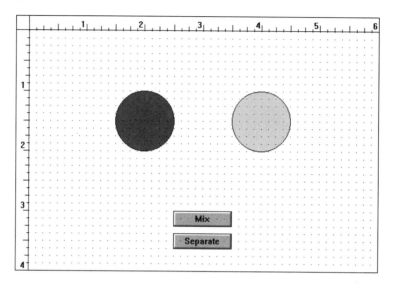

Figure 9.7

Position of objects for sample exercise. Circles are separated
(and in their original positions).

Select the Mix button. Now start the recording (Edit and Start Recording). Single-click on the magenta circle. This action will select this object (it is *very important* to select the object before moving it to the first position). Next, press the mouse button and drag the circle to the right 1/8 inch, then release the mouse button. Now press the mouse button again and move the circle to the right another 1/8 inch. Repeat this until you have moved the magenta circle to the right a total of six times (its left margin will be at 2-1/4 inches after six moves). Now select the yellow circle by single-clicking on it (this initial selection is *critical*). Then, press the mouse button and drag the yellow circle to the left 1/8 inch, and release the mouse button. Repeat this procedure until you have moved the yellow circle to the left a total of six times (its right margin will be at 3-3/4 inches after six moves). Notice the blended color of red. (If your circles are opaque, this is because you did not check the Transparent option in the Draw menu.) Now stop the recording (Edit and Stop Recording). Your screen should look similar to the one in Figure 9.8. Next select the Mix button. Select Object

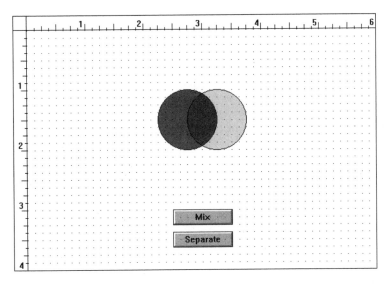

Figure 9.8

Position of circles after they have been "mixed."

and Button Properties. Select Script and when the dialog box appears, select Edit and Paste Recording to paste that recording to the Mix button. Save the script. It should look like the script below (if it doesn't, it may not work properly):

> to handle buttonUp
> select ellipse "magenta circle"
> move the selection to 2340, 1440
> move the selection to 2520, 1440
> move the selection to 2700, 1440
> move the selection to 2880, 1440
> move the selection to 3060, 1440
> move the selection to 3240, 1440
> select ellipse "yellow circle"
> move the selection to 4860, 1440
> move the selection to 4680, 1440

move the selection to 4500, 1440
move the selection to 4320, 1440
move the selection to 4240, 1440
move the selection to 4960, 1440
end buttonUp

Notice that there should be a "select ellipse..." statement for each circle before each set of positions to ensure that the specified circle is moved. If this statement is not there for both circles, the animation may not work properly. Also note that the script that results from a recording does not have indentations (as we have been entering with the scripts we have typed in). Indentations, although making the scripts easier to read, do not affect the performance of the scripts in any way.

Now, we will reverse the movements of the two circles and paste this recorded script to the Separate button. Select the Separate button, and then select Edit and Start Recording. Now select the magenta circle (single-click on it). Then press the mouse button, move the magenta circle to the left 1/8 inch and release the mouse button. Repeat this until you have moved it to the left a total of six times (it should be at its original position when the movement is completed). Now single-click on the yellow circle to select it. Press the mouse button, and move the circle to the right 1/8 inch and release the mouse button. Continue this until you have moved the yellow circle to the right six times (to its original position). Then select Edit and Stop Recording. Next select the Separate button, click on Object, Button Properties, and Script. Click on Edit and Paste Recording. Its script should look like the one below (or else it may not work properly):

to handle buttonUp
select ellipse "magenta circle"
move the selection to 3060, 1440
move the selection to 2880, 1440
move the selection to 2700, 1440
move the selection to 2520, 1440
move the selection to 2340, 1440

> move the selection to 2160, 1440
> select ellipse "yellow circle"
> move the selection to 4140, 1440
> move the selection to 4320, 1440
> move the selection to 4500, 1440
> move the selection to 4680, 1440
> move the selection to 4860, 1440
> move the selection to 5040, 1440
> end buttonUp

Save your script. Your screen should again look like the one in Figure 9.7. Now let's test the animation you just created. Go to reader level. Now click on the Mix button. The two circles should come together smoothly. Click on the Separate button. The two circles should move apart smoothly and be positioned at their original coordinates. If you encounter problems, repeat the steps above and be sure that your scripts look like the ones listed in this exercise. Also be sure that you selected Draw and that Transparent was checked and Draw Direct was not checked.

> **Caution:** If your script is missing one of the "select ellipse..." statements, this is because you failed to select the object before moving it. Be sure you single-click on the object before you move it to its first position.

Completing the Sample Exercises

Be sure you feel comfortable with the above exercises before moving on to the application exercises. You may want to save the last sample exercise if your animation worked properly. This way you may go back to this file at a later time and examine the script. This may be helpful if you have problems creating other animation.

Application Exercises

Once you've gone through the sample exercises, you're ready to apply what you've learned to "The Color Book" application. We will create the second section of the book, called "Nature of Color." This section has two pages, which are shown in Color Plates 9 and 10. Color Plate 11 shows the result of the animation for the second page in this section. Display the grid (with the "Snap to grid" feature) and rulers. Maximize the window and move the tool palette to the far right. Open your application file (File and Open) and go to page 2 ("Physics of Color").

> **Shortcut:** To move quickly from page to page at author level, hold down the **Control** key while pressing the right or left cursor arrows on the keyboard.

Exercise #1: Building Page Three (Hue, Saturation, and Brightness)

The third page of the book is the first page of the section entitled "Nature of Color." This section title will be displayed on the two pages we will create for that section. The first of these pages uses the colors shown in the color tray labeled "3" in Color Plate 16. The finished page you create in this exercise should look like Color Plate 9, and its layout is shown in Figure 9.9.

Step 1. Creating a New Page

Create a new page by clicking on Page and New Page. The status box should now indicate that this is page 3 of 3. Notice that the background objects are displayed on this page.

Step 2. Entering the Title of the Section

To enter the title of the section on the top of page 3, we will follow the same procedures used for the "Physics of Color" page. Double-click on the blue record

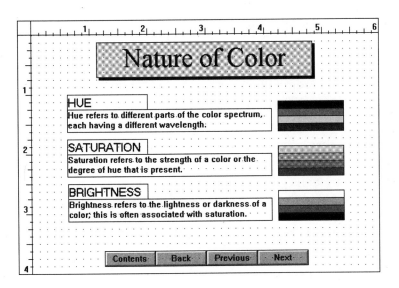

Figure 9.9

Layout of the third page of the book (including background and foreground objects).

field. When the vertical cursor appears, enter four leading spaces followed by **Nature of Color**.

The leading spaces should center the text in the record field. If yours isn't centered, experiment with the spaces until it is centered. Click on the selection arrow in the tool palette to exit from text input mode.

Step 3. Creating and Coloring the Rectangular Graphics

Three sets of rectangles are displayed on this page. Let's begin by creating a single narrow rectangle. Select the rectangle tool from the tool palette. Place the cross-hairs at 4-1/4 inches on the horizontal and 1-1/8 inches on the vertical. Draw a rectangle that extends to 5-3/8 inches horizontally and 1-1/4 inches vertically (see Figure 9.9). Now copy that rectangle to the clipboard and paste three copies on top of the original. Drag each copy down and position it so that it is touching the rectangle above. Your four rectangles should look like the upper set in Figure 9.9.

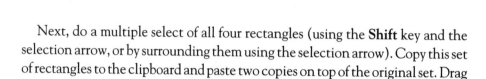

Next, do a multiple select of all four rectangles (using the **Shift** key and the selection arrow, or by surrounding them using the selection arrow). Copy this set of rectangles to the clipboard and paste two copies on top of the original set. Drag the two copies down, separating each set by 1/4 inch on the vertical (see Figure 9.9).

Open the color tray by pressing the **Control** key while double-clicking on the tool palette (while pointing to any object except the selection arrow or the zoom tool). Or you can open the color tray by clicking on Window and Palettes and checking Color tray. Select each narrow rectangle and individually apply a fill color so that your rectangles look like those in Color Plate 9. Refer to the color tray labeled "3" in Color Plate 16 for a better indication of the colors used.

Step 4. Creating the Fields and Text

Next, we need to create the fields that hold the text for hue, saturation, and brightness (see Figure 9.9). Begin by selecting the field tool in the tool palette. Place the cross-hairs at 5/8 inch on the horizontal and 1 inch on the vertical. Draw a field that extends to 2 inches horizontally and 1-1/4 inches vertically. Select this field, and click on Object and Field Properties. In the dialog box, select the following properties:

- Single line text
- Activate scripts

We'll change the border style to "None" later on. Click OK. Now while the field is still selected, choose a fill color of white and a stroke color of dark blue (see Color Plate 16 for the dark blue used for the stroke of this field). Now that you have assigned the properties to this field, you should copy it to the clipboard and paste two copies onto the original. Drag the first copy so that it is directly below the original, and its top margin is at 1-3/4 inches on the vertical. Drag the second copy so that its top margin is at 2-1/2 inches on the vertical.

Double-click on the top field and enter the word "HUE" (without the quotes). The text should be dark blue (the color you selected for the stroke). This is also the color of the field's outline, but this will disappear once we change the border style to None. Go to the next field down, and enter the word "SATURATION" (without the quotes). In the last field, enter the word "BRIGHTNESS" (again, without the quotes). We have just three more fields to create.

With the field tool selected, position the cross-hairs at 5/8 inch on the horizontal, and 1-1/4 inches on the vertical. Draw a field that extends to 4-1/8 inches horizontally and 1-5/8 inches vertically. Select this field, click on Object and Field Properties, and check the "Activate scripts" box. Be sure the field type is kept at the default of "word-wrap text." As with the other fields, we'll change the border style of this field to None in the next step. Using the color tray, select a fill color of white and a stroke color of black. Now, copy this field to the clipboard and paste two copies onto the original. Drag each copy down so that it is positioned as shown in Figure 9.9.

Select the top copy of this field, and enter the following text:

Hue refers to different parts of the color spectrum, each
having a different wavelength.

Let the text automatically wrap inside the field instead of entering a carriage return after the first line. Select the next copy of the field, and enter the following text:

Saturation refers to the strength of a color or the
degree of hue that is present.

In the last copy of the field, enter the following:

Brightness refers to the lightness or darkness of a
color; this is often associated with saturation.

Your screen should now look like the one in Figure 9.9.

Step 5. Changing the Border Style of the Fields

Finally, we want to change the border style of all of the fields to None. To do this using the shortcut method given in the last chapter, select the six fields that contain text (be sure you don't also select the rectangles that are filled with color) using a multiple select operation. When all fields are selected, click on Window and Command, and in the command window, enter the following command:

set borderstyle of selection to none

Then press the **Enter** key. Close the command window after this operation. (Alternatively, you may change each field's border individually, but this is more time-consuming.)

> **Shortcut:** Instead of clicking on Window and Command, you could press **Shift+F3**. This will open the command window, allowing you to enter a command.

Step 6. Naming the Page

This page must be named for two reasons. It is the page that starts the section called "Nature of Color," and in order for the hot object on the contents page to be able to access this section, we must name this page. Second, in a later section of the application, the words "hue" and "saturation" will be defined as hotwords. We need to name this page so that if the reader clicks on these words, they can access this page for more information.

To name this page, click on Object and Page Properties. In the dialog box, enter a page name of "nature" (without the quotes). Then click OK.

Step 7. Saving the Page and Checking it at Reader Level

Click on File and Save to save your work. The dialog box informs you of the amount of time remaining for this application. Press **F3** to go to reader level. Your page should look like the one shown in Color Plate 9. We'll test its performance with the rest of the book after we create the next page. Press **F3** to return to author level.

Exercise #2: Building Page Four (Color Mixture)

The fourth page of the book is shown in Color Plate 10. This page involves an animated sequence in which three colors can be mixed and separated. The result of mixing is shown in Color Plate 11. The basic layout of this page is shown in Figure 9.10. The layout with the "mixed" circles is shown in Figure 9.11.

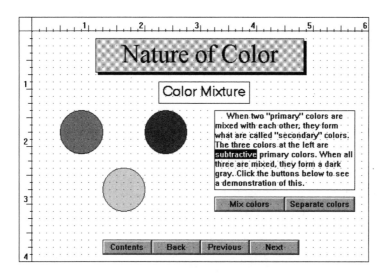

Figure 9.10

Layout of the fourth page of the book prior to the animation that moves the circles together. Background and foreground objects are shown.

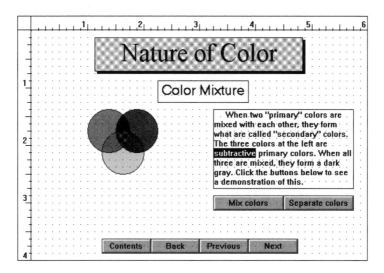

Figure 9.11

Positions of circles after they have been moved for the animated sequence.

Step 1. Starting a New Page

First, we need to begin a new page. To do this, be sure you are in author level and on page 3 (as indicated in the status box). Click on Page and New Page. You should now be on page 4 of 4, with the background objects displayed.

Step 2. Entering the Title of the Section

We need to again enter the section title, since we are on the second page of the same section. Double-click on the blue record field. When the vertical cursor appears, enter four leading spaces followed by **Nature of Color**. It should appeared centered in the record field. Click on the selection arrow in the tool palette to exit from text input mode.

Step 3. Creating the Fields with Text

There are two fields on this page. One contains the subtitle "Color Mixture"; the other contains information explaining color mixture, and has a hotword, which will be defined in the step after this one. First, let's create the field for the subtitle.

Select the field tool in the tool palette. Position the cross-hairs at 2-1/4 inches on the horizontal and 7/8 inch on the vertical. Draw a field that extends to 3-7/8 inches horizontally and 1-1/4 inches vertically. Select this object, click Object and Field Properties, and in the dialog box, select the following properties:

- Single line text
- Activate scripts

Click OK to close the dialog box and save your selections. With the field still selected, click on Text and Character and select a font of MS Sans Serif with a point size of 18. Click OK. Double-click on the field, and enter the words "Color Mixture" (without the quotes).

Next, let's create the larger field that contains the wrapping text. Click on the field tool in the tool palette. Place the cross-hairs at 3-1/4 inches horizontally and 1-3/8 inches vertically. Draw a field that extends to 5-3/4 inches horizontally and 2-3/4 inches vertically. Select this field, click on Object and Field Properties, and check the "Activate scripts" box. Click OK to save this property. We don't need to change the text style, since we will use the default font and point size. Now double-click on the field and enter the following text (with five leading spaces):

When two "primary" colors are mixed with each other, they form what are called "secondary" colors. The three colors at the left are subtractive primary colors. When all three are mixed, they form a dark gray. Click the buttons below to see a demonstration of this.

This text should fit inside the field. In the next step, we will create a hotword.

Step 4. Creating a Hotword

Notice in Figure 9.10 that the word "subtractive" is highlighted. While the vertical cursor is still inside this field, place it just before the word "subtractive" and highlight the word by pressing the left mouse button and dragging it over the word. Release the mouse button when the word is highlighted. Click on Text and Create Hotword. Then click on Object and Hotword Properties and in the dialog box, name this hotword "subtractive" (without the quotes). Next click on Script and enter the following lines of script:

```
to handle buttonUp

        request "A subtractive color selectively absorbs certain
wavelengths of light."

        end buttonUp
```

Save the script (**Control+S**, or Script and Exit/Update), and click OK in the dialog box.

Step 5. Creating Two Additional Buttons

This page has two additional buttons that will be used to mix and separate the colored circles. Select the button tool in the tool palette. Place the cross-hairs at 3-1/4 inches on the horizontal and 2-7/8 inches on the vertical. Draw a button extending to 4-1/2 inches horizontally and 3-1/8 inches vertically. Copy this button and paste the copy to the right as illustrated in Figure 9.10. Select the button on the left, click on Object and Button Properties, and label this button

"Mix colors" (without the quotes). Click OK. Select the button on the right, click on Object and Button Properties, label this button "Separate colors" (without the quotes), then click OK. Soon you will record some animation and paste the recordings to these two buttons.

Step 6. Creating and Coloring Transparent Circles

You next want to create the three circles shown in Figure 9.10. Begin by selecting the ellipse tool in the tool palette. Click on Draw, and be sure that Transparent is checked and that Draw Direct is *not* checked. Place the cross-hair at 1/2 inch on the horizontal and 7/8 inch on the vertical. While pressing the **Control** key on the keyboard, draw a circle that extends to 1-1/4 inches horizontally. It will automatically make a symmetrical ellipse (or circle) that extends to 2-1/8 inches on the vertical. Now copy this object to the clipboard and paste two copies onto the original. Drag the first copy so that its left border is at 2 inches on the horizontal and its top margin is at 1-3/8 inches on the vertical. Drag the second copy so that its left border is at 1-1/4 inches on the horizontal and its top margin is at 2-3/8 inches. The layout of your circles should look like those in Figure 9.10. Now open the color tray (if it is not already open), and color the three circles cyan, magenta, and yellow. Refer to Color Plate 10 and the color tray labeled "4" in Color Plate 16 for the colors you should use.

Now you must label these three circles. Select the circle on the upper left, click on Object and Graphic Properties, and give this circle the label of "cyan circle." Select the circle on the upper right and label it "magenta circle." Select the lower circle and label it "yellow circle." (None of the labels should include quotes.) Now you are ready to animate these circles.

Step 7. Creating Animation

You have already performed the basic steps in animating these circles in the sample exercise in which you moved two circles together (and apart) and assigned the animation scripts to buttons. What we will do here is essentially the same, but this step will involve a third circle.

Be sure that the grid is showing and that the "Snap to grid" feature is selected. Start the recording by clicking on Edit and Start Recording. Then single-click on the cyan circle (on the upper left) to select it. (Remember from the sample exercise that this initial selection is very important.) Then drag the circle to the right 1/8 inch. Release the mouse button to record its position. Depress the mouse button again, and drag the circle to the right another 1/8 inch. Record its position by releasing the mouse button. Repeat this procedure two more times (to move it to the right a total of four times). Now single-click on the magenta circle (in the upper right) to select it. Move it in 1/8-inch increments to the left, recording its position after each 1/8 inch, moving it a total of four times. Finally, single-click on the yellow circle to select it. Then move it up five times in 1/8-inch increments, recording its position along the way. Note that the yellow circle gets moved one more time than the other circles. When you have completed this movement, click on Edit and Stop Recording. Now select the "Mix colors" button. Click on Object, Button Properties, and Script. When the script window opens, click on Edit and Paste Recording to paste the recorded script to the dialog box. The script should look exactly like the one below:

```
to handle buttonUp
select ellipse "cyan circle"
move the selection to 900, 1980
move the selection to 1080, 1980
move the selection to 1260, 1980
move the selection to 1440, 1980
select ellipse "magenta circle"
move the selection to 2700, 1980
move the selection to 2520, 1980
move the selection to 2340, 1980
move the selection to 2160, 1980
select ellipse "yellow circle"
move the selection to 1800, 3240
move the selection to 1800, 3060
move the selection to 1800, 2880
move the selection to 1800, 2700
```

move the selection to 1800, 2520

end buttonUp

When you are satisfied that your script looks like the one above (including the statements to "select ellipse..." for each of the three circles), save your script, then click OK in the button's dialog box. (If it looks different, you can modify your script using standard word processing techniques, rather than rerecording these movements.)

You have created the animation to mix colors. Now you will create the animation to separate them. Begin by selecting Edit and Start Recording. First select the cyan circle by single-clicking on it. Then move it to the left in 1/8-inch increments, recording its position after each 1/8 inch move by releasing the mouse button. Be sure you move it to the left four times. Then select the magenta circle by single-clicking on it. Move it to the right four times in 1/8-inch increments, recording its position after each 1/8 inch. Finally, select the yellow circle, and move it down five times in 1/8-inch increments, recording its position every 1/8 inch. Click on Edit and Stop Recording. Then select the button labeled "Separate colors." Click on Object, Button Properties, and Script. When the script window opens up, click on Edit and Paste Recording. Your script should look like the one below:

to handle buttonUp

select ellipse "cyan circle"

move the selection to 1260, 1980

move the selection to 1080, 1980

move the selection to 900, 1980

move the selection to 720, 1980

select ellipse "magenta circle"

move the selection to 2340, 1980

move the selection to 2520, 1980

move the selection to 2700, 1980

move the selection to 2880, 1980

select ellipse "yellow circle"

```
move the selection to 1800, 2700
move the selection to 1800, 2880
move the selection to 1800, 3060
move the selection to 1800, 3240
move the selection to 1800, 3420
end buttonUp
```

If your script looks like the one above, save the script and click OK in the button's dialog box. If your script looks different, either repeat the recording steps or modify your script to match the one above. We have just one more step to complete this page.

Step 8. Changing the Border Style of the Fields

We still need to change the border style of the two fields we created. It's probably just as fast to do this individually, since there are only two fields. Select the field with the subtitle ("Color Mixture"). Click on Object and Field Properties and click on a border style of None. Then click OK to save this change. Now select the other field, and change its border style to None.

Step 9. Saving and Testing the Book

Save your file (File, Save). Now let's test the various additions you just made. Press the **F9** key so that any hotwords are displayed. Switch to reader level (press **F3**). You will probably be on the page you just created. Click on the Contents button to get to the first page of the book. Now try the following:

- Click on the "Nature of Color" field. The screen should now display the first page of this section.

- Click on the "Next" button. This should take you to the "Color Mixture" page.

- Click on the "Mix colors" button. The three circles should converge smoothly.

- Click on the "Separate colors" button. The three circles should separate smoothly to their original positions.

- Click on the hotword "subtractive." A dialog box with a message about subtractive color should be displayed.

- Click on the "Next" button. You should see the dialog box that warns you that you are on the last page of the book.

- Click on the "Previous" button. This should take you to the previous page, which is the "Nature of Color" page with information about hue, saturation, and brightness.

- Click on the "Back" button. This should return you to the "Color Mixture" page.

If you are satisfied that you have successfully completed these application exercises, you're ready to complete the book in the next chapter. If you have run into some problems, you might check the following to remedy them:

- Be sure you assigned the name of "nature" to the first page of the "Nature of Color" section.

- Check to be sure that the animation scripts look exactly like those listed above, and that they are assigned to the appropriate buttons. If you are missing any of the three statements to "select ellipse…" with the circle's name, you may run into problems.

- Be sure that the names of the three circles correspond with the names in the animated scripts.

Summary

In this chapter, you learned how to copy and paste multiple objects. You also learned how to create circles and squares using the **Control** key, how to apply transparent color, and how to animate objects on the screen. And you created two more pages for the application "The Color Book." In the next chapter, we'll complete "The Color Book" and add sound.

Glossary

draw direct   A property of an object that when true (or checked on the Draw menu), causes that object to appear in front of other objects. This should be set to false (or unchecked on the Draw menu) for an animated object to prevent flickering.

opaque object   An object that does not show other objects behind it.

transparent object   An object through which you may see other objects behind it.

Completing the Application and Adding Sound

In this chapter, you will complete "The Color Book" application, and add sound (an optional exercise, applicable only if you have a sound board). You'll also learn some other techniques such as creating scrolling fields, and copying and pasting "widgets" from the Multimedia Mini Widgets Book. And you'll learn a little more about "grouping" objects and manipulating them on the screen.

An Overview of the "Perception of Color" Section

The last section of the book consists of three pages that use the same background as the last two sections. These pages are shown in Color Plates 12, 13, and 14.

The last page (Color Plate 14) has a interesting exercise that illustrates an optical illusion using one of Multimedia ToolBook's three-dimensional "widgets," so if you plan to skip one of the pages in this section (perhaps because you lack sufficient time to complete "The Color Book"), you might want to consider skipping one of the first two instead of the third.

As we did in the last two chapters, let's go through some sample exercises to give you a feel for some of the techniques we'll be using to develop the last section of the application.

Sample Exercises

Exercise #1: Grouping Objects

In the last two chapters, you learned how to select multiple objects so that you could quickly move or copy all of them as a single unit. Recall that this operation is temporary. As soon as you click outside the selection handles surrounding the selected objects, the objects are no longer grouped together. In this exercise, you learn how to group objects more permanently so that even if you click outside the selection handles, the objects are still grouped together.

Open ToolBook, and begin a new file. You may either display grids and rulers for this exercise or not, depending on your preference. We won't really need them here. Now select the rectangle tool in the tool palette. Draw a rectangle that is about 1-1/4 inches wide and 1 inch high. Now copy the rectangle and paste a copy on top of the original. Drag the copy to the right until it is next to (and touching) the original. Open the color tray, and fill the rectangle on the left with a color, leaving the copy on the right filled with white. Your drawing should look similar to the one in Figure 10.1.

Now select both rectangles by pressing the **Shift** key while you click on both rectangles. The selection handles should surround both rectangles. To illustrate that this multiple selection is temporary, click anywhere on the page outside these handles. Now click on one of the rectangles, and notice that it is not

Figure 10.1

Illustration of two rectangles created in sample exercise.

grouped with the other one anymore. Now select both rectangles again. To group them together permanently, click on Object and Group. Now if you click anywhere on the page outside the selection handles, the objects will stay grouped. Try this, and then click on one of the rectangles. Note that both rectangles are surrounded by handles, and that the icon in the title bar of the tool palette indicates that the selected object is a group. They will remain "grouped" until you "ungroup" them. To ungroup a set of objects, select the group, then click on Object and Ungroup. Now if you click on one of the objects, the others will not be selected along with it.

Exercise #2: Manipulating Draw Objects

ToolBook calls the graphic objects that you create using the drawing tools in the tool palette "draw objects." The rectangle you drew in the last exercise is a draw object. In this exercise, you'll learn to manipulate these objects so that they are oriented differently on the screen.

Begin by making sure the two rectangles you created are grouped and selected. Copy this group and paste a copy onto the original. Now drag the copy down below the original so that its upper margin is just touching the lower margin of the rectangles above. With this copy still selected, click on Draw and Flip Horizontal. Your drawing should now look like the one in Figure 10.2 on the next page.

In order to see some of the other manipulations better, you should change the color of one of the rectangles. Begin by selecting the lower group of rectangles. Ungroup them by clicking on Object and Ungroup. Notice that the icon in the title bar of the tool palette indicates several objects that are now separated or

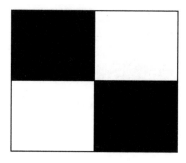

Figure 10.2

Illustration of double set of rectangles created in sample exercise.

ungrouped. With the selection arrow, click anywhere on the screen so that the rectangles are not multiply selected. Now select the colored rectangle on the right and fill it with a different color. Be sure that your two colored rectangles are different colors.

Now let's select all of the rectangles on the screen (there are four of them) using the selection arrow, and group them into a single group by clicking on Object and Group. Your selected drawing should look similar to the one in Figure 10.3. Experiment with its orientation by clicking on the following:

- Draw, Flip Vertical
- Draw, Flip Horizontal
- Draw, Rotate Left
- Draw, Rotate Right

Note that in each of these procedures, you are changing the orientation of the objects as a single unit because they are grouped.

Exercise #3: Recording a Manipulation

Now that you feel comfortable changing the orientation of a draw object, let's record some of these changes, and assign the recording to a button. You already have an object on the screen that we can use for this exercise—a set of rectangles.

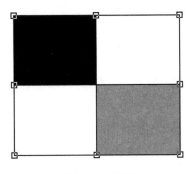

Figure 10.3

Illustration of grouped rectangles.

Before we start, select the rectangles (they should still be grouped). Click on Object and Group Properties and give the group a name of "rectangles" (without the quotes), then click OK. Now, create a button below the rectangles and label it "Rotate."

Now start recording by clicking on Edit and Start Recording. Now select the set of rectangles, and click on Draw and Rotate Right. Then click on Edit and Stop Recording.

> **Shortcut:** You can use the **F8** key to toggle between Start Recording and Stop Recording.

Now select the button, and click on Object, Button Properties, and Script When the script window opens up, click on Edit and Paste Recording. Your script should look like the one below:

    to handle buttonUp
    select group "rectangles"
    send RotateRight
    end buttonUp

In fact, you could have typed in this script instead of recording it as we did. Save the script (either by pressing **Control+S**, or by clicking on Script and Exit/Update).

Now switch to reader level, and test your button. Each time you click on it, the set of rectangles should rotate to the right.

Exercise #4: Copying and Pasting Widgets

Recall from Chapter 7 that Multimedia ToolBook provides you with a set of "widgets" that you can copy and paste into your application. Many of these objects have their own scripts, which also get pasted into your application. Other widgets require that you write your own scripts. In this sample exercise, we'll copy a horizontal slider into a sample application. It won't be functional, but it will give you some experience in copying widgets.

Begin with a new file (or simply a new page). To run the Multimedia Mini Widgets application (without exiting from the one you are currently working on), you may click on File and Run. From the menu of ToolBook files, select the file called "mwidget.tbk" (see Figure 10.4). The opening screen of the Mini Widgets Book will be displayed. Two buttons on this screen allow you either to go directly to the "map" of available widgets, or to "continue," which will display some introductory information before taking you to the map of widgets (see Figure 10.5). On the map, you will see a list of widgets that you may paste into your application. Only those shown in white are available in the Evaluation Edition. All of these widgets are available in the full version of Multimedia ToolBook. Notice that the icons are animated. The full version also allows you to incorporate these animated widgets into your application.

To see the horizontal sliders, single-click on this widget (it is under the "Generic Control" category—see Figure 10.5). A variety of sliders is displayed along with instructions telling you how to copy them into your application. To copy a slider, click on the button labeled "Click me to copy an object" (see Figure 10.6 on page 224). A green window opens up that instructs you to "Click an object to copy it to the clipboard." Simply point to the top horizontal slider, and single-click on it. The green window closes and the slider is now on the clipboard waiting to be pasted into your application. Close the Mini Widgets Book by clicking on File and Exit. (You could also double-click on the control-menu box, but *be sure* that you click on the correct box, or else you will close ToolBook instead!)

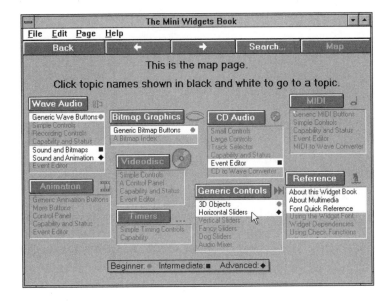

Figure 10.4

Dialog box with list of files to run.

Figure 10.5

Map of Multimedia Mini Widgets Book; available widgets
are shown in white.

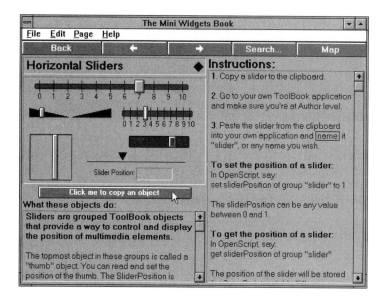

Figure 10.6

Illustration of window displaying horizontal sliders.

Now with the ToolBook screen displayed, click on Edit and Paste. The horizontal slider you selected should be displayed on your screen. You may now resize it or move it to a different position. You may even want to test this slider by switching to reader level. Move the slider by pointing to the button and dragging it up and down the scale. In an actual application, you would need to write some script to link this slider to some function such as going to a particular spot in a sound clip or an animated sequence. This particular widget does not have any script associated with it (you may check this by selecting this object and clicking on Object, Group Properties, and Script). In a later exercise, we'll copy a widget and write some script for it. And when we add a button for sound, the widget we copy will have its own script.

Completing the Sample Exercises

You might want to look at some of the other widgets in the Mini Widgets Book to see what they look like and do. Once you have gone through the sample exercises and feel comfortable with the new techniques you have learned, you are ready to move on to the exercises to complete "The Color Book" application.

Application Exercises

In the next few exercises, you'll apply what you learned in the sample exercises, and build the last section of the book, called "Perception of Color." This section has three pages, shown in Color Plates 12, 13, and 14. As I mentioned earlier in this chapter, if you choose to skip one of these pages for lack of time remaining in your application, you might consider skipping one of the first two. The last page, although not very colorful, has an interesting exercise illustrating an optical illusion.

Begin by displaying the grid and rulers. Maximize the window and move the tool palette to the far right. Open the file containing "The Color Book" application. Go to the last page of the book (this should be page 4) using the **Control** and right arrow keys. You should have the last page of the "Nature of Color" section displayed on the screen.

Exercise #1: Building Page Five (Color Contrast)

The fifth page of the book is shown in Color Plate 12, and has a subtitle of "Color Contrast." Its layout is illustrated in Figure 10.7 on the next page.

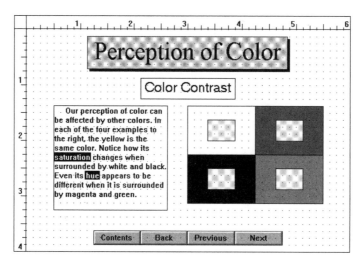

Figure 10.7

Layout of the fifth page of the book (including background and foreground objects).

Step 1. Starting a New Page

Create a new page by clicking on Page and New Page. The status box should indicate that you are on page 5 of 5. Notice the background objects are displayed.

> **Note:** If you accidentally create a new page in the wrong place, you can delete the page by clicking on Edit and Select Page. Then click on Edit again, and Clear. This will remove the page from the book.

Step 2. Entering the Title of the Section

Using the selection arrow, double-click on the blue record field. When the vertical cursor appears, type a single leading space followed by **Perception of Color**. The title should appear centered in the record field. If you enter more than one leading space, the entire text will not appear in the field.

Step 3. Creating and Coloring the Rectangular Graphics

There are eight rectangles on this page—four small ones lying on top of four larger ones. Let's create the four large ones first. Select the rectangle tool in the tool palette. Position the cross-hairs at 3 inches on the horizontal and 1-3/8 inches on the vertical. Draw a rectangle that extends to 4-1/4 inches horizontally and 2-1/4 inches vertically. Copy the rectangle to the clipboard and then paste three copies of it onto the original. Drag the copies to the positions illustrated in Figure 10.7. Open the color tray, and apply a fill color to each of them as shown in Color Plate 12. Refer to the color tray labeled "5" in Color Plate 16 for the specific colors used.

Now we will draw the smaller rectangles. Select the rectangle tool in the tool palette. Begin drawing the first small rectangle at 3-3/8 inches on the horizontal and 1-5/8 inches on the vertical. The rectangle should extend to 3-7/8 inches horizontally and 2 inches vertically. Because we want all four of the small rectangles to be the same color, let's apply a color to this before we copy it. Color this rectangle the pale yellow color circled in the fifth color tray in Color Plate 16. Now copy the rectangle and paste four copies on the original. Then drag each small rectangle to the center of the larger ones, as illustrated in Figure 10.7.

> **Note:** If you copy the larger rectangle by mistake, you can delete it, or any object, by selecting it and clicking on Edit and Cut.

The rectangles on your screen should now look like those shown in Color Plate 12.

Step 4. Creating the Fields with Text

There are two fields containing text on this page. Let's first create the smaller one that contains the subtitle "Color Contrast." Select the field tool in the tool palette. Draw a field that extends from 2-1/8 inches horizontally and 7/8 inch vertically to 3-7/8 inches horizontally and 1-1/4 inches vertically. Select this field, click on Object and Field Properties, and select the following:

- Single line text

- Activate scripts

Click OK to close the dialog box and save your selections. With the field still selected, click on Text and Character and select a font of MS Sans Serif with a point size of 18. Click OK. Double-click on the field, and enter a leading space followed by **Color Contrast**. The subtitle should appear centered in the field.

Select the field tool again, and draw a field that extends from 1/2 inch horizontally and 1-3/8 inches vertically to 2-5/8 inches horizontally and 3-1/4 inches vertically. Select the field, click on Object and Field Properties, and check the box to "Activate scripts." Click OK to save your selection. We will use the default text style, so we don't need to change that. Now double-click on the field and enter the following (with five leading spaces):

> Our perception of color can be affected by other colors. In each of the four examples to the right, the yellow is the same color. Notice how its saturation changes when surrounded by white and black. Even its hue appears to be different when it is surrounded by magenta and green.

Be sure you allow the text to wrap inside the field and that you don't enter any carriage returns. Stay in text input mode until you complete the next step—creating hotwords.

Step 5. Creating Hotwords

There are two hotwords in this paragraph of text: "saturation" and "hue." Place the vertical cursor just in front of the word "saturation." Press the left mouse button, and drag the cursor over the word to highlight it (as illustrated in Figure 10.7). Now click on Text and Create Hotword. Then click on Object and Hotword Properties. Name this hotword "saturation" (without the quotes). Then click on Script, and enter the following lines of script:

```
to handle buttonUp

    go to page "nature"

end buttonUp
```

Recall that the other hotwords we have defined use the "request" statement to open a dialog box and display some line of information about the hotword. In this example, we already have information about saturation (and hue) on another page in the book. So we can take the reader to that page to provide additional information. Save the script and click OK in the Hotword Properties dialog box.

Next, highlight the word "hue," click on Text and Create Hotword, and then Object and Hotword Properties. Name this hotword "hue" (without the quotes), and give it the same script you gave to the hotword "saturation," because this should take the reader to the same page. Save the script and click OK in the dialog box.

Step 6. Changing the Border Style of the Fields

Select the field containing the subtitle ("Color Contrast"), click on Object and Field Properties, select a border style of None, then click OK. Do the same for the larger field with the paragraph of text.

Step 7. Naming the Page

Because this is the first page of the section "Perception of Color," we need to name it so that if the user clicks on this topic on the contents page, this page will be displayed. Click on Object and Page Properties and name this page "perception" (without the quotes).

Step 8. Saving the Book

Before testing the page, be sure to save your work by clicking on File and Save.

Step 9. Testing the Page and Hotwords

Before we move on to the next page, let's test this one so you can see how the hotwords you just created work. Press **F3** to switch to reader level. Also press **F9** to show the hotwords, and **F11** to center the page on the screen. The page you just created should be displayed. Now move the cursor over the word "saturation." The cursor should look like a small rectangle and when you click on the word, the page you created in the last chapter (with hue, saturation, and brightness) should be displayed. To return to the page that contained the hotword, click on the Back button. This demonstrates how the "bookmark" feature works. Now try this again, clicking on the word "hue." Again, you should see the page with information about hue, saturation, and brightness. Click on the Back button to return to the page you just created.

> **Note:** If the hotwords do not take you to the right page, be sure that the scripts for these hotwords look exactly like the one given on page 228, and that the page with the information on hue, saturation, and brightness has been named "nature" (without the quotes).

Exercise #2: Creating Page Six (Afterimages)

The sixth page of the book, shown in Color Plate 13, deals with afterimages. Figure 10.8 illustrates its layout.

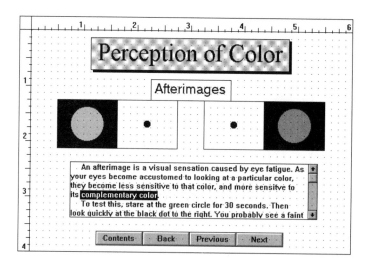

Figure 10.8

Layout of the sixth page of the book (including background and foreground objects).

Step 1. Creating a New Page

Be sure you have switched back to author level. Create a new page by clicking on Page and New Page. The status box indicates that you are on page 6 of 6, and the background objects are displayed.

Step 2. Entering the Title of the Section

Although you entered the title to the section on the last page, you must enter it again on this page. Double-click on the blue record field. When the vertical cursor appears, enter a single leading space followed by **Perception of Color**. The title should be centered in the record field.

Step 3. Creating the Subtitle Field

Select the field tool, and draw a field that extends from 2-1/4 inches horizontally and 7/8 inch vertically to 3-3/4 inches horizontally and 1-1/4 inches vertically. Select the field, and give it the following properties:

■ Single line text

■ Activate scripts

■ Border style of None

In this example, we have set the border style to None prior to entering text. You should not have problems in this particular case. Now, select Text and Character and choose a font of MS Sans Serif with a point size of 18. Double-click on the field, and enter a leading space followed by **Afterimages**. The text should be centered in the field (indicated only by the selection handles).

Step 4. Drawing the Graphics

Begin by selecting the rectangle tool in the tool palette. Position the cross-hairs at 1/2 inch on the horizontal and 1-1/4 inches on the vertical. Draw a rectangle that extends to 1-5/8 inches horizontally and 2-1/8 inches vertically. Now create a copy of the rectangle and paste the copy adjacent to it on the right side (see Figure 10.8). The two rectangles should be touching. Now fill the rectangle on the left with a black color.

Next, we need to draw two circles. Select the ellipse tool. For the rectangle on the left, place the cross-hairs at 3/4 inch horizontally and 1-3/8 inches vertically. While holding down the **Control** key on the keyboard (to force the ellipse to form a circle), draw a circle until the cross-hairs are at 1-3/8 inches on the horizontal and 2 inches on the vertical. Your circle should look like the one shown in Figure 10.8. Now we need to draw the small circle on the rectangle to the right. Position the cross-hairs at 2-1/8 inches horizontally and 1-5/8 inches vertically. Hold down the **Control** key, and draw a circle until the cross-hairs are at 2-1/4 inches horizontally and 1-3/4 inches vertically.

> **Note:** If either circle you have drawn is not the right size or not in the right position, you may resize it using its handles (and the **Control** key to force it into a circle), or move it by dragging it to the proper position.

Now using the color tray, fill the small circle with black. After you are satisfied that your drawing looks like the one on the left in Figure 10.8, you are ready to copy it. You have just created four objects (two rectangles and two circles). Let's first select all of these and then group them. Choose the selection arrow in the tool palette. Now draw a rectangle that surrounds the outside perimeter of the two rectangles. Notice that this has selected all of these objects. Now click on Object and Group. Now you are working with a single object, which will make the following operations simpler. First copy this object and paste the copy onto the original. Next, drag the copy to the right until its left margin is at 3-1/4 inches. While the grouped object is still selected, click on Draw and Flip Horizontal. This should produce what looks like a mirror image of the first set of objects.

Now we need to ungroup both sets of objects so we can color the larger circles. Select the group to the left. Click on Object and Ungroup. Now click outside the perimeter of the group to unselect them. Select the large circle on the left. With the color tray open, select a fill color of green (see the green in Color Plate 13, and in the sixth color tray of Color Plate 16). Now ungroup the objects on the right, click outside the perimeter of the objects to unselect them, select the large circle on the right, and fill it with red. Your drawings should look like those in Color Plate 13.

Step 5. Creating the Scrolling Field with Text

The last field on the page is a scrolling field, which is created just like any other field—only its border is different. Select the field tool, and create a field that extends from 3/4 inch on the horizontal and 2-3/8 inches on the vertical to 5-3/8 inches horizontally and 3-3/8 inches vertically. Select the field, and enter the following properties:

- Activate scripts
- Border style of scroll bar

Click OK to save these properties. Note that the field has a scroll bar on the right. You will enter more text than can be displayed in the field, but the scroll bar will allow the reader to scroll down and read the remaining text.

We'll keep the default type style. Double-click on the field and enter the following text (with the leading spaces as illustrated):

An afterimage is a visual sensation caused by eye fatigue. As your eyes become accustomed to looking at a particular color, they become less sensitive to that color, and more sensitive to its complementary color.

To test this, stare at the green circle for 30 seconds. Then look quickly at the black dot to the right. You probably see a faint afterimage of a magenta circle (green's complementary color). Do the same with the red circle. When you look at the black dot next to it, you will see an afterimage of a blue-green circle (red's complementary color). Some people have to try this several times before they perceive the effect.

You will want to enter a carriage return at the end of the first paragraph, but otherwise let the text wrap in the field.

Step 6. Creating a "Hot Phrase"

We can create a hot object out of more than one word, and this might be called a *hot phrase*. Place the cursor just in front of the word "complementary" in the first paragraph. Highlight the two words, "complementary color" (see Figure 10.8). Then click on Text and Create Hotword. Then click on Object and Hotword Properties. Name this hotword "complementary color" (without the quotes). Then enter the following script:

> to handle buttonUp
>
> > request "Complementary colors are widely separated in the color spectrum. Examples are green and magenta, red and blue-green, and yellow and blue."
>
> end buttonUp

Don't enter carriage returns in the "request" statement. If you do, you will get a syntax error when you try to save the script. Your text will extend far to the right in the script window, but this is fine. Save the script, then click OK in the dialog box.

Step 7. Coloring the Field

Now we want to fill this field with a pale yellow color to offset it from the rest of the page. Be sure you are out of text input mode (click on the selection arrow in the tool palette). With the color tray open, fill this field with the pale yellow indicated in the color tray labeled "6" in Color Plate 16.

Step 8. Saving the Book

Before we begin the last page of the book, let's save our work (click on File and Save).

Exercise #3: Creating Page Seven (Optical Illusions)

This is the last page of the book, and although it is not very colorful, it has an interesting example of an optical illusion using one of ToolBook's three-dimensional widgets. The page is shown in Color Plate 14, and its layout is illustrated in Figure 10.9.

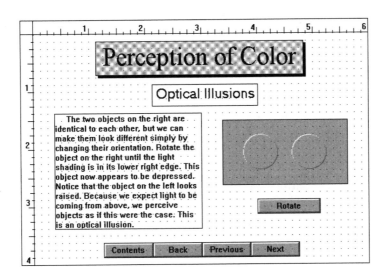

Figure 10.9

Layout of the seventh page of the book (including background and foreground objects).

Step 1. Creating a New Page

Be sure you are still at author level. Create a new page by clicking on Page and New Page. The status box should indicate that you are on page 7 of 7.

Step 2. Entering the Title of the Section

As with the other two pages of this section, you must again enter the section title on this page. Double-click on the blue record field, and enter a single leading space followed by **Perception of Color**.

Step 3. Creating the Subtitle Field

Select the field tool and place the cross-hairs at 2-1/8 inches on the horizontal and 7/8 inch on the vertical. Draw a field that extends to 4 inches horizontally and 1-1/4 inches vertically. Select the field and give it the following properties:

■ Single line text

- Activate scripts

Click on OK in the dialog box to save these properties. Now select Text and Character. Choose a font of MS Sans Serif and a point size of 18. Click OK. Now double-click on the field and enter a leading space (to center the subtitle in the field) followed by **Optical Illusions**.

Step 4. Creating the Large Text Field

Select the field tool again, and place the cross-hairs at 3/8" horizontally and 1-3/8 inches vertically. Draw a field that extends to 3 inches on the horizontal and 3-3/8 inches on the vertical. Click on Object, Field Properties, and the "Activate scripts" box. Click OK in the dialog box. We will use the default type style. Double-click on the field and enter the following text (with five leading spaces):

> The two objects on the right are identical, but we can make them look different simply by changing their orientation. Rotate the object on the right until the light shading is in its lower right edge. This object now appears to be depressed. Notice that the object on the left looks raised. Because we expect light to be coming from above, we perceive objects as if this were the case. This is an optical illusion.

The text should fit in the field you drew, and look like that shown in Figure 10.9.

Step 5. Creating the Rectangular Graphic

Select the rectangle tool in the tool palette. Draw a rectangle that extends from 3-3/8 inches horizontally and 1-1/2 inches vertically to 5-5/8 inches horizontally and 2-5/8 inches vertically. Fill this rectangle with the gray color circled in the color tray labeled "7" in Color Plate 16. It is important that you use this gray, because this will affect the three-dimensional appearance of the circular objects we will copy to its surface.

Step 6. Copying and Pasting a Widget

Now we will copy one of the three-dimensional widgets from ToolBook's Multimedia Mini Widgets Book. First open up the Mini Widgets Book by clicking on File and Run. Select the file named "mwidget.tbk" from the list of files (either double-click on the file name or highlight the file and click OK). When the opening screen is displayed, click on the button labeled "Map" to go directly to the map page. Single-click on "3D Objects" under the heading "Generic Controls." A window with various three-dimensional objects will be displayed. Single-click on the button labeled "Click me to copy an object." Another message window is now displayed telling you to "Click an object to copy it to the clipboard." Refer to Figure 10.10 for the widget you should click on. It is the circle on the right that appears to be raised. After you have clicked on this object, close the Mini Widgets Book by double-clicking on its control-menu box, or by selecting File and Exit from its menu bar. (Be sure you do not close the ToolBook window behind it.)

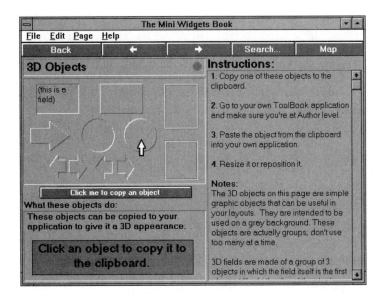

Figure 10.10

Screen display indicating the widget to copy for the application.

Once you have the ToolBook window displayed again (and are on page 7), click on Edit and Paste. This will paste the circular widget onto the screen (in the same position it occurred in the Mini Widgets Book). Notice that it has selection handles surrounding it. Now we want to change its properties. While it is still selected, click on Draw and if Draw Direct is not checked, click on it to set this to true (or checked).

Now drag the circle onto the gray rectangle so that it is positioned like the left-hand circle in Figure 10.9.

> **Note:** If you find that you cannot keep the circle on top of the gray rectangle (because it goes behind the rectangle when you try to drag it to that position), this is because you don't have the circle's Draw Direct property checked. Click on Draw and be sure that there is a checkmark next to the Draw Direct property. Also be sure that the Transparent property (in the Draw menu) for this object is *not* checked.

When the circle is correctly positioned, its left margin should be at 3-3/4 inches on the horizontal ruler, and its upper margin should be at 1-3/4 inches on the vertical ruler. Next, copy the circle and paste the copy on top of the original. Drag the copy to the right so that its left margin is at 4-5/8 inches on the horizontal and its top margin is even with the circle on the left.

Because we want to manipulate the circle on the right (by rotating it), let's name this circle. Actually, as you will soon see, this circle is a "group" of three circles that are overlapped to give it a three-dimensional appearance. Do *not* ungroup this object. Now, be sure the right circle is selected. Click on Object and Group Properties and name this group "right circle" (without the quotes). Then click OK to save this name.

Step 7. Creating a Button to Rotate the Right-hand Circle

Next, we need to create the "Rotate" button shown in Figure 10.9. Select the button tool in the tool palette. Place the cross-hairs at 4 inches on the horizontal and 2-7/8 inches on the vertical. Draw a button that extends to 5-1/8 inches horizontally and 3-1/8 inches vertically. Select the button, click on Object and Button Properties, and label this button "Rotate" (without the quotes). Click OK.

Now we will record a script for that button. Click on Edit and Start Recording. Click on the right-hand circle to select it. Then click on Draw and Rotate Right. A dialog box is displayed asking, "Repair 3D object after resizing?" Respond "No" to this question. (Otherwise, ToolBook will return the circle to its original orientation.) Now click on Edit and Stop Recording. Select the Rotate button and click on Object, Button Properties, and Script. When the script window is displayed, click on Edit and Paste Recording. Your script should look like the one below:

```
to handle buttonUp
select group "right circle"
send RotateRight
end buttonUp
```

If yours is slightly different, you should edit it to match the one above. Save your script, then click OK in the Button Properties dialog box. Let's rotate this right-hand circle back to its original position by clicking on Draw and Rotate Left (but don't record this procedure). The two circles should look like those in Figure 10.11a.

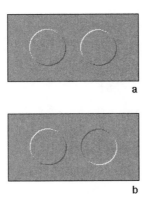

a

b

Figure 10.11

(a) Both objects appear to be raised; (b) the object on the right appears to be depressed.

Step 8. Changing the Border Style of the Fields

Select the field containing the subtitle for the page. Change its border style to None by clicking on Object and Field Properties, checking the border style box labeled None, and clicking OK. Select the larger field containing the paragraph of text, and change its border style to None.

Step 9. Saving and Testing the Book

Once you are satisfied that your page matches the one in Color Plate 14, save your book (File and Save). Next, switch to reader level to test the pages you created. Press **F9** to show hotwords, and **F11** to center the page on the screen. Try the following tests:

- With the "Optical Illusions" page displayed, click on the "Rotate" button to be certain that the right-hand circle rotates. Rotate the circle until the light shading is in its lower right edge (see Figure 10.11b). The circle should now appear to be depressed. Rotate it two more times until it matches the circle on the left (see Figure 10.11a).

- Click on the "Next" button to verify that the dialog box with the warning indicating that this is the last page of the book is displayed.

- Click on the "Contents" button; this should take you to the contents page.

- Click on the light green field with the section title "Perception of Color." This should take you to the first page of that section (with the "Color Contrast" subtitle).

- Click on the hotword "hue." This should take you to the page with explanations of hue, saturation, and brightness. Now click on the "Back" button to return to the "Color Contrast" page.

- On the "Color Contrast" page, click on the "Next" button. This should take you to the "Afterimages" page. Try the exercise described in the scrolling window to see the afterimages described. This will also test the scroll bar.

- Click on the hot phrase "complementary color" to be sure that the dialog box opens with explanatory text.

- Click on the "Next" button to go to the next (and last) page (with the "Optical Illusions" subtitle). Test the "Rotate" button again.

If your book does not respond as indicated above, pay close attention to any dialog boxes that warn you of an error. These can help you determine where the problem is. Be sure your scripts match those provided in the application exercises and that you have correctly named the necessary pages and objects.

If your book responds as expected, congratulations! If you don't plan to add sound, you have completed the book. Whether or not you add sound, you may now go through the book's various sections to see how it all looks. And hopefully, you still have plenty of time left to work on the application. If you have a sound board, you will use some of this time to add sound to your application. If you don't have a sound board, you might want to modify the book or add to it in any way you choose.

In the next chapter, you will learn how you can further explore multimedia, using ToolBook and also using Windows' multimedia capabilities for narrating a "wave" file.

If you plan to add sound, continue with the next exercise. If you don't want to add sound, go on to the next chapter.

Exercise #4: Adding Sound

Your book is nearly complete. We will now add the final element of multimedia— sound. If you do not have a sound board, you should skip this exercise and go on to the next chapter. If you do have a sound board, we will add to the contents page a button that will play a tune when clicked.

Although the full version of Multimedia ToolBook has a special widget (in its Mini Widgets Book) that allows you to record sound, this widget is not available in the Evaluation Edition. Therefore, in this exercise, we will use a pre-made sound file that has been provided with the Evaluation Edition. The next chapter will provide an exercise in which you can provide your own narration (if you have a microphone) using the capabilities of Windows with multimedia extensions.

Before beginning, be sure you are at author level and are on the first (contents) page of the book.

> **Shortcut**: You can quickly jump to the first page of the book by clicking on Page and First. You may similarly go to any of the other pages listed in the Page menu.

Step 1. Copying and Pasting a Button from the Mini Widgets Book

We will copy and paste a button from the Multimedia Mini Widgets Book and position it below the field containing the text "Click on topic." Figure 10.12 shows the position of this button (labeled "Click for Sound") on the contents page.

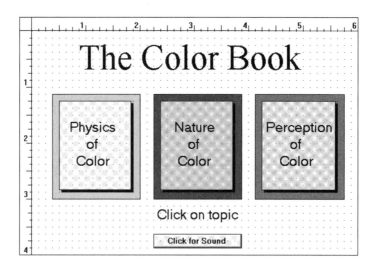

Figure 10.12

Position of the sound button on the contents page.

Click on File and Run. Double-click on the file "mwidget.tbk." On the opening display of the Multimedia Mini Widgets Book, click on the button labeled

"Map." On the map page, the first category is called "Wave Audio." There are several selections under this category, but only three are available in the Evaluation Edition. Notice that one of the options *not* available in this category is "Recording Controls." This is the option you would select with the full version of Multimedia ToolBook if you wanted to copy a widget to record your own sound. In this Evaluation Edition, we will instead incorporate a pre-made sound file.

Single-click on the topic called "Generic Wave Buttons." Two generic wave buttons are displayed. Double-click on the one labeled "Play and Wait." A dialog box will open that instructs you to choose a wave file for this button. A wave file is a sound file with a particular format, and has a file extension of .WAV. A list of wave files is displayed. Select the file named "passport.wav" (see Figure 10.13 on the next page). This wave file will be played, and it is now linked to the "Play and Wait" button. (An error message will be displayed if you don't have a sound board, or if you have not correctly installed its driver(s) in Windows.)

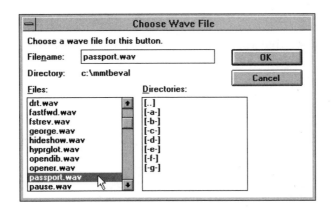

Figure 10.13

Screen display indicating wave file to select for sound button.

Now single-click on the button labeled "Click me to copy a button." A green window opens and displays the message "Click an object to copy it to the clipboard." Single-click on the "Play and Wait" button. Close the Mini Widgets Book window by double-clicking on its control-menu box. When you are back on the contents page of "The Color Book" application, click on Edit and Paste to paste the button to the screen. Drag the button to the position shown in Figure 10.12 and in Color Plate 7. Its left margin should be at 2-1/4 inches and its top margin should be at 3-5/8 inches. Resize the button so that its right margin is at 3-7/8 inches on the horizontal and its bottom margin is at 3-7/8 inches on the vertical. It should now be placed symmetrically on the page.

Step 2. Renaming the Button

Finally, let's change the button's label. With the button selected, click on Object and Button Properties. Enter a label of "Click for Sound" (without the quotes), and leave its name as it is. You might want to click on Script to see the script that was pasted into your application along with this button. It is more complex than the script we have been entering so far.

> **Caution:** If you choose to look at the script, do *not* make any changes to the script, or the button may not function properly. To ensure that you do not save any changes, close the script window by clicking on Script and Exit/Cancel. This will keep the script in its original form. Click OK in the Button Properties dialog box to save the button's new label.

Step 3. Saving the Book and Testing the Sound Button

Save the application (File and Save), and then switch to reader level. Press **F11** to center the page on the screen. Now click on the "Click for Sound" button. The wave file you selected should now play the music stored in the "passport.wav" file. (An error message will be displayed if you don't have a sound board, or if you have not correctly installed its driver(s) in Windows.)

Note: If you later want to substitute a different wave file, such as the narrative we will create in the next chapter, you may do so by clicking on the "Click for Sound" button (at reader level) using the *right* mouse button. A selection of wave files will be displayed. When you select a new wave file, its file name will be linked to the "Click for Sound" button, so that when you click on this button, the new wave file will be played.

Summary

In the last three chapters, you have created a multimedia application incorporating all of the components of multimedia—text, graphics, animation, and sound. Except for the wave file, you have created all of these components from scratch using the built-in features of Multimedia ToolBook. In this chapter, you learned how to manipulate graphic objects on the screen and how to incorporate sound (or "wave") files into your application. In the next chapter, we will explore some other techniques for adding pre-made graphics and text files to a ToolBook application, and for recording a narration using Windows's multimedia capabilities.

Glossary

draw object   A graphic object in ToolBook that is created using one of the draw object tools.

group   A set of objects that can be manipulated as a single object.

hot phrase   A hot object consisting of two or more words.

wave file   A sound file with a particular format that is saved in a file with an extension of .WAV.

Chapter

11

Further Exploring

In the previous four chapters, you have learned the basics of using an authoring software package—Multimedia ToolBook. The techniques you learned using this software will be useful no matter what authoring software you use, because the concepts are very similar from one authoring tool to the next—just as word processing concepts are similar in the various word processing packages. In the application you built, you learned how to apply those concepts to build a multimedia "book" incorporating text, graphics, animation, and sound. You built all of these components (except sound) using Multimedia ToolBook's built-in development features. There is certainly a lot more to ToolBook than we touched on in this book.

In this chapter, we will do some further exploring. You will learn how to copy some clip art from ToolBook's clip art book. And you will learn to create text, graphics, and sound files using Windows's accessory programs and how to import these files into ToolBook. This chapter will round out your experience in building a multimedia program.

Exercise #1: Copying and Pasting ToolBook Clip Art

In previous exercises, you copied "widgets" from ToolBook's Multimedia Mini Widgets Book. Another useful book that is provided with the Evaluation Edition is a book of clip art that contains numerous graphics that you can copy into your application.

Open a new file in ToolBook (File and New). Now click on File and Run. When a list of files is displayed, select the file named "clipart.tbk" (see Figure 11.1). This is ToolBook's Clip Art Book. The opening screen displays two scrolling windows—one with instructions on copying clip art to your book, and one with a list of available clip art. (The full version of Multimedia ToolBook has a larger set of clip art.)

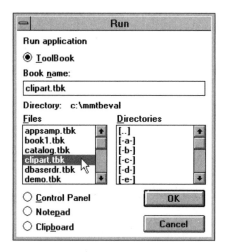

Figure 11.1

Dialog box that displays list of ToolBook files to run. The file "clipart.tbk" runs ToolBook's Clip Art Book.

Let's try the following. Double-click on the clip art "Fish" from the scrolling menu in the right-hand window. You will now see several "objects" displayed on the screen. Single-click on the large, colorful fish on the right (see Figure 11.2). Now, close the Clip Art Book by double-clicking on its control-menu box. When your ToolBook page is again displayed, click on Edit and Paste to paste this fish onto your page. With the object selected, you may now move it to a new place on the page, or resize it. You could integrate any of ToolBook's clip art with your applications, and even animate these objects by moving them across the screen and recording their positions. (You could try this with the fish you just pasted onto your ToolBook page.)

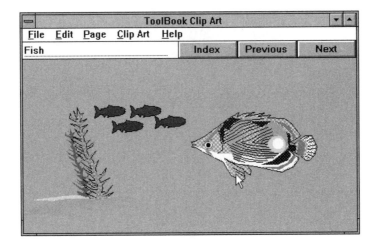

Figure 11.2

Clip art with several objects. The chapter's exercise uses the large fish on the right.

Exercise #2: Importing a Text File

There may be times when you want to import text that was created using a package other than your authoring tool. For example, you may have a list of names and addresses that was created in a database package that you would like to import into ToolBook to build an interactive address book. This exercise will show you how to import a text file. We will use Windows's Write program to create the lines of text, and then import that text into ToolBook.

Begin a new file. Now, minimize this window by single-clicking on the minimize box (with the down arrow) in the upper right-hand corner of the ToolBook window. Notice that the ToolBook window is now represented by a small icon (see Figure 11.3) in the lower left corner of your screen. Now open up the Accessories window by double-clicking on the icon labeled "Accessories" in

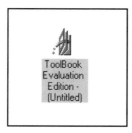

Figure 11.3

The ToolBook icon that is displayed when ToolBook's window is minimized.

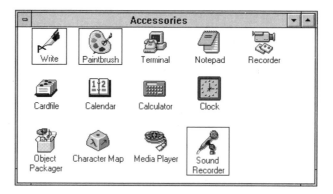

Figure 11.4

Icons surrounded by rectangles indicate the three Windows programs used in this chapter for creating text, graphics, and sound.

the Windows's Program Manager window. Figure 11.4 indicates the three icons (surrounded by rectangles) we will be using in the following exercises to create text, graphics, and sound. With the Accessories window open, double-click on the "Write" icon to open Windows's word processor. In the Write window, enter the following names and addresses, entering a carriage return after each one:

Sarah Demere,111 S. 15th St.,New York,NY,10011,(212)555-2437

Cary Matthews,222 West Ave.,San Diego,CA,92019,(619)555-2436

John Peterson,333 Main St.,Santa Clara,CA,95055,(408)555-2438

Note that each line of text contains six "units" of information (such as city, state, and zip code) separated from each other with a comma, and that there are no spaces between these units of information. This is the format that most database packages use when saving a database file in ASCII format. In this example, each unit of information represents a database "field," and each line of information for a person and their address represents a database "record." To save this file, click on File, Save As, and in the dialog box (see Figure 11.5 on the next page), be sure to specify the following:

- file name of "names.txt" (without the quotes)

- file type of Text Files (*.TXT) (you will need to click on the down arrow in this box and scroll to the proper file type)

- the drive and subdirectory where ToolBook is loaded (such as C:\MMTBEVAL)

Then click OK to save this file. Now close the Write window by double-clicking on its control-menu box. (If you do not close the Write window, you will get a "sharing" error message when you try to import the "names.txt" file in ToolBook.) To restore the ToolBook window, you may either double-click on its icon (which is in the lower left-hand corner of the screen), or single-click on the icon, and click on "Restore" in the resulting menu.

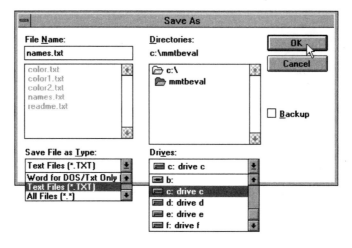

Figure 11.5

*Dialog window indicating the selections you should make to save your
text file (assuming ToolBook is loaded in the subdirectory
"c:\mmtbeval" on your computer).*

With a new ToolBook file open, click on File and Import. Change the File Name
template to read "*.TXT" (rather than "*.ASC"), be sure the proper drive and
subdirectory are selected, and click OK. You should see the file you just created
in the list of files that are displayed. Double-click on the file "names.txt." Notice
that the status box on the ToolBook page indicates that you are now on page 1
of 3, and displays six record fields, each containing one of the units of information
for each line of text that you entered (see Figure 11.6). You could switch to the
background, and move and/or resize these record fields. When ToolBook
imports text files, it places each line of text (delimited with a carriage return and
line feed) on a separate page. This can be very useful when you are using a flat-
file database, such as the one used in our example. ToolBook reads each line as
a record, and places that information on a separate page. In the example we just
completed, you could create an address book (with each person on a separate
page), similar to the one in ToolBook's tutorial ("Learning ToolBook"). You could
also add other elements such as photographs and hotwords.

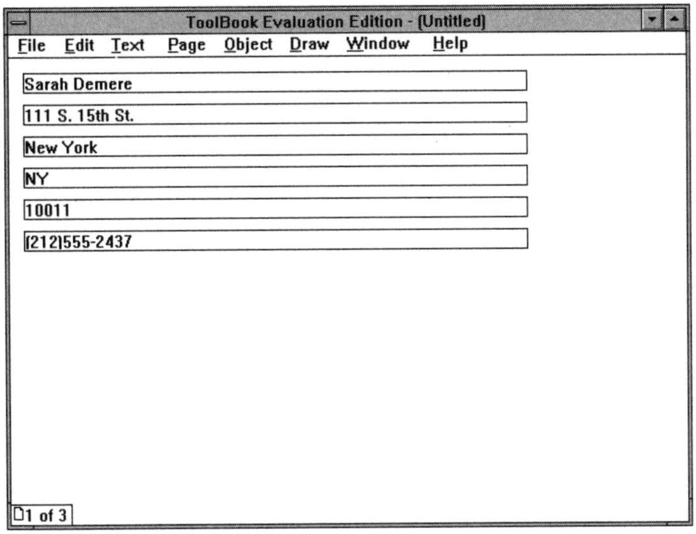

Figure 11.6

*ToolBook screen display resulting from importing a text file created
in Windows's Write program.*

This exercise has also illustrated the convenience of using the Windows
environment. Its multitasking capabilities allowed you to work in one software
package (Write) while keeping the other (ToolBook) open. And you may have
noticed that Write's menu bar operations are very similar to those of ToolBook's
(and other Windows applications). These points will be illustrated again in the
examples that follow.

Example #3: Creating and Importing a Graphic File

Next we will use Windows's Paintbrush program to create a graphic image, and
then we will import that graphic into ToolBook. Begin a new file in ToolBook,
and then minimize the ToolBook window by single-clicking on its minimize box.
Open the Paintbrush program by double-clicking on its icon in the Program

Manager's Accessories window (the same window that contained the "Write" icon used in the last exercise; see Figure 11.4). Figure 11.7 shows the screen that is displayed when you first open up Paintbrush. Notice that the drawing tools are displayed on the left (in a "toolbox"), and the color palette is displayed at the bottom. The line width is shown in the "linesize box."

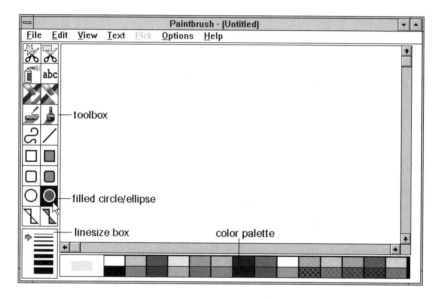

Figure 11.7

Screen display of Windows's Paintbrush program.

We first want to specify a fairly small size for the image. To do this, click on Options (in Paintbrush's menu bar), and Image Attributes. Change the width to 2.0 inches and the height to 2.0 inches (see Figure 11.8), and be sure that "in" (inches) is selected for Units, and that Colors is selected (vs. Black and White). Then click OK. Note that your drawing area has been reduced.

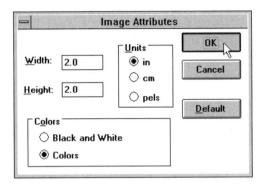

Figure 11.8

*Dialog box for selecting image attributes of a
graphics file in Paintbrush.*

Select a color such as blue by clicking on that color in the color palette. Next, select the "filled circle/ellipse" drawing tool (shown highlighted in Figure 11.7). Draw a couple of filled circles. (In Paintbrush, you force an ellipse to form a circle by holding down the **Shift** key instead of the **Control** key.) Paintbrush is an example of a different type of drawing package than the one you used in ToolBook, which was very object-oriented. In ToolBook, you work with an entire object, whereas in Paintbrush, you work with sets of pixels. To move a circle in Paintbrush, you must select the "scissors" tool or the "pick" tool (the two icons represented by scissors at the top of the toolbox). Using one of these tools, you surround the object or portion of the object that you want to work with (for instance, to move). You should refer to your Windows manual for more information on using Paintbrush. You may later go back into Paintbrush and experiment with its other tools.

For this exercise, we will save the graphic. Click on File and Save As. In the dialog window, be sure to specify the following:

- file name of "circles.bmp" (without the quotes)
- file type of "16 Color bitmap (*.BMP)"
- the drive and subdirectory where ToolBook is loaded (such as C:\MMTBEVAL)

Click OK to save the file. Now close Paintbrush by double-clicking on its control-menu box, or by clicking on File and Exit. Restore the ToolBook window by double-clicking on its icon in the lower left-hand corner of the screen. With the ToolBook window displayed, click on File and Import Graphic. The dialog box that is displayed should look like the one in Figure 11.9. If yours looks different, be sure that you have selected a .BMP format, and that the drive and subdirectory displayed are the ones in which you saved the graphic file. Double-click on the file "circles.bmp" to import this file. Notice that the entire graphic image is treated as a single object that you may move to a new position, or resize using its handles.

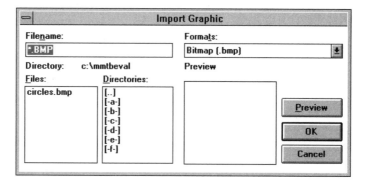

Figure 11.9

Dialog box for selecting a graphic file to import.

Using similar steps, you could create a graphic (or animated) image using another software package, or scan an image into the computer and save it as a file, and then import this graphic into ToolBook.

Exercise #4: Creating a Narrative Using Windows's Sound Recorder

Now you will learn how to create your own sound file using Windows's Sound Recorder. You may then substitute the resulting "wave" file for the musical wave file we used in the "Click for Sound" button in "The Color Book" application. You may only do this exercise if you have a microphone plugged into your sound board. You should plan a short narration before starting out. You might want to give a brief introduction to "The Color Book" to tell the reader what the application is about. Try to keep your narration short (perhaps 30 seconds or less) because the longer the narration, the larger will be the resulting sound file.

Begin by minimizing the ToolBook window. Double-click on the Sound Recorder icon in the Program Manager's Accessories window (see Figure 11.4) to open the Sound Recorder window. Figure 11.10 illustrates this window with its buttons and wave box. When you first open the Sound Recorder, the "Record" button (with the microphone icon) is the only active button. Be sure your microphone is turned on. Now, click on the Record button to start recording. (Note that the Stop and Rewind buttons are now active.) Record your narration by speaking into the microphone. The length of your narration is indicated in seconds, and the sound level is indicated in the "wave box." When you have finished, click on the Stop button (activating the Play button). Click on the Rewind button to go to the beginning of the recording. Then click on Play to play back your narration.

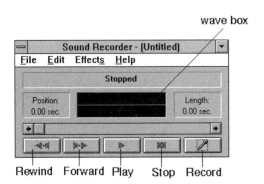

Figure 11.10

Sound Recorder window, illustrating its buttons and wave box.

The scroll bar and position counter indicate your position in the sound file. You may click Forward to go to any position or stop the playback at any position. You may record on top of your present recording by rewinding, or you may record new sound at any position in the file. Or you may go to the end of the file and continue recording from that position. There are many other things you may do to modify the sound. For example, you could click on Edit in the menu bar, and include sound from other files (using Insert File or Mix with File). You may even add some special effects by clicking on Effects. Options including changing the speed of the recording, or adding an echo effect. You may even play the recording in reverse.

Once you are satisfied with your recording, click on File and Save As. In the dialog box, be sure to select the following:

- file name (such as "color.wav," without the quotes)
- file type of "sounds (*.wav)" (you will need to click on the down arrow in this box and scroll to the proper file type)
- the drive and subdirectory where ToolBook is loaded (such as C:\MMTBEVAL)

Click OK to save the wave file. Close the Sound Recorder window by double-clicking on its control-menu box. In the next exercise, we will incorporate this sound file in "The Color Book."

Exercise #5: Adding the Narration to ToolBook

In the last chapter, you created a sound button (if you have a sound board), and linked this button to a wave file called "passport.wav." We will now substitute your narration for this wave file so that when the reader clicks on the "Click for Sound" button on the contents page of the book, your narration will be played.

Restore the ToolBook window. Now open up "The Color Book" application that you built in the last few chapters. Be sure you are on the first (contents) page of the book. Switch to reader level (press **F3**). Now click on the "Click for Sound" button with the *right* mouse button (if you click on it with the left mouse button, it will play the wave file you assigned to the button in the last chapter). A dialog window opens asking you to choose a wave file. Your narration file (such as "color.wav") should appear in the list of files. (If it does not, you probably saved it in a different subdirectory.) Now select your narration file. Then, click on the "Click for Sound" button with the *left* mouse button. Your narration should play. Remember that clicking with the left mouse button will play the wave file assigned to that button. Clicking with the right mouse button will allow you to select a different wave file and assign it to that button so that in the future, that sound file will be played each time the button is clicked. Be sure to save "The Color Book" file if you want this new sound file to be used in the future.

From the few exercises in this chapter, you've learned how to create files using other packages and incorporate them into ToolBook. This capability will provide you with much more flexibility and power when creating your multimedia applications.

Summary

This book has introduced you to the exciting world of multimedia, and if you have followed the exercises, you have learned first-hand how a multimedia program with its various components is built. With the knowledge you have now, your future explorations should be much more informative and rewarding. Appendix C provides you with a list of resources available to help you along. There are several multimedia magazines and newsletters, as well as organizations you can join. Many of these organizations publish their own newsletters and other publications. User groups are another excellent way to learn about multimedia, so you should check to see if your area has a multimedia user's group. Other very good sources of information are CompuServe's multimedia forums. There are many files you may download for free (except for on-line CompuServe charges). These files may contain graphics, animation, or sound. In addition, many of the newsletters listed in the resource list (in Appendix C) are downloadable from CompuServe.

There is so much to learn about multimedia. And no matter what you do with it, two things are certain—you'll never be bored, and you'll enjoy developing your own useful applications.

Glossary

database field   A "unit" of information of a database record that is stored in a database file; in an ASCII file, it is delimited from other database fields by a character such as a comma.

database record   A collection of database fields; in an ASCII file, it is often separated from other records by a carriage return and line feed.

filled circle/ellipse tool   Drawing tool in Windows's Write program used to create ellipses and circles.

linesize box   Box in Windows's Paintbrush program used to select line width.

Paintbrush	Windows's accessory program used to create and modify graphic images.
pick tool	Tool in Windows's Paintbrush program used to surround a graphic image with a rectangle so that the image may be moved or modified in some way.
scissors tool	Tool in Windows's Paintbrush program used to surround a graphic image with an irregular outline so that the image may be moved or modified in some way.
Sound Recorder	Windows's accessory program used to create and modify wave sound files.
toolbox	Collection of tools in Windows's Paintbrush program.
wave box	Box in Windows's Sound Recorder that indicates the relative volume of recorded sound.
Write	Windows's accessory program for word processing.

Appendix
A

Glossary

<u>**101-key enhanced keyboard**</u>	Standard keyboard having 101 keys including 12 function keys and separate cursor movement keys; requirement of MPC standard.

A

<u>**access time**</u>	Amount of time it takes a CD-ROM drive to locate specified information; measured in milliseconds.
<u>**actor**</u>	An individual object that moves in an animation sequence; also called "cast member."
<u>**ADC**</u>	Analog to Digital Converter; converts analog sound to digital information; standard feature on an MPC sound board.

<u>animation</u>	Refers to moving graphic images; usually involves the simulation of movement by sequentially displaying several frames showing a progression of movement.
<u>animation clip software</u>	Software that provides a library of animation sequences that can be included in a multimedia application.
<u>animation software</u>	Permits user to create and control animation sequences and incorporate sound to accompany the animation.
<u>architecture</u>	The overall structure and design of a computer system.
<u>ASCII</u>	American Standard Code for Information Interchange; standard character format that allows various computers and programs to exchange character information.
<u>author level</u>	The mode in ToolBook in which the user develops a program or "book" by creating objects, foregrounds, and backgrounds.
<u>authoring software</u>	Specialized software used to develop computerized books and multimedia applications; uses interactive links to connect associated information.
<u>auto-hypertext</u>	An automatic hypertext facility; using auto-hypertext, the program recognizes text that has more information associated with it and automatically displays that information.

B

<u>background</u>	A template consisting of objects and properties that are shared by pages in the book.
<u>balloon help</u>	Feature of some software that causes explanatory information to be displayed when the mouse pointer is moved over certain words, without the need to click on the mouse button.
<u>Bernoulli Drive</u>	An external storage device using cartridges capable of storing large amounts of data.

board (or interface card)	A component that fits into the expansion slot of the system unit and expands the capabilities of the computer; many allow the computer to communicate with an external hardware device such as a CD-ROM.
book	Another name for a ToolBook program or application consisting of a group of pages with which the user interacts.
bookmark	A facility that allows the user to return to the previous screen or starting point after jumping to associated information.
bps	Bits per second; a measurement of speed used with modems, such as 2400-bps or 9600-bps.
bus	Set of wires that transfers information in a computer.
bus mouse	A type of mouse that connects to a separate board in the computer.
button	A screen object with a label indicating what action it activates.

C

camera	An external hardware device that, along with a video board, is used to capture video images.
cartridge	A removable, high-capacity disk used with an external storage device such as a Bernoulli drive.
cast member	An individual object that moves in an animation sequence; also called an "actor."
cast-based animation	Animation that involves the creation and control of individual objects ("cast members" or "actors") that move across a background.
CD-ROM drive	Compact Disk Read Only Memory; a high-capacity storage device that can store up to 600 MB of data; it does not allow user to save information, but only to read stored data;

required by the MPC standard to have a transfer rate of at least 150 KB per second.

click Term for the rapid press and release of the mouse button.

clip art Software with a collection of simple graphic images that can be incorporated into other applications.

clock speed Number of clock cycles per second at which information is sent through the computer's bus; measured in millions of clock cycles per second, or megahertz (MHz).

clone A computer system that is a copy of another's architecture.

color tray One of the color palettes (the other is the spectrum palette) used to color objects.

communications software Software that allows a computer to communicate with another computer.

compatibility The ability of hardware and software to work together; compatibility is dependent on the computer's architecture and operating system.

CPU Central Processing Unit; the computer's electronic brain which controls the processing of the computer and allows it to perform instructions; sometimes called the microprocessor; the MPC standard requires at least a 386SX CPU.

D

DAC Digital to Analog Cor.verter; converts digital information to analog sound; standard feature on an MPC sound board.

database field A "unit" of information of a database record that is stored in a database file; in an ASCII file, it is delimited from other database fields by a character such as a comma.

database record	A collection of database fields; in an ASCII file, it is often separated from other records by a carriage return and line feed.
debugger	A facility that helps developers locate errors in a program, and may suggest how to correct these errors.
dialog box	A window that either communicates a message or requests specific information.
DOS	Disk Operating System; the operating system most commonly used on personal computers.
double-click	Term for two rapid clicks of the mouse button.
dragging	A mouse operation that involves pointing to an object and moving the mouse while holding down the mouse button, thus moving the object to another position.
Draw Direct	A property of an object that when true (or checked on the Draw menu), causes that object to appear in front of other objects. This should be set to false (or unchecked on the Draw menu) for an animated object in order to prevent flickering.
draw object	A graphic object in ToolBook that is created using one of the draw object tools.
driver	A software program that tells the computer how to control or operate a hardware device.
Dynamic Data Exchange (DDE)	Feature that allows user to exchange data quickly and easily among various Windows programs.
Dynamic Link Libraries (DLL)	Feature that allows user to control other Windows applications from within a single Windows program.

E

EGA	Enhanced Graphics Adapter; graphics adapter capable of displaying 640 x 350 pixels with 16 colors (or gray scales).

EISA
: Extended Industry Standard Architecture; the architecture used by most major brands of PC-compatible computers with 386 and 486 microprocessors; this is the same architecture as the IBM-PC/XT computer.

event-driven software
: Software that is driven by events or program actions as a result of clicking on menu options or buttons, or other objects.

expansion port
: The opening in the back of the computer that corresponds to an expansion slot.

expansion slot
: A connection in the computer into which various interface boards are plugged.

extended graphics
: Graphics adapters with capabilities beyond Standard VGA; examples are 640 x 480 with 256 colors, 800 x 600, and 1024 x 768.

F

field
: An object that generally holds text entered by either the author or the reader.

fill icon
: Used to assign color to the inside of an object.

filled circle/ellipse tool
: Drawing tool in Windows's Write program used to create ellipses and circles.

flat-file database
: Simple database that is not associated with any other database.

floppy disk drive
: A magnetic storage device that allows you to save data on a floppy disk; most common sizes are 5.25 inch and 3.5 inch disks; the MPC standard requires a 3.5 inch floppy disk drive with 1.44 MB capacity.

foreground
: Element of a page that consists of objects specific to that page.

frame-based animation
: Animation that is created by designing each frame individually as it will be displayed.

G

Graphical User Interface (GUI)	The graphic environment used by some software such as Windows, and which displays easy to understand menus and symbols (or icons).
graphics	The display of images on a computer monitor; images may be still or full-motion video.
graphics accelerator board	Special graphics board that controls not only resolution and the number of colors the computer can display, but speeds up the refresh rate for displaying graphic images.
graphics board	Hardware device that allows the computer to display graphic images; the type of graphics board (such as EGA, VGA, and Super VGA) determines the resolution of images; the MCA standard requires a Standard VGA graphics board capable of displaying 640 x 480 pixels on a screen and 16 colors.
graphics memory	Memory attached to a video graphics card that increases the display speed and the number of colors that can be displayed.
group	A set of objects that can be manipulated as a single object.

H

hard disk drive	A high-capacity magnetic storage device that allows you to save data; the MCA standard requires a minimum hard disk capacity of 30 MB.
headphones	Allows you to listen to sound via connection to the CD-ROM drive or the sound board; required by the MPC standard.
hot objects	Any object that when clicked on initiates some action; examples are hypertext (or hotwords) and hypergraphics.
hot phrase	A hot object consisting of two or more words.

hotwords	Words that have associated information that is accessible to the user; sometimes called "hypertext."
hypermedia	Integration of text, graphics, animation, and sound into a multimedia program using interactive links.

I

icon	A small symbol displayed on the screen that, when clicked on with a mouse, carries out some action.
integrated software	Software that integrates several types of applications such as word processor, spreadsheet, and database.
interactive links	Connections that allow user to jump from one topic to another in a nonlinear way.
ISA	Industry Standard Architecture; the architecture used in earlier IBM-PC and -XT computers with 8086 or 286 microprocessors.

J

joystick	Used to control object movements, especially in games; required by the MPC standard.
joystick port	Port to accommodate the joystick; generally part of the sound board and interchangeable with the MIDI port; required by the MPC standard.

L

layer	The relative order of objects on a background or foreground. Each object has its own layer, with the most recently created object having the highest layer number.

line palette	Palette used to select width of lines and outlines.
linesize box	Box in Windows's Paintbrush program used to select line width.

M

maximize button	Button used to expand a window to its maximum dimensions.
MCA	Micro Channel Architecture; the architecture used by most newer models of IBM PS/2 computers.
memory (RAM)	Random Access Memory; the electronic storage of the computer which is temporary; information stored in the computer's memory is lost when the computer is turned off; the MPC standard requires a minimum of 2 MB of memory.
microphone	Device used to input sound into the computer's sound board.
microprocessor	The electronic brain of the computer; see also CPU, or Central Processing Unit.
MIDI	Musical Instrument Digital Interface; an international standard developed for digital music; the MIDI standard determines the cabling and hardware and communications protocol needed to transfer information, or music, between electronic musical instruments or recording equipment and a computer. The MPC standard requires that the sound board have a MIDI in port, a MIDI out port, and a MIDI synthesizer.
minimize button	Button used to shrink a window to an icon.
modem	Hardware device that, along with special software and a phone line, allows your computer to communicate with another computer.
monitor	A device that displays computer output; must be compatible with the graphics board.
mono	Sound recorded on a single channel.

mouse Device used to point to and select screen options; required by the MPC standard.

MPC standard Multimedia PC standard; popular standard developed to ensure that a computer system has all the necessary capabilities to run multimedia software; developed by Microsoft Corporation in cooperation with various hardware manufacturers, this refers specifically to PCs running under Windows with multimedia capabilities, and also ensures that any separately sold hardware or software carrying the MPC logo will be compatible.

multimedia Any form of communication that uses more than one medium to present information; computer program integrating text, graphics, animation, and sound.

Multimedia PC A computer meeting the MPC standard.

multiple selection Procedure for selecting more than one object for some operation, such as moving.

multisync monitor A monitor that can display images using various graphics adapters such as EGA, VGA, and Super VGA.

multitasking The ability of a computer to run multiple software packages at one time.

N

navigation A term that refers to the user's progress through a multimedia application.

NTSC National Television Standards Committee; standard signal output by televisions in North America and Japan, and by many video cameras such as VCRs.

O

object	Any "thing" that is displayed on the screen, including buttons, fields, text, or graphics.
object-oriented software	Software that is based on the creation and manipulation of objects.
OCR software	Optical Character Recognition; software used to interpret scanned characters as text information rather than as meaningless shapes.
opaque object	An object that does not show other objects behind it.
OpenScript	The programming or scripting language of ToolBook.
operating system	The basic software that controls how the computer operates.
optical storage device	Storage device that uses a laser beam to read information from the disk; a CD-ROM is an optical storage device.

P

page	The basic unit of a book that is made up of objects on a background and a foreground.
page layout	A term that refers to the layout of the screen in a computerized book.
Paintbrush	Windows's accessory program used to create and modify graphic images.
painting/drawing software	Allows you to create and modify graphic images.
PAL	Phase Alternate Line; standard signal output by televisions in most countries outside of North America and Japan.

parallel port   Port commonly used to connect a computer to a printer; required by the MPC standard.

pattern palette   Palette used to select the pattern of objects.

pen   A useful device for inputting information, by touching either a screen or a special input pad.

pick tool   Tool in Windows's Paintbrush program used to surround a graphic image with a rectangle so that the image may be moved or modified in some way.

pixel   Short for "picture element," which is a unit of measurement across a computer screen.

platform   A crucial factor determining hardware and software compatibility; it is defined by the computer's architecture and operating system.

polygon palette   Used to select the number of sides of a polygon.

presentation software   Software used to present information in the form of graphs, charts, and diagrams.

properties   Unique attributes of an object that control how it appears on the screen and how it behaves in the program.

prototype   A model or mock-up of an actual program that often is used to illustrate sample screen displays.

public-domain software   Software that may legally be used by the public without a fee having to be paid to the owner or developer.

R

RAM   Random Access Memory; another term for memory.

reader level   The mode in ToolBook in which the user reads a program or "book" and interacts with it using hot objects; the user may also enter text in specified fields to be stored with the book.

record field	A special field that is associated with the background and allows the developer or reader to enter different text in the same field on every page of the book.
refresh rate	The speed at which graphic images are "painted" or displayed onto the screen.
restore button	Button used to shrink a window to its original size.
RGB	Red, Green, and Blue; type of output used by some cameras.
runtime system	Feature that allows an application to be run on a computer without the complete program software used to develop the application.

S

sampling rate	Number of sound "samples" the sound board takes per second; measured in kilohertz (KHz); the MPC standard requires a sound board with a recording sampling rate of at least 11 KHz and an output rate of 11 and 22 KHz.
sampling size	Determines the range of sound adjustment; the MPC standard requires a sound board with a sampling size of at least 8 bit for both input and output.
scanner	A hardware device used to digitize photographs and drawings so that they may be displayed on the computer; may be a large "flatbed" model or a small hand scanner.
scanning software	Software that allows the user to scan graphics or text and store them as digitized information.
scissors tool	Tool in Windows's Paintbrush program used to surround a graphic image with an irregular outline so that the image may be moved or modified in some way.
screen capture software	Captures graphic images displayed on the computer screen and saves them as graphic image files.

scripting language	Programming language used by authoring software that controls the application.
SCSI interface	Small Computer System Interface; an interface that allows several hardware devices to be connected in a "daisy chain" configuration.
selection arrow	A tool that is used to select specific objects for some operation.
serial mouse	Type of mouse that connects to the computer using the serial port.
serial port	Port that connects the computer to a variety of hardware devices such as a modem, mouse, or serial printer; required by the MPC standard.
single-tasking	The ability of a computer to run only one program at a time.
sliders	Objects that control the playback of multimedia elements such as sound and animation.
sound board	Hardware device that records and plays sound used in multimedia applications; the MPC standard requires a sound board with a MIDI in port, a MIDI out port, and a MIDI synthesizer.
sound clip software	Software that provides a library of sound effects and/or music that can be included in a multimedia application.
Sound Recorder	Windows's accessory program used to create and modify wave sound files.
speakers	Hardware used to amplify sound from the sound board or CD-ROM drive; required by the MPC standard.
spectrum palette	One of the color palettes (the other is the color tray) used to color objects.
standard keyboard	Original IBM 83-key keyboard with 10 function keys and no separate cursor movement keys.

Standard VGA	Standard Video Graphics Array; graphics adapter capable of displaying 640 x 480 pixels with 16 colors (or gray scales); required by the MPC standard.
stereo	Sound recorded on two channels.
storage	Refers to the means whereby information is saved when the computer is turned off; may mean magnetic disks (either floppy or hard) that allow you to add your own information to them, or optical disks (such as CD-ROM) that don't allow you to write files to them.
storyboard	A visual outline (with simple sketches, notes, and instructions) of the actions, sounds, and images that will appear or occur during the course of a multimedia program.
stroke icon	Used to assign color to the outline and text of an object.
Super VGA	Super Video Graphics Array; graphic adapter with a resolution of 800 x 600.
supporting software	Software that is used in addition to an authoring tool that provides more powerful capabilities to create certain types of files or performs some other function useful in developing an application.
surge suppressor	A device that prevents electrical surges from damaging electrical equipment that is plugged into it.
system unit	The main body of the computer that contains most of the electronics (such as the CPU) and internal hardware.

T

text searching	Feature that allows user to search quickly for a word and access associated information.

<u>**title bar**</u>	The wide bar along the top of a window that displays a title such as a file name or name of the window; the title bar is used to drag the window to a new position on the screen.
<u>**tool palette**</u>	The set of icons displayed at author level that allows the developer to create and work with objects.
<u>**toolbox**</u>	Collection of tools in Windows's Paintbrush program.
<u>**touch screen**</u>	Device that allows user to input information by touching the screen.
<u>**transfer rate**</u>	The rate at which the CD-ROM drive can transfer located information to the computer; measured as kilobytes per second; the MPC standard requires a transfer rate of at least 150 KB per second.
<u>**transition effects**</u>	Special effects used in animation such as fade-in and fade-out, layering, and rotation of objects.
<u>**transparent object**</u>	An object through which you may see other objects behind it.

V

<u>**VGA**</u>	Video Graphics Array; see Standard VGA and Super VGA.
<u>**video capture board**</u>	Hardware device that captures still graphic images, animation, or live motion video and saves this information in a file.
<u>**video monitor**</u>	Monitor that allows you to observe live video images as you are capturing them on the computer.
<u>**virtual reality**</u>	Computer technology involving a glove and goggles that allows the user to experience three-dimensional interaction with the computer.

W

wave box
Box in Windows's Sound Recorder that indicates the relative volume of recorded sound.

wave file
A sound file with a particular format that is saved in a file with an extension of .WAV.

widgets
Pre-made ToolBook objects that the developer can copy into an application such as buttons and sliders; any associated scripts controlling these objects are also copied into the application.

Windows
A software package that provides a Graphical User Interface and overcomes many of the limitations of DOS.

Write
Windows's accessory program for word processing.

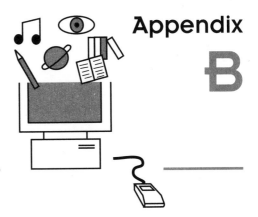

ToolBook Tips and Common Scripts

I n Part II of this book, you learned some basics about using ToolBook. These chapters provided you with some tips, shortcuts, and common scripts, which are consolidated in this appendix. This will make it easier for you to refer to them in the future when you build other applications.

Tips

Function keys

Many ToolBook commands can be quickly performed using the function keys below and on the following page.

F1   Accesses help with any ToolBook operation.

F3   Toggles between reader and author level.

F4   Toggles between background and foreground.

F5	Searches for text within the book's pages.
F6	Accesses window to select character style.
F7	Accesses window to select paragraph style.
F8	Toggles between Start Recording and Stop Recording.
F9	Shows hotwords (that is, surround a hotword with a rectangle).
F11	Centers the page on the screen.

Control key

- Holding down the **Control** key while using the zoom tool demagnifies the page.

- You may call up the color tray by pressing the **Control** key (on the keyboard), positioning the mouse arrow on any tool in the tool palette *except* the selection arrow and the zoom tool, and double-clicking the left mouse button.

- The **Control** key is useful to constrain several types of drawing tools so that, for example, rectangles have sides of equal lengths, ellipses form circles, and lines are perfectly horizontal or vertical.

- To move quickly from page to page at author level, hold down the **Control** key while pressing the right or left cursor arrows on the keyboard.

- You can press **Control+S** to quickly save a script.

Shift key

- Depressing the **Shift** key while clicking on subsequent objects will perform a "multiple select."

- To move from one entry field to another in a dialog box, you can use the **Tab** and **Shift+Tab** keys instead of clicking on each field with the mouse pointer. This can be faster when you are entering information using the keyboard and don't want to switch back to the mouse to get to another field.

■ You can paste an object by pressing **Shift+Insert** on the keyboard.

■ **Shift+F3** will open the command window and may be used instead of clicking on Window and Command.

Space Bar

■ You may select the object you just drew by pressing the space bar. The space bar toggles you from the last tool you've used to the selection of the last object you've drawn.

Common Scripts

"Next" Button

This script takes the reader to the next page:

```
to handle buttonUp
        go to next page
end buttonUp
```

The following script is useful to prevent cycling:

```
to handle buttonUp
        if this page is the last page of this book
                request "This is the last page of the book."
        else
                go to next page
        end
end buttonUp
```

"Previous" Button

This script is used to take the reader to the previous page:

to handle buttonUp

    go to previous page

end buttonUp

The following script is useful to prevent cycling:

to handle buttonUp

    if this is the first page of this book

        request "This is the first page of the book."

  else

        go to previous page

  end

end buttonUp

"Back" Button

This script takes the reader back to the page prior to clicking on the "Back" button:

to handle buttonUp

    send back

end buttonUp

"Contents" Button

This script can be used to take the reader to any page named on the button. Just substitute "contents" with the page's name. This could also be used with a hotword to take the reader to a page in the book.

```
to handle buttonUp
        go to page "contents"
end buttonUp
```

Hotword

This is used to open a dialog box with a message (specified in quotes):

```
to handle buttonUp
        request "This is the hotword message."
end buttonUp
```

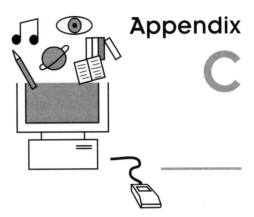

Appendix

C

Resources

Getting started in any new area can be difficult when you don't know what resources are available, or whom to call. This appendix provides you with a list of resources that can help. The list does not include every company or resource available, nor does it include all of the types of hardware and software discussed in this book, but it will certainly help you get started in multimedia.

General Resources

Magazines

<u>InfoWorld</u> (a good source for the latest information on hardware and software)
InfoWorld Publishing Inc.
155 Bovat Rd., Suite 800
San Mateo, CA 94402
(415) 572-7341

MPC World
Subscription Services
P.O. Box 55400
Boulder, CO 80322
(800) 274-2815 or (303) 447-9330

New Media
Hypermedia Communications Inc.
901 Mariner's Island Blvd., Suite 365
San Mateo, CA 94404
(415) 573-5170

Newsletters

The companies that publish the following newsletters also provide many other publications on multimedia. In addition, you should check the organizations listed in the next category because many of them publish their own monthly newsletters for members.

DiscNews—a GUI newsletter downloadable from CompuServe's MULTIMEDIA forum (enter "GO MULTIMEDIA").

Multimedia and Videodisc Monitor
Monitor Information Services
Future Systems Inc.
P.O. Box 26
Falls Church, VA 22040
(800) 323-3472 or (703) 241-1799

Multimedia Computing and Presentations, and New Media in Education and Entertainment
Simba Information Inc.
213 Danbury Rd.
Box 7430
Wilton, CT 06897
(203) 834-0033

Organizations

Many of these organizations publish a monthly newsletter as well as other multimedia publications.

International Communications Industries Association (produces multimedia publications and has a yearly trade show called Infocomm)
3150 Spring St.
Fairfax, VA 22031-2399
(703) 273-7200

International Interactive Communications Society (has many local chapters throughout the United States and abroad)
P.O. Box 1862
Lake Oswego, OR 97035
(503) 649-2065

Interactive Multimedia Association
3 Church Circle, Suite 800
Annapolis, MD 21401
(410) 626-1380

Multimedia Business Communications (corporate training seminars)
1580 Oakland Rd., Suite C206
San Jose, CA 95131
(408) 453-3950

Multimedia Computing Corp.
3501 Ryder St.
Santa Clara, CA 95051
(408) 737-7575

Simba Information Inc.
213 Danbury Rd.
Box 7430
Wilton, CT 06897
(203) 834-0033

CD-ROM Sources

CD-ROM, Inc.
1667 Cole Blvd., Suite 400
Golden, CO 80401
(303) 231-9373

Nautilus
7001 Discovery Blvd.
Dublin, OH 43017-3299
(800) 637-3472

NewMedia Source
3830 Valley Centre Dr., Suite 2153
San Diego, CA 92130
(800) 344-2621

UniDisc
4401 Capitola Rd., Suite 4
Capitola, CA 95010
(408) 464-0707

Bulletin Board Services

CompuServe—there are several forums for general multimedia information and files (enter "GO MULTIMEDIA") and for specific multimedia vendors (enter "GO MULTIVEN"), including Asymetrix Multimedia ToolBook.

Microsoft BBS—this provides access for Microsoft products, including its Multimedia Development Kit (MDK).

Hardware

Multimedia computer systems

CompuAdd Corp.
12303 Technology Blvd.
Austin, TX 78727
(800) 627-1967 or (800) 456-3116

CCSI
Computer and Control Solutions Inc.
1510 Stone Ridge Dr.
Stone Mountain, GA 30083
(800) 782-3525

Dolch Computer Systems
372 Turquoise St.
Milpitas, CA 95035
(800) 538-7506 or (408) 957-6575

IBM Corp.
1133 Westchester Ave.
White Plains, NY 10604
(800) 426-9402 or (914) 642-4662

Media Vision Inc.
47221 Fremont Blvd.
Fremont, CA 94538
(800) 845-5870 or (510) 770-8600

NEC Technologies Inc.
1414 Massachusetts Ave.
Boxborough, MA 01719
(800) 632-4636 or (508) 254-8000

Newmarket Technologies
6140 Variel Ave.
Woodland Hills, CA 91367
(800) 223-7288

Packard Bell
9425 Canoga Ave.
Chatsworth, CA 91311
(818) 886-4600

Philips Consumer Electronics Co.
1 Philips Dr.
P.O. Box 14810
Knoxville, TN 37914
(800) 722-6224 or (615) 521-4316

Samsung Information Systems America Inc.
3655 North First St.
San Jose, CA 95134
(800) 446-0262 or (408) 434-5400

Swan Technologies
3075 Research Drive
State College, PA 16801
(800) 468-9044

Tandy Corp.
1800 One Tandy Center
Forth Worth, TX 76102
(817) 390-3011

Zenith Data Systems
2150 East Lake Cook Rd.
Buffalo Grove, IL 60089
(800) 553-0331 or (708) 808-5000

Multimedia upgrade kits

CompuAdd Corp.
12303 Technology Blvd.
Austin, TX 78727
(800) 627-1967, (800) 456-3116, or (512) 250-1489

Creative Labs. Inc.
1901 McCarthy Blvd.
Milpitas, CA 95035
(800) 544-6146

Headland Technology Inc.
46221 Landing Pkwy.
Fremont, CA 94538-5016
(800) 238-0101, (800) 962-5700 (CA), or (510) 623-7857

Media Resources
640 Puente St.
Brea, CA 92621
(714) 256-5000

Media Vision Inc.
47221 Fremont Blvd.
Fremont, CA 94538
(800) 845-5870 or (510) 770-8600

NEC Technologies Inc.
1414 Massachusetts Ave.
Boxborough, MA 01719
(800) 632-4636 or (508) 254-8000

Samsung Information Systems America Inc.
3655 North First St.
San Jose, CA 95134
(800) 446-0262 or (408) 434-5400

Swan Technologies
3075 Research Drive
State College, PA 16801
(800) 468-9044

Tandy Corp.
1800 One Tandy Center
Fort Worth, TX 76102
(817) 390-3011

Turtle Beach Systems
Cyber Center, Unit 33
1600 Pennsylvania Ave.
York, PA 17404
(717) 843-6916

CD-ROM drives

Chinon America Inc.
660 Maple Ave.
Torrance, CA 90503
(800) 441-0222 or (213) 533-0274

Hitachi Home Electronics (America) Inc.
401 West Artesia Blvd.
Compton, CA 90220
(800) 369-0422 or (213) 537-8383

NEC Technologies Inc.
1414 Massachusetts Ave.
Boxborough, MA 01719
(800) 632-4636 or (508) 254-8000

Panasonic
2 Panasonic Way
Secaucus, NJ 07094
(800) 742-8086

Peripheral Land Inc.
47421 Bayside Pkwy.
Fremont, CA 94538
(800) 288-8754

Sony Corp.
3 Paragon Drive
Montvale, NJ 07645-1735
(800) 352-7669

Texel America Inc.
1080-C East Duane Ave.
Sunnyvale, CA 94086
(800) 886-3935

Toshiba America Consumer Products
1010 Johnson Drive
Buffalo Grove, IL 600089
(800) 253-5429

Graphics boards

Actix Graphics Engine
Actix Systems Inc.
3016 Tasman Drive
Santa Clara, CA 95054
(800) 927-5557 or (408) 986-1625

Cardinal VGA
Cardinal Technologies Inc.
1827 Freedom Road
Lancaster, PA 17601
(800) 233-0187

Diamond Stealth VRAM
Diamond Computer Systems Inc.
532 Mercury Drive
Sunnyvale, CA 94086
(408) 736-2000

Genoa Windows VGA
Genoa Systems Corp.
75 E. Trimble Road
San Jose, CA 95131
(408) 432-9090

Orchid Fahrenheit
Orchid Technology Inc.
45365 Northport Loop West
Fremont, CA 94538
(800) 767-2443

Paradise
Western Digital Imaging
800 E. Middlefield Rd.
Mountain View, CA 94043
(800) 356-5787 or (415) 960-3360

STB Wind/X Ultra
STB Systems Inc.
1651 N. Glenville, Suite 210
Richardson, TX 75801
(800) 234-4334

Targa
Truevision
7340 Shadeland Station
Indianapolis, IN 46256
(800) 344-8783

Thunder and Lightning Card
Media Vision Inc.
47221 Fremont Blvd.
Fremont, CA 94538
(800) 348-7116 or (510) 770-8600

X8 Color Graphics Controller Card
Microfield Graphics Inc.
Beaverton, OR 97005
(503) 626-9393

Sound boards

Audioport (an external device serving the same function as an internal sound board), and **Thunder and Lightning** (combined graphics and sound card)
Media Vision Inc.
47221 Fremont Blvd.
Fremont, CA 94538
(800) 348-7116 or (510) 770-8600

MultiSound
Turtle Beach Systems
Cyber Center, Unit 33
1600 Pennsylvania Ave.
York, PA 17404
(717) 843-6916

Port Blaster (an external device serving the function of an internal sound board)
Creative Labs Inc.
1901 McCarthy Blvd.
Milpitas, CA 95035
(800) 544-6146 or (408) 428-6600

Pro AudioSpectrum
Media Vision
47221 Fremont Blvd.
Fremont, CA 94538
(510) 770-8600

Sound Blaster
Creative Labs Inc.
1901 McCarthy Blvd.
Milpitas, CA 95035
(800) 544-6146 or (408) 428-6600

Sound Master II
Convox Inc.
675 Conger St.
Eugene, OR 97402
(503) 342-1271

Sounding Board
Artisoft Inc.
691 East River Road
Tucson, AZ 85704
(800) 846-9726 or (602) 293-4000

Video capture boards

MultiSound
Turtle Beach Systems
Cyber Center, Unit 33
1600 Pennsylvania Ave.
York, PA 17404
(717) 843-6916

New Media Graphics
780 Boston Rd.
Billerica, MA 01821-5925
(508) 663-0666

Targa
TrueVision
7340 Shadeland Station
Indianapolis, IN 46256
(800) 344-8783

Video Blaster
Creative Labs Inc.
1901 McCarthy Blvd.
Milpitas, CA 95035
(408) 428-6600

VIP video capture subsystem
Ventek Corp.
31336 Via Colinas, Suite 102
Westlake Village, CA 91362-9897
(818) 991-3868

Amplified speaker systems

Acoustic Research
330 Turnpike St.
Canton, MA 02021
(800) 969-2748 or (617) 821-2300

Altec Lansing Consumer Products
P.O. Box 277
Milford, PA 18337-0277
(800) 258-3288 or (717) 296-4434

Bose Corp.
The Mountain
Framington, MA 01701
(800) 444-2673 or (508) 879-7330

Koss Corp.
4129 North Port Washington Ave.
Milwaukee, WI 53212
(800) 872-5677 or (414) 964-5000

Sony Corp.
3 Paragon Drive
Montvale, NJ 07645-1735
(800) 352-7669

Flatbed color scanners

Advanced Vision Research Inc.
562 S. Milpitas Blvd.
Milpitas, CA 95035
(408) 956-0350

Epson America Inc.
20770 Madrona Ave.
Torrance, CA 90509
(800) 922-8911 or (310) 782-0770

Hewlett-Packard Co.
19310 Pruneridge Ave.
Cupertino, CA 95014
(800) 752-0900

Howtek Inc.
21 Park Avenue
Hudson, NH 03051
(603) 882-5200

Microtek Lab Inc.
680 Knox St.
Torrance, CA 90502
(800) 654-4160 or (213) 321-2121

Mustek Inc.
15225 Alton Parkway
Irvine, CA 92718
(800) 366-4620 or (714) 833-7740

Sayett Technology Inc.
17 Tobey Village
Pittsford, NY 14534
(716) 264-9250

Sharp Electronics Corp.
Sharp Plaza MS 1
P.O. Box 650
Mahwah, NJ 07430
(800) 237-4277 or (201) 529-9593

UMAX Technologies Inc.
3170 Coronado Drive
Santa Clara, CA 95054
(800) 562-0311 or (408) 982-0771

Hand-held scanners

Computer Friends Inc.
14250 Northwest Science Park Dr.
Portland, OR 97229
(800) 547-3303 or (503) 626-2291

Intel Corp.
CO3-7
5200 Northeast Elam Young Pkwy.
Hillsboro, OR 97124
(800) 525-3019 or (503) 629-7354

KYE International Corp.
2605 E. Cedar St.
Ontario, CA 91761
(800) 456-7593 or (714) 923-3510

Logitech Inc.
6505 Kaiser Drive
Fremont, CA 94555
(800) 231-7717 or (510) 795-8500

Touch-screen and Pen input

InkWare NoteTaker
Ink Development Corp.
1300 South El Camino Real, Suite 201
San Mateo, CA 94402
(415) 573-6565

NCR 3125 pen system
NCR Corp.
1700 S. Patterson Blvd.
Dayton, OH 45479
(800) 225-5627 or (513) 445-5000

ThinkPad (pen input)
IBM Corp.
1133 Westchester Ave.
White Plains, NY 10604
(800) 426-9402 or (914) 642-4662

TouchMate
Visage Inc.
1881 Worcester Rd.
Framingham, MA 01701
(508) 620-7100

TouchMonitor
Elographics Inc.
105 Randolph Rd.
Oak Ridge, TN 38730
(615) 482-4100

TruePoint touch monitor
MicroTouch Systems Inc.
55 Jonspin Rd.
Wilmington, MA 01887
(508) 694-9900

WriteAway
Arthur Dent Associates
500 Clark Rd.
Tewksbury, MA 01876-1639
(508) 858-3742

Extra storage

Bernoulli drives
Iomega Corp.
1821 West 4000 South
Roy, Utah 84067
(800) 456-5522

Data Traveler
Kingston Technology Corp.
17600 Newhope Street
Fountain Valley, CA 92708
(714) 435-2600

Mercury removable hard drives
Mega Drive Systems
489 South Robertson Blvd.
Beverly Hills, CA 90211
(310) 247-0006

Portable hard drives
Vision Logic
283 E. Brokaw Rd.
San Jose, CA 95112
(408) 437-1000

SCSI Interfaces

CorelSCSI
Corel Systems Corp.
1600 Carling Ave.
Ottawa, Ontario K1Z 8R7, Canada
(800) 836-7274 or (613) 728-8200

MiniSCSI
Trantor Systems Ltd.
5415 Randall Pl.
Freemont, CA 94538-3151
(510) 770-1400

Software

Multimedia authoring tools

AskMe 2000
Innovative Communication Systems Inc.
112 Roberts St., Suite 14
Fargo, ND 58102
(701) 293-1004

Authorware Professional for Windows
Authorware Inc.
275 Shoreline Drive, 4th Floor
Redwood City, CA 94065
(415) 595-3101

HyperCASE
Interactive Image Technologies
700 King St. W., Suite 815
Toronto, Ontario M5V 2Y6, Canada
(416) 361-0333

HyperWriter
Ntergaid Inc.
2490 Black Rock Turnpike, Suite 337
Fairfield, CT 06430
(203) 368-0632

IconAuthor
AimTech Corp.
20 Trafalgar Square
Nashua, NH 03063-1973
(800) 289-2884 or (603) 883-0220

LinkWay
IBM Multimedia Information Center, Dept. 7EY
4111 Northside Pkwy. HO4L1
Atlanta, GA 30327
(800) 426-9402

Multimedia ToolBook
Asymetrix Corp.
110 110th Avenue NE, Suite 700
Bellevue, WA 98004
(800) 448-6543 or (206) 637-1500

Microsoft Multimedia Development Kit
Microsoft Corp.
1 Microsoft Way
Redmond, WA 98052-6399
(800) 227-4679, (800) 426-9400, or (206) 882-8080

Plus
Spinnaker Software Inc.
One Kendall Square
Cambridge, MA 02139
(617) 494-1200

Storyboard Live
IBM Multimedia Information Center, Dept. 7EY
4111 Northside Pkwy. HO4L1
Atlanta, GA 30327
(800) 426-9402

Works
Microsoft Corp.
One Microsoft Way
Redmond, WA 98052-6399
(800) 541-1261

Other software with multimedia capabilities

There are many software packages on the market that incorporate multimedia capabilities. The following are just a few.

Knowledge Pro
Knowledge Garden Inc.
12-8 Technology Drive
Setauket, NY 17333
(516) 246-5400

Realizer
Within Technologies Inc.
Laurel Corporate Center, #201 South
8000 Midlantic Dr.
Mt. Laurel, NJ 08054-5080
(609) 273-8881

Thinx
Bell Atlantic
575 E. Swedesford Rd., 3rd Floor
Wayne, PA 19087
(800) 688-4469 or (215) 768-5787

Visual Basic
Microsoft Corp.
1 Microsoft Way
Redmond, WA 98052-6399
(800) 541-1261

Painting/drawing/image creation software

Most of the software packages listed also provide other capabilities such as format conversion and scanning.

Aldus PhotoStyler
Aldus Corp.
411 First Ave. South
Seattle, WA 98104-2871
(206) 628-2320

CorelDRAW!
Corel Systems Corp.
1600 Carling Ave.
Ottawa, Ontario K1Z 8R7, Canada
(800) 836-7274 or (613) 728-8200

Harvard Graphics
Software Publishing Corp.
P.O. Box 54983
Santa Clara, CA 95056-0983
(408) 988-7518

Juggler
Jewell Technologies
130 Nickerson St., Suite 105
Seattle, WA 98109
(206) 285-6860

PC Paintbrush (DOS), Publisher's Paintbrush (Windows), Photo Finish
ZSoft Corp.
450 Franklin Rd., Suite 100
Marietta, GA 30067
(800) 444-4780 or (404) 428-0008

Picture Publisher
Micrografx Inc.
1303 Arapaho
Richardson, TX 75081
(800) 733-3729 or (214) 234-1769

Capture and conversion of image formats

These software packages may also provide other capabilities such as image creation.

Collage Plus
Inner Media Inc.
60 Plain Road
Hollis, NH 03049
(603) 465-3216

Conversion Artist
North Coast Software
P.O. Box 343
Barrington, NH 03825
(603) 332-9363

HiJaak
Inset Systems
71 Commerce Drive
Brookfield, CT 06804-3405
(203) 740-2400

Image-In-Color Professional
Image-In Inc.
406 East 79th St.
Minneapolis, MN 55420
(800) 345-3450 or (612) 888-3633

SnapIt!
Window Painters Ltd.
7275 Bush Lake Rd.
Minneapolis, MN 55439
(612) 897-1305

WinRix
Rix SoftWorks Inc.
18023 Skypark Circle, Suite J
Irvine, CA 92714
(714) 476-8266

Art, animation, and sound software

Most of the following packages allow you to create your own art, animation, or sound, as well as providing you with "clips."

Animation Clips
Media in Motion
P.O. Box 170130
San Francisco, CA 94117
(800) 395-2547

Animation Works Interactive
Gold Disk Inc.
5155 Spectrum Way, Unit5
Mississauga, Ontario L4W 5A1, Canada
(416) 602-4000

AutoDesk Multimedia Explorer, Animator Pro
AutoDesk Inc.
2320 Marinship Way
Sausalito, CA 94965
(800) 525-2763, (800) 445-5415, or (415) 332-2344

ClickArt
T/Maker Co.
1390 Villa St.
Mountain View, CA 94041
(415) 962-0195

Clip Artist
PC Publishing
58 Charles St.
Cambridge, MA 02141
(800) 634-4555

Corel Artshow
Corel Systems Corp.
1600 Carling Ave.
Ottawa, Ontario K1Z 8R7, Canada
(800) 836-7274 or (613) 728-8200

DigiSound, Sound Solution
Presentation Graphics Group
270 N. Canon Drive, Suite 103
Beverly Hills, CA 90210
(800) 468-9008 or (213) 277-3050

Images with Impact
3G Graphics Inc.
114 Second Ave. South, #104-E
Edmonds, WA 98020
(800)456-0234 or (206)774-3518

MacroMind Directory, FilmMaker, Action
MacroMedia Inc.
600 Townsend St.
San Francisco, CA 94105
(415) 442-0200

Midisoft Studio for Windows
Midisoft Corp.
P.O. Box 1000
Bellevue, WA 98009
(800) 776-6434 or (206) 881-7176

MusicBytes
Prosonus
11126 Weddington St.
North Hollywood, CA 91601
(800) 999-6191 or (818) 766-5221

Picture Pak
Marketing Graphics Inc.
4401 Dominion Blvd., Suite 210
Glen Allen, VA 23060-3379
(804) 747-6991

Presentation Task Force
New Vision Technologies
38 Auriga Dr., Unit 13
Nepean, Ontario K2E 8A5, Canada
(613) 727-8184

Tempra Pro, Tempra GIF
Mathematica
402 S. Kentucky Ave.
Lakeland, FL 33801
(800) 852-6284 or (813) 682-1128

Totem Graphics Inc.
6200 Capitol Blvd. SE, #F
Tumwater, WA 98501
(206) 352-1851

Wave for Windows
Turtle Beach Systems
Cyber Center, Unit 33
1600 Pennsylvania Ave.
York, PA 17404
(717) 843-6916

Presentation software

Act III
Informatics Group/PSI
100 Shield St.
West Hartford, CT 06110
(203) 953-4040

Aldus Persuasion
Aldus Corp.
411 First Ave. South
Seattle, WA 98104-2871
(206) 628-2320

Freelance Graphics
Lotus Development Corp.
55 Cambridge Pkwy.
Cambridge, MA 02142
(800) 343-5414 or (617) 577-8500

HSC Interactive
HSC Software
1661 Lincoln Blvd., Suite 101
Santa Monica, CA 90404
(310) 392-8441

MacroMind Action

MacroMind-Paracomp Inc.
600 Townsend St., Suite 310W
San Francisco, CA 94103
(415) 442-0200

Tempra Show

Mathematica
402 S. Kentucky Ave.
Lakeland, FL 33801
(800) 852-6284 or (813) 682-1128

Scanning software

DeskScan

Hewlett-Packard Co.
19310 Pruneridge Ave.
Cupertino, CA 95014
(800) 752-0900

Ofoto

Light Source Inc.
17 E. Sir Francis Drake Blvd., Suite 100
Larkspur, CA 94939
(415) 461-8000

Optical character recognition (OCR) software

OmniPage

Caere Corp.
100 Cooper Court
Los Gatos, CA 95030
(800) 535-7226

Perceive
Ocron Inc.
3350 Scott Blvd., Bldg. 36
Santa Clara, CA 95054
(408) 980-8900

Readright
OCR Systems Inc.
1800 Byberry Road, Suite 1405
Huntingdon Valley, PA 19006
(800) 233-4627

Recognize
Dest
1015 E. Brokaw Road
San Jose, CA 95131
(408) 436-2700

TypeReader
ExperVision Inc.
3590 N. First St.
San Jose, CA 95134
(800) 732-3897

WordScan
Calera Recognition Systems Inc.
475 Potrero Ave.
Sunnyvale, CA 94086
(408) 720-8300

Note to Readers:

If you prefer to use the Evaluation Edition from 3.5-inch disks rather than the CD-ROM packaged with this book, you may exchange the single CD-ROM disk provided for a set of six disks by contacting Asymetrix at the address below. Or take advantage of the following special offer.

Now that Linda Tway has introduced you to multimedia and you ve experimented with the evaluation edition packaged with this book, you ll want to go all the way with *Multimedia ToolBook*!

Special Coupon

Now you re ready to construct your own multimedia world with a full development copy of *Multimedia ToolBook* from Asymetrix.

Receive a 25% discount off the suggested list price by sending the coupon below. Call (800) 448-6543 for price and further details.

Mail To: Multimedia ToolBook Sales Offer
Asymetrix Corporation
110 - 110th Avenue, NE, Suite 700
Bellevue, WA 98004

Phone: (800) 448-6543 or (206) 637-1500

Int'l Fax: 001-206-637-1504

Ship To:

Name_____ Phone # ( ) _____
Street _____ Fax # ( ) _____

City/State _____ Zip _____
Country _____

Payment Method:

❑ Check enclosed (payable to Asymetrix Corp.)
❑ MC/VISA Card #_____ Exp Date _____
❑ AMEX #_____ Exp Date _____

Authorized Signature _____

MIS: Press

NOTE: THIS IS A LEGAL AGREEMENT BETWEEN YOU (EITHER AN INDIVIDUAL OR ENTITY), THE END USER, AND ASYMETRIX CORPORATION. IF YOU DO NOT AGREE TO THE TERMS OF THIS AGREEMENT, PROMPTLY RETURN THE DISK PACKAGE WITH THE SEAL INTACT AND WITH ALL ACCOMPANYING MATERIALS AND YOUR MONEY WILL BE REFUNDED. BY EXERCISING THE RIGHTS GRANTED TO YOU IN THE AGREEMENT, YOU AGREE TO BE BOUND BY ITS TERMS.

ASYMETRIX MULTIMEDIA TOOLBOOK EVALUATION EDITION LICENSE AGREEMENT

Copyright. The enclosed Asymetrix software program ("Program") and any Asymetrix user manual(s) ("Manual") that accompany it are copyrighted and remain the property of Asymetrix or its suppliers. You may not copy or otherwise reproduce any part or all of the Program or Manual, except that you may either (a) make one copy of the Program solely for backup or archival purposes, (b) transfer the Program to a single hard disk provided you keep the original solely for backup or archival purposes. You may not copy the Manual.

License. Asymetrix grants you a license to use one copy of the Program on a single computer which you own or operate. If you are a licensed user of Multimedia ToolBook, you may also modify the application portion of the Program provided that you:

(i) do nothing with the modified Program except what you are permitted to do with the Program pursuant to this agreement;

(ii) include Asymetrix's copyright notice and restricted government rights notices on the modified Program;

(iii) agree to indemnify, hold harmless and defend Asymetrix from and against any claims or lawsuits, including attorneys' fees, that arise or result from the use of the modified Program; and

(iv) use such modified Program only for internal use, and do not let anyone else have a copy. If you are interested in distributing the modified Program, contact Asymetrix regarding its distribution licenses.

The "ToolBook Files" are TOOLBOOK.EXE and those files which have names beginning with "TB". You may not modify the ToolBook Files. The application portion of the Program are the files other than the ToolBook Files.

Other Restrictions. You may not rent or lease the Program. However, you may transfer this license together with the original copy of the Program, all Program updates and the Manual; on a permanent basis so long as the transferee agrees to be bound by the terms of this Agreement and you destroy all copies of all or any portion of the Program and all updates that you do not transfer to the transferee. Except as provided above, you may not sublicense, assign or transfer the License or the Program. Any attempt to do so shall terminate the License.

You may not reverse engineer, decompile or disassemble the ToolBook Files or any portion of them or otherwise attempt to determine the underlying source code of them or to permit any such actions.

LIMITED WARRANTY. Asymetrix warrants only that under normal use for a period of 90 days from the date of delivery to you the unaltered Program will operate substantially as described by the Manual.

YOU MUST ASSUME FULL RESPONSIBILITY FOR THE SELECTION OF THE PROGRAM TO ACHIEVE YOUR INTENDED PURPOSES, FOR THE PROPER INSTALLATION AND USE OF THE PROGRAM AND FOR VERIFYING THE RESULTS OBTAINED FROM USE OF THE PROGRAM, ASYMETRIX DOES NOT WARRANT THAT THE FUNCTIONS CONTAINED IN THE PROGRAM WILL MEET YOUR REQUIREMENTS, OR THAT THE OPERATION OF THE PROGRAM WILL BE INTERRUPTION OR ERROR FREE.

If the program fails to operate substantially as described in the Manual within the 90-day warranty period, then return the defective diskette to Asymetrix at the address indicated below within such 90-day period together with the receipt showing the price and date of purchase of this license. Asymetrix will, upon verification of the defect or error, at Asymetrix's option, either repair or replace the defective copy or refund the amount you paid for this license (the "License Fees"). If Asymetrix elects to provide a refund, upon the date you receive notice of such election this license shall terminate and you must destroy all copies of all or any portions of the Program. No action for any breach of warranty may be commenced more than one year following the expiration of such warranty.

ASYMETRIX EXPRESSLY DISCLAIMS ALL OTHER WARRANTIES, WHETHER ORAL OR WRITTEN, EXPRESS OR IMPLIED, INCLUDING WITHOUT LIMITATION WARRANTIES OF MERCHANTABILITY, FITNESS FOR A PARTICULAR PURPOSE, TITLE OR INFRINGEMENT. ALL WARRANTIES SHALL TERMINATE 90 DAYS FROM DATE OF DELIVERY OF THE PROGRAM TO YOU.

Some states do not allow limitation on how long an implied warranty lasts, so the above limitation may not apply to you. This limited warranty gives you specific legal rights and you may have other rights which vary from state to state.

EXCLUSIVE REMEDY. YOUR EXCLUSIVE REMEDY AND ASYMETRIX'S ENTIRE LIABILITY ARISING FROM OR IN CONNECTION WITH THE PROGRAM, PROGRAM MANUAL AND/OR THIS LICENSE (INCLUDING WITHOUT LIMITATION FOR BREACH OF WARRANTY OR INFRINGEMENT) SHALL BE, AT ASYMETRIX OPTION, THE REPAIR OR REPLACEMENT OF PROGRAM DISKETTES OR REFUND OF LICENSE FEES.

LIMITATIONS OF LIABILITY

A. IN NO EVENT WILL ASYMETRIX BE LIABLE TO YOU FOR ANY INDIRECT, INCIDENTAL, CONSEQUENTIAL, SPECIAL OR EXEMPLARY DAMAGES, ARISING OUT OF OR IN CONNECTION WITH YOUR USE OR INABILITY TO USE THE PROGRAM OR MANUAL, THE BREACH OF ANY EXPRESS OR IMPLIED WARRANTY, OR OTHERWISE IN CONNECTION WITH THE PROGRAM, THE PROGRAM MANUAL, AND/OR THIS LICENSE EVEN IF ASYMETRIX HAS BEEN ADVISED OF THE POSSIBILITY OF SUCH DAMAGES. Some states do not allow limitation or exclusion of incidental or consequential damages, so that above limitation or exclusion may not apply to you.

B. IN NO EVENT SHALL ASYMETRIX'S TOTAL LIABILITY FOR AND DAMAGES, DIRECT OR INDIRECT, IN CONNECTION WITH THE PROGRAM, THE PROGRAM MANUAL, AND/OR THIS LICENSE EXCEED THE LICENSE FEES PAID FOR YOUR RIGHT TO USE THIS COPY OF THE PROGRAM WHETHER SUCH LIABILITY ARISES FROM ANY CLAIM BASED UPON CONTRACT, WARRANTS, TORT OR OTHERWISE.

Allocation of Risks. Provisions of this Agreement such as the warranty limitations, exclusive remedies and limitations of liability are unrelated, independent allocations of risks between you and Asymetrix. Unenforceability of any such allocations shall not affect the enforceability of other such allocations. Asymetrix's pricing reflects the allocations of risk contained in this Agreement.

U.S. GOVERNMENT RESTRICTED RIGHTS. Use, duplication, or disclosure by the Government is subject to restrictions as set forth in subparagraph (c) (i) (ii) of the Rights in Technical Data and Computer Software clause at DFARS 252.227-7013 (Oct. 1988) and FAR 52.227-19 (June 1987). Contractor is Asymetrix Corp., 110-110th Avenue Northeast, Suite 700, Bellevue, Washington, 98004.

YOU AGREE THAT THIS AGREEMENT IS THE COMPLETE AND EXCLUSIVE STATEMENT OF THE AGREEMENT BETWEEN YOU AND ASYMETRIX AND SUPERCEDES ANY PROPOSAL OR PRIOR AGREEMENT OR ANY COMMUNICATIONS RELATING TO THE USE OF THE PROGRAM. This agreement shall be governed by the internal laws of the State of Washington, and venue in the event of any suit, proceeding or claim shall be in the Courts located in King County, Washington. If you have questions regarding this Agreement, you may contact Asymetrix by writing to Asymetrix Corporation, 110—110th Avenue N.E., Suite 700, Bellevue, WA 98004.